CONTEMPORARY SOCIAL THEORY

General Editor: ANTHONY GIDDENS

This series aims to create a forum for debate between different theoretical and philosophical traditions in the social sciences. As well as covering broad schools of thought, the series will also concentrate upon the work of particular thinkers whose ideas have had a major impact on social science (these books appear under the sub-series title of 'Theoretical Traditions in the Social Sciences'). The series is not limited to abstract theoretical discussion – it will also include more substantive works on contemporary capitalism, the state, politics and other subject areas.

CONTEMPORARY SOCIAL THEORY

General Editor: ANTHONY GIDDENS

Published titles

Tony Bilton, Kevin Bonnett, Philip Jones, Ken Sheard, Michelle Stanworth and Andrew Webster, *Introductory Sociology*
Anthony Giddens, *A Contemporary Critique of Historical Materialism*
Anthony Giddens, *Central Problems in Social Theory*
Ali Rattansi, *Marx and the Division of Labour*
Gerry Rose, *Deciphering Sociological Research*
Steve Taylor, *Durkheim and the Study of Suicide*
John Urry, *The Anatomy of Capitalist Societies*

Forthcoming titles

Martin Albrow, *Weber and the Construction of Social Theory*
Clive Ashworth, Chris Dandeker and Terry Johnson, *Theoretical Sociology*
David Brown and Michael Harrison, *Industrial Sociology*
Simon Clarke, *Marx, Marginalism and Modern Sociology*
Emile Durkheim, *The Rules of Sociological Method* (intro. by Steven Lukes)
Boris Frankel, *The Modern State*
Anthony Giddens, *Between Capitalism and Socialism*
Anthony Giddens, *Sociology: A Brief but Critical Introduction*
David Held, *Bureaucracy, Democracy and Socialism*
Geoffrey Ingham, *Capitalism Divided*
Jorge Larrain, *Marxism and Ideology*
Claus Offe, *Structural Problems of the Capitalist State*
John Scott, *The Development of the British Upper Class*
John B. Thompson and David Held (eds), *Habermas: Critical Debates*

Theoretical Traditions in the Social Sciences

Published title

Barry Barnes, *T. S. Kuhn and Social Science*

Forthcoming titles

Ted Benton, *Althusser and the Althusserians*
David Bloor, *Wittgenstein and Social Science*
Chris Bryant, *Positivism in Social Theory*
John Forrester, *Jacques Lacan*
John Heritage, *Garfinkel and Ethnomethodology*
Athar Hussain, *Foucault*
Bob Jessop, *Nicos Poulantzas*
Julian Roberts, *Walter Benjamin*
James Schmidt, *Maurice Merleau-Ponty and Social Theory*
Dennis Smith, *Barrington Moore and Historical Sociology*
Robin Williams, *Erving Goffman*

Marx and the Division of Labour

Ali Rattansi

Lecturer in Sociology
University of Leicester School of Education

First published 1982 by
THE MACMILLAN PRESS LTD
London and Basingstoke
Companies and representatives throughout the world

ISBN 0 333 28555 7 (hard cover)
ISBN 0 333 28556 5 (paper cover)

Typeset in 10/12pt Times by
ILLUSTRATED ARTS

Printed in Hong Kong

For my parents

Contents

Acknowledgements

This book is a condensed and revised version of a Doctoral thesis submitted to the University of Cambridge in 1978. I am greatly indebted to Anthony Giddens for supervising the original work and for his continuing encouragement and guidance. I have also learnt much from other friends, and for giving so generously of their time, and for sharing their ideas with me, I would especially like to thank Mehmet Dikerdem, Norman Geras, John Hoffman, Terry Johnson, Gavin Mackenzie, Graham Murdock, Doug Smith, Hillel Steiner, Dominic Strinati and Sallie Westwood, to whom I owe much more besides. I am also very grateful to Gerry Bernbaum for his encouragement and support and to Dorothy Brydges for converting a series of illegible manuscripts into impeccable typescripts.

January 1981 M.A.R.

Introduction

This book is primarily about Marx's theorisation of the division of labour, and his analysis of its historical forms. Despite the recent growth of Marx scholarship of a very high order, a general resurgence of interest in Marxist ideas and, more specifically, something of a rediscovery of the concept of division of labour itself, this subject has not in fact received adequate treatment. I hope that this book will therefore rectify a notable anomaly in the secondary literature on Marx. And although this is a point that will obviously emerge in the pages to come, it is worth remarking at this stage that notwithstanding the absence of detailed discussions by commentators on Marx's thought, the concept of division of labour does play a very significant role in his work and merits the extended treatment I have sought to provide in this work.

However, the discussion of Marx presented here is not intended as a simple exercise in exegesis and synthesis, a pulling together of quotations to yield a unified, transparent discourse; recent debates have decisively established the existence of important transformations in Marx's thinking as well as the radically unfinished nature of his intellectual project. Although controversy continues to rage over the precise character of these changes and absences, it is clear that they can no longer be glossed over and I hope to show that this is as much the case for his conceptualisation of the division of labour as it is for other elements of his discourse. Thus I have endeavoured to document important discontinuities and ambiguities in his theorisation, although not without attention to some important recurrences. In addition, I have attempted to indicate the existence of serious limitations in Marx's views which continue to bedevil and hamper contemporary Marxist discussions of the division of labour.

This is particularly the case when the analysis of the division of labour is considered in relation to the closely implicated subject of exchange, a theme I shall remark upon in more detail in this introduction. Before doing so, however, it is appropriate to add an explanation concerning the mode of entry into the central discussion of Marx and the division of labour.

I have chosen to analyse Marx's conception of the division of labour through a consideration of one significant interpretational issue: the idea of the abolition of the division of labour. That Marx believed throughout his life in the necessity and possibility of the abolition of the division of labour *tout court* is taken as a cardinal principle in two rather different traditions of Marx interpretation, one largely hostile and the other mainly sympathetic to Marx. Both rely primarily upon accentuating relatively unambiguous propositions in his early works, for example the *Economic and Philosophic Manuscripts* and *The German Ideology*, where Marx insists upon the complete dissolution of the division of labour as a central organising principle for future society. The first school uses these statements to demonstrate the essentially utopian, indeed religious nature of Marxian socialism and thus to discredit the whole movement. The second, sometimes forged in opposition to and in justified criticism of the bureaucratic brutalism of the Soviet Union, deploys Marx's early pronouncements to hold out what it sees as a humane and libertarian vision still capable of generating political commitment, although rendering Marxism vulnerable to the charge of utopianism. Ironically, neither in scholarly nor in political discussion has the question of Marx's continuing belief in the abolition of the division of labour been given any serious, sustained treatment. I have therefore sought to organise much of my own discussion around this issue, and I have attempted to secure the thesis that Marx's mature thought on this subject cannot be assimilated to the romantic, almost visionary passages to be found in some of the early writings. At the same time, the book incorporates a general interpretation of Marx's intellectual development which is employed to explain the transformation in his views on the abolition of the division of labour.

No interpretation of Marx can hope to be definitive. It is to be expected that the thesis I am advancing will generate debate and criticism, although if it establishes the necessity for a serious discussion of what Marxian socialism entails, and if it undermines the strongly held but crippling view that such discussions are utopian, that they should be postponed until some more appropriate future time, then this book will have fulfilled some of the author's primary intentions. Those Marxists who are convinced by the interpretation of Marx offered here will be able to shed a variety of beliefs which some of them have long been uncomfortable about defending, while those hostile to Marx will, I hope, find it more difficult to caricature and dismiss his thought as essentially eschatological.

This is an appropriate point at which to say something about the vexed question of the relationship between Marx and Engels. For a long time now opinion has been divided about the precise nature of the convergences and disagreements – overt or implicit -- between the two collaborators.[1] However, it is my belief that in matters of historical, social and economic analysis there are no differences between Marx and Engels fundamental enough to necessitate separate treatment in a book on their conception of the division of labour. Thus, while I have written primarily about Marx, I have often referred to works by Engels either for clarification or for additional material where this has been necessary. On the other hand, I have not hesitated in pointing to a significant discursive divergence between the two authors on the question of the abolition of scarcity in their mature texts.

Historically, discussions of the division of labour have almost always been tied to analyses of exchange, and Marx's discourse is no exception. The idea of the abolition of the division of labour in his thought is closely allied to the idea of the elimination of relations of exchange and the production of commodities, and quite properly forms an important element of this book. In this context I have tried to secure three main theses: first, that Marx continued to espouse throughout his life a belief in the necessity and possibility of the abolition of exchange relations; second, that in so far as much of Marx's argument here rests upon presuppositions concerning the abolition of scarcity, his thought must be judged unsatisfactory; and third, that the experience of 'state socialist' societies is acutely relevant here and further reinforces the theorem that Marx's views on the abolition of exchange relations and commodity production stand in need of revision.

The last of these propositions is liable to prove especially contentious and the form of argument which sustains it merits some preliminary elaboration. While there are of course several different standpoints both within and outside Marxism concerning the relevance of existing state socialist systems for the validity of Marx's work, there are three – often combined in a single discourse – which my discussion particularly seeks to undermine. One tends to regard analyses of exchange relations and the market in state socialist societies as essentially technical matters best left to specialist economists; a second takes the view that because the origins of these social formations lie in conditions far removed from those envisaged by Marx, nothing that happens in, say, eastern Europe, carries any significance for the substantive propositions embodied in his vision of socialism; the third suggests that only a comprehensive implementation of Marx's (unrevised) vision will liberate these societies, although some changes, especially the abolition of relations of exchange and the division of labour, will have to await the further development of the forces of production. Each of these propositions contains more than a grain of truth, but each if adopted as it stands is highly misleading and constitutes an obstacle to the development of Marxist thought. Again, my intention in the last section of the book is to open up this area for serious discussion away from the forum of specialised economics and Soviet studies journals on the one hand, and the dogma of Marxist political pamphleteering on the other.

The exploration of Marx's theorisation of the division of labour is preceded by a brief consideration of pre-Marxian conceptions. I cannot emphasise too strongly that this first section does not attempt to provide a comprehensive history of concepts of division of labour before Marx; it is merely an outline in which I have tried to set out some of the main developments which together comprise the intellectual backdrop against which Marx's own theorisation must be understood. The account I offer also suffers from other limitations which can only be remedied by another sort of project: it necessarily contains little specification of the social and political conditions of existence of differing conceptions of the division of labour and it gives to individual authors a privileged status which a more theoretical history might be inclined to deny. My purpose in providing these 'materials for a history', which is all they are, is two-fold: to rescue them from the obscurity of specialist papers which only consider special aspects of the subject, and to detach them from histories of economic thought which usually fail to provide connected discussions of differing conceptions of the division of labour and, moreover, unduly restrict the discourse to so-called 'economic' relevance. In contrast I have attempted to demonstrate the interpenetration of 'division of labour' with much broader themes, especially those of forms of property, the determination and historical evolution of successive socio-economic formations, and conceptions of the 'just' social order. Inevitably, this has led to selective emphases which to some extent are the obverse of those found in the standard histories of economic thought: for example, the account offered here contains little on conceptions of productive and unproductive labour, which a more comprehensive study would need to elucidate.

I have not thought it appropriate in this book to discuss recent analyses of the capitalist division of labour and labour process in any detail.[2] Much of the research being undertaken in this area is of exceptional interest, but to have given it the consideration it merits would have meant writing an additional book. Nevertheless, two sets of remarks are perhaps in order here. Note, first, the endemic confusion in the usage of 'division of labour' in these texts: although it has become obligatory to distinguish between the 'technical' and the 'social' division of labour, the meaning of these concepts varies considerably between texts, while the relationship between 'division of labour' and other relevant concepts, such as 'relations of production' and 'mode of production', is rarely clarified.[3] Second, as Burawoy has pointed out, there has been a tendency in this type of research to operate with a theorisation in which the essence of the capital relationship permeates the entire social formation, in turn producing misleadingly reductionist forms of analysis.[4] *Marx and the Division of Labour* will, I hope, serve to remedy both types of discursive limitation: the first, because it specifies some of the confusions underlying Marx's own conceptualisation of the division of labour and thus lays bare the roots of many contemporary obscurities; the second, because the book documents the existence of an alternative, non-reductionist discourse in the original texts, and which Marx himself deploys in his mature analysis of the division of labour and its historical forms.

Note to the reader. Although the sections within each part of the book begin on fresh pages, they are not separate chapters but part of a more interconnected argument and should be read as such.

Part I

'Division of Labour' before Marx: Materials for a History

1
Concepts of Division of Labour

The term 'division of labour' came to be widely used only in the eighteenth century when it emerged as a central theme in the writings of the school of 'conjectural history' during the period of the Scottish Enlightenment. In their discussion of the division of labour the Scots and other Enlightenment thinkers made some reference back to writings from classical antiquity and at first sight it appears reasonable to suggest that the roots of the concept of division of labour have to be sought in the social thought of classical Greece, and especially in the work of Plato, Aristotle and Xenophon. There is, indeed, a well-established tradition in the history of ideas which delights in finding remote origins and tracing direct chains of continuity across vast historical periods, and the concept of division of labour has not been immune to this form of treatment.[1]

In recent years, however, a variety of important theoretical departures have problematised notions of continuity and recurrence in the history of ideas.[2] The meaning of concepts, it has been pointed out, is governed by the overall structure of theories in which they are embedded and cannot be understood apart from the discursive space they occupy in relation to other concepts. Moreover, theories – or 'paradigms' (Kuhn), 'problematics' (Bachelard), 'discursive formations' (Foucault) – could well exhibit relations of incommensurability which make the exercise of conceptual and theoretical translation redundant.[3] Whatever the internal difficulties of discontinuist accounts, it is clear that their theorems can no longer be ignored in the sort of project attempted here despite the qualifications that have already been introduced concerning its limited scope.

Whether the Greeks actually possessed or employed a precise

equivalent for the term 'division of labour' is itself difficult to establish and this is reflected in differences in translation from the original language. Jowett uses the term in a well-known translation of Plato's *The Republic*:

> And the division of labour which required the carpenter and the shoemaker and the rest of the citizens to be doing each his own business, and not another's, was a shadow of justice, and therefore of use?[4]

Other translators, however, have not followed Jowett's usage, although it is evident that Plato often used the terms 'division' and 'distribution' when discussing occupations and 'arts'.[5]

Bearing in mind that the absence of a term does not necessarily signify the absence of a concept, but also that concepts only acquire meaning within the architecture of particular discursive formations, it is possible to argue that the Greeks possessed *a* conceptualisation of the division of labour by which was designated, primarily, a division of crafts and occupational specialisation. This is articulated with other notions, especially exchange, in a discourse with two central objects of analysis which intersect at various levels: *oikos* (household) and *polis* (city-state). Their theorisation is underpinned by a set of propositions concerning the admissibility of organic and other analogies, the classification of occupations and arts into 'liberal' and 'mechanical' or 'servile', the existence of innate talents and dispositions among individuals, and the importance of improvements in the quality of goods as an overriding goal of changes in methods of production. Together, these assumptions and objects of analysis create a theoretical field within which, on the one hand, their conceptualisation of the division of labour acquires its meaning and, on the other, differentiates it from subsequent usages. This discourse therefore is also the site of conceptual absences – for example, the 'economy' – which do not characterise later theories, and this makes it difficult to speak of *the* concept of division of labour *tout court*, despite the identification of certain networks of continuity and influence which will be established in the account that follows.[6]

2
Classical Greece: The Division of Labour as Justice

It is not necessary here to provide an exhaustive examination of classical Greek reflections on the division of labour, but merely to elucidate some central themes based mainly on the writings of Plato and Aristotle. Moreover, the obvious epistemological and political differences between these authors are not especially relevant to this discussion, which seeks only to identify a broad discursive structure within which their conceptualisation of the division of labour acquires its significance.

Although Aristotle thought of humans as inherently communal beings both he and Plato located the origins of cooperative social activities, the differentiation of tasks and occupational specialisation in the exigencies of subsistence and the absence of self-sufficiency: 'Society originates . . . because the individual is not self-sufficient, but has many needs which he can't supply himself.'[7] And they were both aware of the advantages of occupational specialisation for the improvement of quality and an increase in productivity:

> Quantity and quality are therefore more easily produced when a man specialises more appropriately on a single job for which he is naturally fitted.[8]

The needs of subsistence, innate differences in ability and the advantages of occupational specialisation allowed Plato and Aristotle to deduce the need for an elaborate differentiation of crafts. Beginning with the most basic needs – food, dwelling and clothing – and postulating the necessity for a husbandman, a builder and a weaver, Plato went on to add several specialists who would have to make up any 'healthy' state, including manual workers possessed of little 'powers of mind' who market their physical strength for wages 'and in consequence are usually called wage earners'.[9]

Organicist analogies are more clearly evident in Aristotle's writings and are reflected in his attempt to outline a set of functional requisites and a corresponding division of labour:

> Now if our chosen subject were not the forms of constitution but the forms of animal life, we should first have to answer the question 'What is it essential for every animal to have in order to live?' . . . We may apply this to the constitutions mentioned; for states too have many parts . . . These are (1) the bulk of the people concerned with food-production, tillers of the soil, (2) the part called banausic, by which we mean people who follow those occupations which are indispensable in the work of a city, (3) the commercial, by which we mean that section which spends its time on buying and selling . . . (4) the hired labourer section, (5) the class which will defend in time of war . . . And surely there also ought to be . . . one whose duty it will be to decide and pronounce upon matters of justice . . . Those who render service by their possessions are a seventh class . . . An eighth class is composed of those who are employed by the state or who render service in connection with offices of government.[10]

The absence of individual self-sufficiency and the division of labour necessarily implied the exchange of products between individuals and social groups, but exchange occupies discursively a subordinate space in Greek social theory. Thus Plato's discussion is based on a reversal of Smith's later proposition that the division of labour is limited by the extent of the market; for Plato it is the extent of the market that is determined by the nature and variety of the division of labour.[11] It is often thought – as Marx did – that in this respect Xenophon was much closer to a Smithian conception, for in his famous remarks on the preparation of food at the Persian court Xenophon points not merely to the significance of specialisation in the kitchens, but also makes the general observation that 'the various trades are most developed in the large cities . . . [where] because many make demands on each trade, one alone is enough to support a man and often less than one . . .'.[12] This view however cannot be assimilated to Smith's for a variety of reasons, of which the most relevant here is that, in common with all other ancient writers,

Xenophon's primary interest is in craftsmanship and quality rather than in increased productivity.

Exchange and accumulation in fact were only seen as legitimate if limited by the needs of maintaining the household and the *polis* rather than as ends in themselves. Aristotle, of course, made a rigorous distinction between use value and exchange value – 'a shoe may be used either to put on your foot or to offer in exchange' – but he insisted that 'exchange should be carried on just so far as to satisfy the needs of the parties'.[13] Hostility to accumulation – an ideology to which Marx was later to ascribe an important influence in preventing capitalist development in antiquity – can only be understood in the wider context of attitudes to labour and the prerequisites for political judgement and participation to which Plato and others subscribed, although there is some dispute concerning the extent to which these views were held by other than an aristocratic minority increasingly insecure in the wake of democratisation and the development of commerce.[14]

'The history of the internal conflict and civil wars in Athens', as Littman has pointed out, 'is the history of the struggles of the lower classes to obtain from the upper classes equal citizenship rights and a full share in the rule of the state.'[15] By the time Plato and Aristotle were composing their major works in the fourth century BC the 'lower orders' had won considerable concessions from the aristocratic oligarchies which dominated throughout the archaic and classical periods. Rights of citizenship and thus political participation in the Assembly had been extended to peasants, craftsmen and labourers, while rich merchants and traders had transformed themselves into considerable landowners. Slaves, moreover, were to be found in all occupations: they were managers of large enterprises, foremen, policemen and mineworkers.

Nevertheless, despite their disagreements on other matters, both Plato and Aristotle insisted that neither traders nor 'mechanics' could be allowed full rights of citizenship in the *polis*. The exclusion of traders should serve as a warning that neither Plato nor Aristotle were simply propounding a distinction between 'manual' and 'intellectual' labour. They discriminated in fact between 'liberal' and 'illiberal' or 'servile' arts, for the fundamental objection was to dependence on others rather than to labour as such. Shame was attached not to building one's own house, for instance, but to dependence on others for a wage or for the sale of products.[16]

Moreover, leisure was seen as an essential precondition for the cultivation of virtue thus excluding traders, peasants, labourers and slaves from citizenship:

> In the best state . . . one that possesses just men the citizens must not live a banausic [i.e. a life of mechanics] or commerical life. Such a life is not noble and not conducive to virtue. Nor will those who are to be citizens live an agricultural life; for they must have leisure to cultivate their virtue and talents, time for the activity of a citizen.[17]

Innate talents and dispositions, as has been said earlier, were seen as the primary determinants of the distribution of individuals to different tasks and this notion undoubtedly played an important part in preventing any rigorous distinction in Greek thought between the differentiation of tasks *per se*, on the one hand, and the existence of occupational specialisation among individuals and groups on the other. Thus in most of the passages that have been exhibited here, it is clear that there is a systematic conflation between the necessity for task differentiation and the justification of occupational specialisation, although arguments for the exclusion of 'mechanics' from citizenship rights also incorporated Xenophon's observation that the 'illiberal arts' not only 'spoiled' the bodies of the workmen, 'forcing them to sit still and live indoors, and in some cases to spend the day at the fire', but also involved 'a serious weakening of the mind' and a diminished capacity for social intercourse and defence of the state.[18]

The doctrine of innate talents also allows the Greek authors to present the division of labour as *naturally* and inextricably involving hierarchy and inequality in the distribution of authority and rewards, a proposition that discursively intersects with a system of classification of 'arts' and 'trades' which, for instance, makes no discrimination between a carpenter, trader, 'agriculturalist' and wage-labourer. While the first is an 'occupation' or craft the other categories cut across occupational classifications by introducing criteria based on the ownership of means of production and a sectoral division in production.

Both Plato and Aristotle were of course acutely aware that inequalities in property were a powerful source of social conflict – Aristotle developed a sophisticated 'sociology' of political forms based on variations in the distribution of ownership – and one passage in *The Politics* introduces a specific distinction between an occupational and a property classification: 'the same people may be soldiers, farmers, craftsmen . . . But the same people cannot be rich and poor, and that is why the prime division of classes in a state is into the well-to-do and the propertyless.'[19] Indeed Aristotle urged the creation of a 'middle-class' state, 'for when one set of people possesses a great deal and the other nothing, the result is either extreme democracy or unmixed oligarchy'.[20] But this should not be allowed to obscure the point that in Greek thought the principles underlying the taxonomy of forms of the division of labour systematically conflated different rules of classification, especially those based on occupation, with others determined by the ownership of property.

Plato – like Socrates before him – made ingenious use of analogies from the division of labour to support his (grossly undemocratic) proposals for the 'healthy' or just state. Justice in social life, he contended, meant each person devoting himself to that which his ability best fitted him, 'keeping to what belongs to one and doing one's job'.[21] Each craft required specialised talents, thus 'mutual interchange and interferences' could only result in 'destruction to our state'. This implied, moreover, that it was wholly inappropriate to allow the framing of laws and the practices of government to be carried out by other than specialists, possessors of the knowledge of good and evil, expert 'physicians of the soul' whose prescriptions for spiritually diseased men and cities carry with them, as Bambrough observes, an absolute and unchallenged authority.[22]

The doctrine of souls and Plato's epistemology of 'forms' combine with this notion of justice as a *techné* to yield the proposition that there must be a special group whose exclusive occupation is to rule. Within each individual, injustice could only arise from a conflict between the elements of the soul, when they 'trespass on each other's functions', or when one of them 'sets itself up to control the whole when it has no business to do so, because its natural role is one of subordination to the control of its superior'.[23] On the other hand, only the expert philosophical intellect can penetrate beyond the layman's world of commonsense experience to apprehend and reveal the essential realities which alone can provide a framework for running the state.[24]

Plato's use of analogies from the ethic of *techné* cannot, however, be employed to attribute to him (or to Socrates and Aristotle) any real respect for ordinary craftsmen and artisans. As Wood and Wood argue, it seems more appropriate to conclude that Plato adapted to his own purposes a widespread respect for craftsmen in Athens; his own antipathy is reflected in the hierarchy of souls where, in a list of nine, craftsmen and farmers are placed seventh, just above sophists, demagogues and tyrants.[25]

3
Prelude to the Enlightenment

Both Roman and medieval social thought were pale echoes of Greek thinking and for present purposes may be dealt with quite briefly, although the paucity and lack of originality of Roman social and scientific theory raises interesting issues for both the sociology and the archaeology of knowledge.[26]

The Romans retained the distinction between 'vulgar' and 'liberal' occupations, only the latter being deemed fit for 'gentlemen' who on no account could engage in hired manual labour or work in 'mechanical' trades. The wage, as Cicero put it, was a pledge of 'slavery' while 'no workshop', he added, 'can have anything liberal about it'. Occupations associated with 'sensual pleasures' – fishmongers, butchers, cooks, poulterers – appear to have been particularly despised in the official doctrine, although Cicero at least suggested that medicine, together with architecture and teaching ('professions in which either a higher degree of intelligence is required or from which no small benefit to society is derived') carried a certain degree of respectability.[27]

Perhaps the most fundamental difference between Greek and Roman thinking is to be found in attitudes to private property. There is little in Roman law, for example, which reflects Aristotle's injunctions against unlimited private acquisition; it is hardly surprising, as Roll remarks, that while Roman law served as an important basis for the legal principles and practices of capitalism, it was Aristotle who became the philosopher of the Middle Ages and one of the sources of the Canon Law.[28] Medieval reflections on the 'just price', in fact, bore the strong imprint of Aristotelian directives against accumulation, although Christian attitudes to work were less restrictive.[29]

The unique constellation of events which broke down the stable hierarchy of the feudal order and created the Reformation, the scientific revolution and capitalism also made for the re-emergence of secular social theory in western Europe.[30] One fundamental contrast between Greek and feudal thought, and the type of theorising which subsequently developed, concerns the discursive primacy of exchange and circulation. Until the publication of Adam Smith's *The Wealth of Nations* in 1776 – and Smith only effected a partial break – post-feudal thought accorded a theoretical centrality to exchange and circulation which decisively separated it from Greek and feudal conceptions on the one hand, and the classical Political Economy of the early nineteenth-century Ricardians on the other.[31]

The discursive primacy of exchange – reflected in a systematic conflation between money and wealth – did not entirely exclude a consideration of production or an analysis of the category of labour, and in the late seventeenth and early eighteenth centuries several works commented on the significance of division of labour, although the term is still not used. These writings also establish other significant departures from Greek feudal thought which came increasingly to mark such discussions in the eighteenth century: an emphasis on productivity rather than quality as an argument for the differentiation of tasks, a concern with divisions *within* rather than merely between 'trades', 'employments' and 'manufactures', and an awareness that the possibilities of exchange limited the level to which the division of labour could be carried out. A good example here is Petty in whose writings all these propositions can be found in one form or another. In *Political Arithmetick* (1690), for instance, he points out that 'those who live in Solitary places, must be their own Soldiers, Divines, Physicians, and Lawyers'; elsewhere he remarks that 'the Gain which is made by Manufactures will be greater, as the manufacture itself is greater and better', and then provides an interesting illustration:

> In the making of a Watch, If one Man shall make the Wheels, another the Spring, another shall Engrave the Dial-plate, and another shall make the Cases, then the Watch will be better and cheaper, than if the whole Work be put upon any one Man.[32]

Similar observations can be found in other works, of which the best known is *The Fable of the Bees* where Mandeville had drawn the conclusion that a society was more 'Rich, Potent and Flourishing' the greater 'the Variety of Trades and Manufactures . . . and the more they are divided in many branches'.[33]

Moreover, the term 'labour' had also begun to acquire, especially in the eighteenth century, a meaning only dimly present in earlier thinking. Labour as a general, abstract category begins at this time to be increasingly conceptualised as the major element in the costs of production, the primary source of the difference in value between input and output which determined national and individual wealth.[34] At the same time, under the impact of an emergent capitalism, 'labour' came more and more to mean a measurable component in the production of commodities for sale on an ever extending market, while the terminological usage already overlapped with the idea of 'labourers' as a special group divorced from the means of production and separate from capital as a component in the production of commodities.[35] It is in the context of these social and conceptual transformations that the re-emergence of the division of labour as a central theme in the social and economic thought of the Scottish Enlightenment should be understood.

Another basic difference between feudal and post-feudal social thought is marked by the appearance in the latter of a figure almost totally absent from feudal (and classical Greek) discourse: the 'individual'.[36] The connections between this conceptual rupture and the development of capitalism are too well known to require detailed elucidation here: it is sufficient to note that a variety of social transformations – the breakdown of localised feudal ties, the rise of the commercial bourgeoisie, the growing encroachment of the market on social relations, the emergence of large numbers of labourers divorced from the means of production – gathered momentum from the end of the fifteenth century to produce what Macpherson has called 'possessive individualism'.[37] On the other hand it must be remarked that there is a tendency to stretch the concept of individualism to a point where it begins to distort historical and discursive specificities. In a recent study, for example, Lukes has pointed out that the term itself embraces a series of eleven analytically distinct meanings.[38] It cannot be assumed, that is, that the 'individual' of Hobbes or Locke is the same 'individual' who appears in Smith or Ferguson, or later in utilitarianism. Thus, while it is clear that without recognising the centrality of conceptions of *individual* self-interest to Enlightenment theories of social order it is impossible to grasp the vast gulf that separates their discourse on the division of labour from that of the Greeks, it is at the same time necessary to urge caution in the use of terms like 'individualism' to telescope and dissolve what were in fact a *series* of theoretical transformations which culminated eventually in utilitarianism and then in neo-classical economics.[39]

The 'individualism' of the Enlightenment, like its conceptualisation of division of labour, derives its meaning and significance within a specific discursive formation some of the elements of which can now be explored.

4
The Scottish Inquiry: The Division of Labour and Modes of Subsistence

It is in the period of the eighteenth-century Enlightenment, one of its foremost historians tells us, that 'the prehistory of the social sciences gives way to its history'.[40] While the development of social science can no doubt be endlessly reconstructed and its origins continually resited from different standpoints – sometimes with scant regard for discursive specifities – Montesquieu's *De l'esprit des lois*, Ferguson's *Essay on the History of Civil Society*, Millar's *The Origin of Ranks* and many other writings do testify to a profound interest, probably without precedent in intellectual history, in the nature of social formations and their evolution.[41] The social thought of the period received a powerful stimulus from the growth in knowledge of other, totally different societies and cultures provided by travellers. Indeed there developed an incipient cultural relativism; the eighteenth century discovered the world to be infinitely more varied and interesting than it had ever been.

It was especially in Scottish 'conjectural history', as it came to be described, that conceptualisations of the division of labour played a central role, although other Enlightenment thinkers – particularly Turgot – were not unaware of its importance.[42] An interest in the immense productive potential of the division and subdivision of tasks had already been generated, as we have seen, by Petty, Mandeville, and Hutcheson; the latter, as Professor of Moral Philosophy at Glasgow from 1730 to 1746 and one of Adam Smith's teachers, was one of the men primarily responsible for the new spirit of enlightenment in Scottish universities – the 'awakening of Scotland' as it has been called – which emerged in the context of rising economic prosperity and rapid social transformation.[43]

It was Smith, however, in his lectures and then in *The Wealth of*

Nations who popularised the concept of division of labour and gave it a theoretical importance and centrality it had never possessed since the decline of the Greek city-state – indeed Schumpeter goes so far as to suggest that nobody either before or after Adam Smith ever thought of putting so heavy a burden on the concept, although as we shall see the same could equally well be said of the young Marx.[44] The first edition of *The Wealth of Nations* was published in 1776; by 1789 the book had gone through five, and had begun to exert an enormous influence both in England and abroad.

The very first sentence of *The Wealth of Nations* announces the central importance of the division of labour:

> The greatest improvement in the productive powers of labour, and the greater part of the skills, dexterity and judgement with which it is anywhere directed, or applied, seem to have been the effects of the division of labour.[45]

Smith immediately adds that it is a mistake to believe that there is a qualitative difference between the division of labour in the workshop and that operative in society as a whole: it is merely the case that the former is more easily visible and thus more striking.[46]

Using as his example the making of pins – an illustration almost certainly borrowed from the 'Epingle' article in the *Encyclopédie* – Smith attributes the great advance in the productivity of labour to three major advantages stemming from 'the separation of different trades and employments from one another'. In the first place, by reducing every individual's task to 'some one simple operation' and making it the 'sole employment of his life', the division of labour is said necessarily to increase his 'dexterity'. The second advantage is consequent upon 'the saving of the time which is commonly lost in passing from one species of work to another', while the third is supposed to flow from the invention of machinery which, according to Smith, is considerably more likely when the whole attention of workers' minds is directed towards a single object 'than when it is dissipated among a great variety of things'.[47] In this context Smith also comments upon the growth of specialisation in intellectual life and the advantages of this are described in the same glowing terms.

Nevertheless, it is worth pointing out that Smith's reasoning is far from flawless. The saving of time, for example, requires only that there is a separation of tasks, not a specialisation by individuals; a pin-maker could spend one day drawing wire, the next day straightening, the next cutting, and so on. There is in Smith's thinking – as there had been in Greek theory – too easy a conflation between the differentiation of tasks and *occupational specialisation*. The notion of increased dexterity, on the other hand, can be questioned on the grounds that the skills Smith refers to were easy to acquire, while his belief in an increased propensity to innovate appears to be contradicted by his own subsequent assertion, to which I shall return, that the specialised labourer 'has no occasion to exert his understanding, or to exercise his invention'.[48] Moreover, it is worth noting that in dissolving the differences between occupational specialisation in general and the specific contours assumed by the division of labour in the workshop, Smith obliterated the possibility of a significant discursive insight – later recovered by Ure and Babbage and then developed by Marx – concerning the social-control functions of the separation of tasks in the factory as part of the reorganisation of work by which capital established its hegemony over labour in the production process.[49] At the same time, Smith erected an obstacle to the recognition of the immense productive potential of a centralised and deliberately coordinated division of labour in the factory, quite unlike the 'spontaneous' differentiation of trades that had grown up in society, coordinated only by the 'invisible hand' of the market.[50]

Indeed, Smith saw the division of labour as rooted in an inherent propensity in human nature to 'truck, barter and exchange one thing for another' rather than in conscious direction by 'human wisdom'.[51] In addition, his discussion was underpinned by the general notion that the division of labour in society coincided with *individual* self-interest, the two being combined into an integrated whole by the process of exchange. Though 'man has almost constant occasion for the help of his brethren', Smith thought it self-evident that the necessary exchange and assistance for 'our dinners', for instance, could not be obtained by appealing to 'the benevolence of the butcher, the brewer, or the baker' but only from 'their regard to their self-interest': 'We address ourselves, not to their humanity but to their self-love and never talk to them of our own necessities but of their advantages.'[52]

Had Smith elaborated his ideas no further, the contrast with Plato's discussion, for example, would have nevertheless been striking: Smith's thinking accords theoretical primacy to an innate tendency for *exchange*, and the division of labour is deduced from this as a necessary consequence; in Plato's theorisation, as we have seen, exchange is a secondary phenomenon derived from the centrality of division of labour as a practice necessitated by the absence of individual self-sufficiency. 'Human nature' is inserted into both schemes as a theoretical device to resolve the problem of the origins of the division of labour, but the discursive space occupied by this category is determined by the differential role played by exchange in the two conceptual systems.

Smith made the break with Greek thought even more radical by explicitly distancing himself from the suggestion that the division of labour reflected differences in natural ability between individuals:

> the very different genius which appears to distinguish men of different professions, when grown to maturity, is not upon many occasions so much the cause, as *the effect of the division of labour*. The difference between the most dissimilar characters, between a philosopher and a common street porter, for example, seems to arise not so much from nature, as from habit, custom and education [my emphasis].[53]

The emergence of this sociologism owed much to the dominant empiricist epistemologies of the time, and especially to the philosophical and educational writings of John Locke who had enunciated the doctrine of the mind as *tabula rasa* at birth, acquiring shape and structure through the absorption of impressions provided by the senses – a doctrine which was, among other things, obviously more supportive of a liberalism struggling to break down the crippling hereditary privileges of feudalism than the Platonic notion of innate human differences could have been.[54]

Smith was not alone in popularising the concept of division of labour; in one form or another most of the eighteenth-century Scottish intellectuals incorporated the idea into their writings, and with a similar sociological sensibility. For instance, John Millar, in his *Historical View* pointed to the fact that:

> in every polished nation, the labour and application of the people is usually so divided as to produce an endless variety of characters in those who follow different trades and professions . . . all those who earn a livelihood by the exercise of separate employments,

> whether liberal or mechanical, are led, by the different objects in which they are conversant, to contract something peculiar in their behaviour and turn of thinking.[55]

Ferguson's *Essay on the History of Civil Society* (1767) is also conceptually organised around the primacy of the division of labour in social and economic life, although it is worth remarking that neither Millar nor Ferguson were able to argue the case for its necessity with the same clarity and forcefulness as Smith, and nor did they attempt to connect up the division of labour in a systematic fashion to problems of exchange and value.

It was Smith who placed at the forefront of his analysis the proposition that the extent of the market limits the degree to which the division of labour can be carried out, thereby neatly overthrowing the assumptions of classical Greek thinking on the subject:

> As it is the power of exchanging that gives occasion to the division of labour, so the extent of this division must always be limited . . . by the extent of the market. When the market is very small, no person can have any encouragement to dedicate himself entirely to one employment, for want of the power to exchange all that surplus part of the produce of his own labour, which is over and above his own consumption.[56]

In this context Smith made a sharp contrast between town and country, the former with its more highly developed commerce allowing for a greater division of employments and trades.[57] In addition Smith regarded the division of labour between agriculture, mainly confined to the country, and manufacture, primarily located in towns, as perhaps the single most important differentiation in production and exchange in the history of any social formation and the one most likely to lead to a self-sustaining process of economic growth:

> The great commerce of every civilized society, is that carried on between the inhabitants of the town and those of the country . . . The gains of both are mutual and reciprocal, and the division of labour is in this, as in all other cases, advantageous to all the different persons employed in the various occupations into which it is subdivided.[58]

The question of exchange, for Smith, naturally led to an inquiry into the basis of prices and thus to a discussion of the 'value' of commodities. He began with the general abstract proposition that in a society characterised by the division of labour and exchange, the exchange of commodities is in essence the exchange of social labour: each individual relies upon the labour of others to provide him with commodities he is unable to produce himself. In this context, the value of any commodity which a person wishes to exchange for other commodities is equal to the quantity of labour which it enables him to buy. 'Labour, therefore, is the real measure of the exchangeable value of all commodities.'[59]

On the basis of this insight Smith developed a notion that was later to be transformed into a theory of exploitation by the early socialists and then by Marx, that the owner of a fortune possesses in essence a 'quantity either of other men's labour, or . . . of the produce of other men's labour, which it enables him to purchase or command'.[60] Smith was also the first to develop what was to become a widely influential model of the class structure of 'commercial' societies, the three-part division into landlords, wage earners and capitalists, reflecting the segmentation of the land and labour of every country into three types of revenue: the 'rents of land', the 'wages of labour' and the 'profits of stock'.[61]

In keeping with the excitement and curiosity of an age that was beginning to discover new forms of social organisation – especially in the New World – the Scots attempted to explore the role of the division of labour and its relation to social inequality by examining the structure of 'primitive' social life; the inquiry was guided by an evolutionary scheme which linked these societies to contemporary western societies in a continuous chain. 'All of a sudden', as Nisbet has said, 'the atmosphere was filled with the words "origins", "stages", "advancement", and "development".'[62] The use of an evolutionary framework was justified on the grounds that extant simple societies were the 'nursery' or 'cradle' of contemporary complex societies, so that to understand the origins of the latter it was necessary to study the former.[63]

Two theoretical propositions underpinned the historical investigations that followed and both bear a resemblance to the principles of historical materialism that Marx and Engels were to advance in the nineteenth century.[64] The first was well stated by William

Robertson, Principal of Edinburgh University:

> In every inquiry concerning the operations of men when united together in society, the first object of attention should be their mode of subsistence. Accordingly as that varies, their laws and policy must be different.[65]

The theorem was firmly embedded in their outline of historical stages, for these all represented different modes of subsistence and, implicitly, levels of technological development. Ferguson referred to this evolution as passing from a 'rude' to a 'polished' state, occurring in three stages: a 'savage' period, characterised by fishing and hunting; 'barbaric' society, defined by herdmanship; and finally 'civil society', embodying the development of commerce and manufactures, an advanced division of labour, and accompanied by a decline in the importance of kinship and the emergence of a complex legal system.[66] Smith distinguished four stages to Ferguson's three, but the basis of the developmental typology was almost identical: hunting, pasturage, agriculture and finally commerce.[67]

The second general principle which informed the Scottish investigations gave to property relations a key role in determining the character of social and political structure. The clearest justification for this procedure was provided by Ferguson, on two major grounds: first, because 'the members of any community, being distinguished among themselves by unequal shares in the distribution of property, the ground of a permanent and palpable subordination is laid'; and second, because 'forms of government take their rise, chiefly from the manner in which the members of a state have been originally classed'.[68]

The discussion of property forms was always included in the delineation of modes of subsistence, together with an analysis of the nature of governmental structures which corresponded to them. Both Smith and Ferguson agreed that there was little private property in hunting societies and no 'government' either, for as Smith rather bluntly put it, 'till there be property, there can be no government, the very end of which is to secure wealth, and to defend the rich from the poor'.[69] Property only becomes important in the pasturage (or 'barbaric') stage, flocks and herds becoming coveted objects; this stage also sees the first beginnings of government. It is in the next stage, agriculture, that property receives its greatest extension because it is then that land, hitherto commonly held, is parcelled out among private individuals. Civil society exhibits the fullest development of private property, and also an extensive 'separation of arts and professions'.

Civil society was seen to embody the greatest extension of individual liberties relative to all other stages, but the Scots were well aware of the inequalities hidden behind this appearance of freedom. Ferguson neatly summed up this view by pointing out that 'the establishments which serve to defend the weak from oppression, contribute, by securing the possession of property, to favour its unequal division', while Smith argued that in the endemic conflict between 'workmen' and 'masters' in commercial society the latter always had the upper hand for they could 'hold out much longer' in any dispute and were 'always and everywhere in a sort of tacit, but constant and uniform combination, not to raise the wages of labour above their actual rate'.[70]

The origins and development of the division of labour remained a constant preoccupation in these historical investigations and the relevant remarks are to be found interwoven with the broader analyses of modes of subsistence and forms of property and inequality. The division of labour between the sexes, to start at the beginning, received extensive treatment in John Millar's *The Origin of the Distinction of Ranks*.[71] In 'rude' and 'barbarous' ages, he argued, there is little private property and thus 'the pride of family' is also unknown, but 'the female character', being unsuited to 'martial employments' and incapable of rivalling the other sex in 'strength and courage' results in the restriction of women to domestic activities.[72]

Nevertheless, if the sexual division of labour was prior to and independent of the development of property, this is not so for occupational specialisation in general as this depends for its extension on the prior establishment of private property. Although hunting societies had chiefs who usually occupied their positions on grounds of courage and ability in war, Millar argues that they were unable to perpetuate their high position because there was little opportunity for acquiring a surplus which could be transmitted.[73] With the invention of taming and pasturing and, subsequently, with the development of agriculture there arises the possibility of a more permanent and stable system of 'ranks' because inequalities can be perpetuated within families; this is especially true of the agricultural stage for it gives rise to property in land and therefore 'the most valuable and permanent species of wealth'.[74] The establishment of private property provides the essential foundation for occupational differentiation. 'The simplicity of early ages', according to Millar, 'admits of little distinction between the master and his servants, in their employments or manner of living . . . By the introduction of wealth and luxury, this equality is gradually destroyed.'[75] Ferguson's explanation of the development of private property and the division of labour parallels Millar's. It is only when men 'are secured in the possession of what they fairly obtain', he argues, that 'the habits of the labourer, the mechanic, and the trader are gradually formed'.[76]

Although the term 'division of labour' was used by Smith, Millar and Ferguson primarily to denote occupational specialisation, it is important to note at this point that as with the Greeks there is no rigorous distinction between 'ranks' and 'orders' on the one hand, and 'occupations' on the other: the terms 'trades', 'employments' and 'professions' embraced a whole variety of groupings from merchants and 'owners of stock' to 'labourers' and 'mechanics'.[77] This conflation of different systems of classification will no doubt be found to have many theoretical and social conditions of existence, but it is worth remarking that in the case of classical Greece and the Enlightenment *one* possible condition can be located in the inherent structure of pre-capitalist modes of production and those in transition to capitalism. In both cases the *absence* of vast numbers of the population divorced from their means of production means that divisions in occupation coincide with divisions in ownership, rendering it unlikely that theoretical importance would be attached to making any systematic distinction between classifications based on occupational specialisation and those based on ownership of the means of production and exchange. Smith's elaboration of a three-part class structure marks the beginning of a break with this particular form of taxonomic assimilation, but it is nowhere coherently integrated into his overall theorisation and, as we shall see, Marx managed to effect a rupture with it only in his later writings.[78]

As I have shown earlier, there are several fundamental discontinuities between Enlightenment and Greek thinking on the division of labour. To these another must now be added: the *critique* of the division of labour. Xenophon had already drawn attention to the harmful effects of 'mechanical' labour, but it is only in the eighteenth century, with the beginnings of the factory system, that the crippling effects of the minute subdivision of tasks became a significant issue of social and moral concern. Smith's famous critique made its appearance in his *Lectures on Justice* and in the second volume of *The Wealth of Nations* in a section on the 'Institutions for the Education of Youth'. In a commercial society with its highly developed division of labour, Smith tells us, the work of most people becomes confined to one or two very simple operations, with disastrous consequences because 'the understandings of the greater part of men are necessarily formed by their employments'. Smith then goes on to describe the effects of the division of labour on 'the understandings' in a remarkable passage that is worth reproducing in some detail:

> The man whose whole life is spent in performing a few simple operations . . . has no occasion to exert his understanding, or to exercise his invention . . . He naturally loses, therefore, the habit of such exertion, and generally becomes as stupid and ignorant as it is possible for a human creature to become. The torpor of his mind renders him, not only incapable of relishing or bearing a part in any rational conversation, but of conceiving any generous, noble or tender sentiment, and consequently of forming any just judgement concerning many even of the ordinary duties of life. Of the great and extensive interests of his country he is altogether incapable of judging; and unless very particular pains have been taken to render him otherwise, he is equally incapable of defending his country in war . . . His dexterity at his own particular trade seems, in this manner, to be acquired at the expense of his intellectual, social, and martial values. But in every improved and civilized society this is the state into which the labouring poor, that is, the great body of the people, must necessarily fall, unless government takes some pains to prevent it.[79]

Smith was not alone amongst the Scottish theorists in remarking upon these consequences; in the *Essay* Ferguson is equally horrified by, and critical of the fact that 'mechanical arts' seem to flourish only by a 'total suppression of sentiment and reason', and succeed most 'where the mind is least consulted, and where the workshop may, without any great effort of imagination, be considered as an engine, the parts of which are men'. And he was quick to note that the consequences were not the same for the *owner* of industry – the latter's work was such as to encourage 'general reflections' and the 'enlargement of thought'; while his 'genius' was cultivated, that of the 'inferior workmen' lay wasted and undeveloped.[80]

In this context one should consider another element introduced by Smith into his discussion of the allocation of labour: the division between 'town' and 'country' and the differently organised subdivision of tasks within each. In keeping with his general critique, he concluded that because the subdivision of tasks in agriculture had not reached the proportions prevalent in industry – the farm worker had often to plough, to sow and to reap, and sometimes even to make and repair his own tools – the agricultural worker remained intellectually much less impoverished. Though he might be less accustomed to 'social intercourse', and his 'voice and language more uncouth', his intelligence, his judgement, and his 'discretions' continued to be far superior to that of the 'mechanic' in the town.

It is important to bear in mind that Smith's critique of the division of labour occurs in the context of a discussion about the education of youth. On the whole Smith was opposed to state education, but his desire to ameliorate the worst excesses resulting from the never-ending subdivision of tasks led him to argue for a minimum provision by the state for educating the children of the labouring poor in reading, writing and 'accounting' (arithmetic). *Smith's motives were not merely altruistic; they were also political.* 'An instructed and intelligent people', he believed, would be much less prone to the 'delusions of enthusiasm and superstition' which could otherwise provoke the most 'dreadful' disorders. A little education would make the labouring poor much more respectful, and in turn would ensure more respect for the people on the part of those in authority. The less educated the people, the more likely that they would be 'misled into any wanton or unnecessary opposition to the measures of government'. 'An instructed and intelligent people are always more decent and orderly than an ignorant and stupid one.'[81] The protagonists in the debate about Smith's 'two views on the division of labour' would do well to bear his political motives in mind.[82]

Smith's remarks demonstrate the fundamentally limited nature of his critique of the division of labour. Politically the Scottish Enlightenment remained wedded to liberalism and the emergent capitalist order, and this is reflected in the scepticism with which its major representatives regarded any schemes for the establishment of egalitarian social relations.[83] In this context perhaps the most interesting argument was Hume's, based on the concept of scarcity, and developing in this regard propositions already powerfully employed by Locke in the previous century for a justification of private property.[84]

'For what purpose', Hume asked rhetorically,

> make a partition of goods where everyone already has more than enough? Why give rise to property, where there cannot possibly be any injury? Why call this object *Mine*, when, upon the seizing of it by another, I need but stretch out my hand to possess myself of what is equally valuable? Justice, in that case, being totally USELESS, would be an idle ceremonial.

But could scarcity be abolished and human equality reign? Hume's views on this were rather ambivalent, for on the one hand he thought that a combination of nature's generosity and human improvement could be sufficient to enable an equitable distribution by which 'every individual would enjoy all the necessaries, and even most of the comforts of life'; on the other hand – and almost in the same breath, as it were – he pronounced ideas of equality 'impractical' and 'pernicious'.[85]

Hume may or may not have been a liberal in any clearly defined sense, but his ambivalence towards equality – like that of Ferguson and Smith – typifies the contradictions of classical liberalism, trapped between having to justify a formal equality of individuals and an inequality of reward and property at the same time, a dilemma made even worse by the development of a sociological sensibility and an empiricist psychology which suggested that differences in ability could well be the *result* rather than the *cause* of contemporary inequalities and the allocation of labour. The fact that at various points in their writings the Scots included sharp critiques of the deleterious effects of the division of labour only adds to their difficulties.

5
Hegel

Smith died only a year after the French Revolution and before the impact of the industrial revolution on restructuring the social order could be fully understood. But he had a profound influence on the generation of thinkers in the early part of the next century who tried to make sense of the social currents unleashed by the French and industrial revolutions. It was especially in Germany – ironically a country yet to experience either a bourgeois or an industrial revolution – that Smith's writings and those of the Scottish Enlightenment had the most influence. Not surprisingly the ideas were viewed, evaluated, absorbed and reworked through an intellectual tradition very different from the hard-headed empiricism of the Scottish Enlightenment. In the process they were transformed to yield a new discourse which combined the traditional preoccupations of German Idealism with a social philosophy more appropriate to the particular, uneven development of the German social formation of the late eighteenth and early nineteenth centuries.

It is both impossible and unnecessary, however, to provide here a detailed consideration of Hegel's social philosophy or metaphysics.[86] The discussion which follows merely attempts to draw out some significant themes from his writings. It is important to understand, in the first place, that for Hegel and his generation of German intellectuals – Goethe, Schiller, Hamann and Hölderlin being the other prominent figures – an overriding ideal was defined by the need to transcend the fragmentation of personal and social life produced by the division of labour and social differentiation, and to recreate a coherent personal experience by the formation of an integrated community.[87] Their writings are permeated by an idealisation of the Greek *polis* which in their romantic vision becomes a culturally homogeneous social entity free from divisions, allowing each individual to develop his potential and to live as a 'whole' man. This integrity of culture and personal life had been destroyed, they argued, by the predominant thrust of specialisation in the modern age; Schiller, for instance, complained that a 'rigid separation of ranks and professions' had destroyed the 'inner harmony of human nature' and had set up a 'disastrous conflict' which 'set the totality of its powers at variance'.[88]

This critique of specialisation and differentiation may well have been a response to the cultural fragmentation and political heterogeneity of contemporary Germany, as Marcuse argues, but it borrowed much of its conceptual vocabulary from the writings of the Scottish Enlightenment.[89] Indeed, Hegel seems to have read Ferguson while still a schoolboy in Stuttgart. In his very early writings he envisaged a solution to the crisis of fragmentation in the creation of a folk-religion built around symbols and ritual deeply rooted in the culture and traditions of the people, integrating the individual once more with society. But this vision was soon tempered by the recognition that any intellectual solution was unlikely to be fulfilled without concomitant changes in social and political conditions. He thus welcomed the French Revolution; but only to be disillusioned by its aftermath. In the period from 1801 to 1807 Hegel seems to have fundamentally altered his perspective: from changing the world to reinterpreting it in a way that would enable individuals to feel at one with it.

Yet there remained an essential continuity in Hegel's general social and economic analysis of the contemporary *malaise*: many of the ideas that appear in the maturer *Philosophy of Right* are prefigured in early writings that remained unpublished in his lifetime – the *System der Sittlichkeit* (1802–3) and the two versions of lectures known as *Realphilosophie* I and II delivered by Hegel at the University of Jena in 1803–4 and 1805–6.[90] One such theme is the postulated relationship between the division of labour, social fragmentation and the individual's lack of control over the social process.[91]

Of crucial significance here is the unique character of Hegel's conception of labour, which also gives a distinctive meaning to his usage of 'division of labour'.[92] For Hegel 'labour' is not merely a category within political economy but a central feature of human existence; it is the instrument through which man comes to know and understand his world; it is the form in which he acquires self-consciousness as well as transforms his environment. It is also used by Hegel to overcome the philosophical problem of the relationship between subject and object: labour becomes in his doctrine the middle term between subject and object. Work, moreover, is seen as a liberating activity; complex networks of social interdependence ensure that individual labour fulfils social needs while at the same time expanding the range of social desires.

Although self-consciousness, freedom and labour are thus interconnected in Hegel's discourse he believed that labour also contained the possibility of man's emasculation, and this in two ways: in the first place, because the division of labour which is necessitated by growing social needs requires for its coordination the development of exchange. Exchange mediates and makes possible the pattern of interdependence and reciprocity characteristic of modern societies, but at the same time means that the individual loses control over his products and work becomes 'an alien power (*eine fremde Macht*) over which he has no control'.[93] The individual within this system fails to understand the way in which he is integrated into a structure which has become a nexus of 'incalculable, blind interdependence'. The domination of social relations by exchange is condemned by Hegel for the way in which economic fluctuations become an endemic feature as a consequence. 'Whole branches of industry which supported a large class of people', Hegel says, 'suddenly fold up because of a change in fashion or because the value of their products fell due to new inventions in other countries.'[94]

Hegel also points to a second form in which labour contains the seeds of its own emasculation: the subdivision of tasks gradually reaches a stage at which much labour becomes dull and mechanical and furthermore is often combined with poverty. The effects of class thus superimpose themselves on the division of labour, and indeed Hegel postulates a natural and automatic transition from the division of labour to the development of classes, as in an important passage in *The Philosophy of Right*:

> The infinitely complex, criss-cross, movements of reciprocal production and exchange, and the equally infinite multiplicity of means therein employed, become crystallised, owing to the universality inherent in their content, and distinguished into general groups. As a result the entire complex is built up into

> particular systems of needs, means, and the types of work relative to those needs, modes of satisfaction and of theoretical and practical education, i.e. into systems, to one or other of which individuals are assigned – in other words, into class divisions.[95]

A polarity between wealth and poverty Hegel regarded as an inevitable feature of commercial society, but in linking poverty with mechanical and stupefying labour Hegel introduced a third term, property, which enables him to link class and alienation at work in a striking manner. Thus he points out that if wealth is 'one side of the picture', the other is 'the subdivision and restriction of particular jobs'. 'This results', Hegel adds, 'in the dependence and distress of the class tied to work of that sort, and these again entail inability to feel and enjoy the broader freedoms and especially the intellectual benefits of society.'[96] The crucial barrier encountered by the poor 'consists of external objects with the special character of being property . . . and hence . . . [their] recalcitrance is absolute'.[97] The extent to which *The Philosophy of Right* in fact prefigures some of the themes of Marx's early works is particularly evident in a remarkable passage:

> Single products of my particular physical and mental skill and of my power to act I can alienate to someone else and I can give him the use of my abilities for a restricted period . . . By alienating the whole of my time, as crystallised in my work, and everything I produced, I would be making into another's property the substance of my being, universal activity and actuality, my personality.[98]

This potentially radical critique of commercial society, however, is not followed by any comprehensive proposals for transforming the social order. Hegel urged state intervention in economic activity to temper the worst excesses of inequality and poverty but regarded the preservation of distinct classes as a crucial antidote to the atomisation endemic in modern society. An individual's membership of a class was seen to mediate between him and the wider context: 'A man with no class is a mere private person and his universality is not actualised.'[99] Part of the responsibility for the limited nature of Hegel's reformism also lies in his view on property.

Despite the link he established at various points in his writings between property and alienating work, and between property and domination, his basic presuppositions were such as to preclude any move towards greater equality through a change in property relations. Hegel saw the development of private property as an inevitable, necessary and desirable process accompanying the application of human labour; the excess that a man produces over and above his needs is transformed into private property, and is a crucial embodiment and extension of the human personality. Private property proclaims man's existence, transforms it from mere subjectivity and is inextricably related to his social acceptance as a person; this is reflected in the fact that other individuals abstain from trespassing upon private property and that legal structures develop to protect its sanctity. 'The rationale of property', Hegel argues, 'is to be found not in the satisfaction of needs but in the suppression of the pure subjectivity of personality. In his property a person exists for the first time as reason.'[100]

But this indissoluble link between property and personality obviously raised the problem of the propertyless in contemporary society: were they to be denied the right to express and affirm their personalities, to transform their existence from 'mere subjectivity'? Hegel regarded the equalisation of property as an unrealisable ideal, but was forced to concede that 'the inference from this (that is, the connection between property and personality) is that *everyone must have property*' [my emphasis].[101]

Expressions such as these support the claim often made that *implicit* in Hegel's writings is a need for the dialectical transcendence of commercial society. Hegel's own thought, however, reached an *impasse*; it was left to the socialists, already flexing their muscles as Hegel's career was drawing to a close to advocate a step that Hegel would have found unpalatable: a fundamental reorganisation of the social order.[102]

6
The Early Socialists

To treat the early socialists as a homogeneous group would be highly misleading. A wide gulf separates Fourier, for example, from Thompson and Hodgskin, or Saint-Simon and the Babouvists. What unites these different strands is their opposition to the individualist liberalism of the day and their critique of *laissez faire*, of the notion that competitive capitalism could be left to regulate itself without conscious intervention, planning and the development of cooperative institutions to counteract the anarchism and egoism of market society.[103] Another commonality also needs emphasis, though it is of a different kind for it serves to distinguish the early socialists from the Marxist tradition: very rarely do their writings contain the argument that the establishment of socialism required the revolutionary expropriation of the bourgeoisie, or that the main actor in this drama would be the mass of propertyless factory labourers or *proletariat*. Suggestions of this kind were hinted at but did not become the core doctrine of any socialist school until the industrial working class began to emerge as a significant political and economic force in Britain and France in the 1830s.

Limitations of space necessitate here a highly selective discussion of the early socialists and this section will revolve mainly around a brief consideration of the ideas of Fourier, Saint-Simon, and the Ricardian Socialists. And in studying the writings and careers of Fourier and Saint-Simon one cannot help observing that the early history of socialism could perhaps be written as the rise to prominence of men whose claims to fame could simply have rested on their eccentricity. As Lichtheim has said of François-Marie-Charles Fourier (1772–1837), 'With the best will the reader of his works cannot altogether discard the impression that the dreamer in him on occasion ventured beyond the merely fantastic.'[104] But his political writings were much admired by Marx and Engels and, as Lichtheim adds, some of Fourier's ideas contained brilliant insights: possibly none more so than the notion that instinctual repression was at the root of much human misery.

The idea that bourgeois industrial civilisation ignored the genuine needs of human nature formed, in fact, the cornerstone of the Fourierist vision. This was regarded as especially true of the repression of sexuality and its corollary, the condition and status of women. Fourier's *phalanstères* – small horticultural communities – were to be based on the complete equality of the sexes and to contain few restrictions on the expression of sexuality. Private property, however, was to be preserved and the organisation of the communities seems to have accommodated a considerable amount of inequality, for reward was proportional not so much to needs as 'work, capital and talent', though Fourier did recommend that a 'social minimum' be guaranteed to all members of the community.[105]

What makes Fourier particularly interesting here is that he was a firm opponent of occupational specialisation and the division of labour; though one should, perhaps, not make too much of the theoretical anthropologism underpinning his opposition, which derived from what he called:

> the eleventh passion, the *Butterfly*, which impels men and women to flit from pleasure to pleasure, to avoid the excesses that ceaselessly plague the people of civilisation who prolong a job for six hours, a festival for six hours (and that during the night) at the expense of their sleep and health.[106]

Fourier's opposition to excessive specialisation seems also to have been a product of his close acquaintance with the condition of textile workers in Lyons, and one of his (seven) conditions for the promotion of 'industrial attraction' was that:

> Work sessions must be varied about eight times a day because a man cannot remain enthusiastic about his job for more than an hour and a half or two when he is performing an agricultural or manufacturing task.[107]

Fourier maintained that there was nothing intrinsically degrading about, say, collecting garbage or labouring on a farm. The work only became unattractive and humiliating if one was forced to *become* a garbage collector, or farm labourer (or clerk).

Fourier's is primarily a critique of industrialism rather than of the specific form it took in early capitalism. Many, indeed, have doubted whether Fourier can properly be called a socialist at all. And one might justifiably entertain the same doubts about Henri Saint-Simon (1760–1825), though the doctrine that came to be associated with his name in the late 1830s was distinctly socialist. In any case, the term 'socialism' itself only acquired popular currency after he had departed from the scene, and he saw himself as a theorist of *industrial society per se*, believing that he had understood the logic of the new form of social organisation that was evolving out of the ruins of agricultural and mercantile Europe.[108]

Not surprisingly – given the emphasis on industrialism – the decisive concept Saint-Simon chose was *production*, and the lines of social conflict he sketched in his analysis derived primarily from a division between 'producers' and 'non-producers'. The famous parable in *L'Organisateur* – contrasting the possible consequences to France of the death of her most eminent industrialists, scientists, artists, and artisans, with the death of all the most important nobles and bureaucrats – is only the most graphic illustration of a theme that always pervaded his grand schemes.[109] This was coupled with an emphasis on 'work', interpreted as almost the only justification for man's existence (Saint-Simon often used it to distinguish 'good' from 'evil' classes).[110]

Though the division of labour between producers and non-producers is a constant *motif* in Saint-Simon's writings, the detailed 'physiology' of classes never remained the same, sometimes changing in response to political events, sometimes in response to rebuffs by members of cherished classes – and sometimes, it seems, for no intelligible reason.[111] The group that suffered most from his prevarication was the class of *savants* (sometimes including both scientists and non-scientists, sometimes composed only of scientists) in whom Saint-Simon had originally placed all his faith as the inaugurators of a new 'Science of Man', a 'Social Physiology', which would eradicate evil and usher in an age of peace and prosperity.[112]

The indifference of the scientists to his schemes infuriated Saint-Simon, and he began to woo industrialists (and later, bankers) to support his schemes. The essential components of his vision were that those who worked and 'produced' should hold the reins of power, and that these producers should cooperate to plan production in a rational and efficient manner. The most typical label applied to the producer was *industriel*, defined in the *Catéchisme des industriels* of 1823 as 'a man who works to produce, or who puts within the reach of different members of society one or more material means of satisfying their needs or their physical tastes'.[113]

The *industriels* included propertied, propertyless, and scientists, but usually pride of place went to industrial entrepreneurs and scientists (hence the justification for labelling Saint-Simon's vision 'technocratic'). Though the amelioration of the condition of the working class formed an important part of his programme, Saint-Simon recognised no conflict of interest between the 'captain of industry' and the labourer. He saw in the division between manual and intellectual labour, however, sufficient grounds for subordination; this is clearly expressed in a speech he composed in 1821 to convince industrialists of the worth of his system, and which workers were to address to their employers:

> You are rich, and we are poor. You work with your brains, we with our hands. As a result of these two fundamental differences between us, we are and should be your subordinates.[114]

Saint-Simon, though a meritocrat, was no egalitarian; he saw inequality as the natural concomitant of differential ability. Hence the division of labour became at one and the same time the basis of, and the justification for, inequality of reward and ownership.

His socialist credentials actually owe much to the radicalisation that his doctrine underwent at the hands of his followers, Enfantin, Bazard, Rodrigues and Leroux: by advocating the abolition of private property they managed to effect a decisive rupture with the liberalism which had in the final analysis continued to hegemonise the discourse of their master although, despite their awareness of the dangers of excessive specialisation, they continued to uphold what they termed 'the three great divisions of the social body' based on the division of labour between fine arts, the sciences and industry.[115] Educational reform occupied an important place in their strategy for social transformation, each individual being entitled, they claimed, to a scheme of instruction divided into 'sympathy', the 'rational faculty' and 'material activity' – the sources of the five arts, the sciences and industry respectively – which would partially overcome a basic division of labour that was inevitable in an industrial society.[116]

In Britain meanwhile the foundations of socialist theory were being laid by an ingenious use of Ricardo's attempted reconstruction of political economy into a rigorous discourse on the nature of production and distribution. In the chapter 'On Value' in his *On the Principles of Political Economy and Taxation* (1817), Ricardo had managed to rid the labour theory of value of most of the confusions which had forced Smith to abandon it; embodied labour could now function as an invariant standard for the value of commodities, besides operating as a theorem in an overall conceptualisation which purported to explain how the 'produce of the earth' came to be divided 'among three classes of the community; namely, the proprietor of the land, the owner of the stock or capital necessary for its cultivation, and the labourers by whose industry it is cultivated'.[117] Ricardo himself was no socialist, but his notion that the values of the instruments of production were themselves dependent on embodied labour left his doctrine open to the interpretation that profits represented a 'deduction' from the produce of labour, consequent upon command over the means of production.[118]

On the other hand, it is clear that the abolition of private ownership of the means of production cannot logically be the only conclusion to follow from this doctrine even if social justice could be said to entail that the labourer received the full produce of his labour, an injunction that could equally be realised by allowing each individual to own whatever instruments he had produced with his own labour. The political indeterminacy of this radicalised version of Ricardian economics is reflected in the fact that the Ricardian Socialists were to be found in a variety of contemporary movements: John Gray (1799–1883), for instance, was for a time an ardent Owenite, while Thomas Hodgskin (1783–1869) defended the right of private property and involved himself in the establishment of a workers' college, the London Mechanics Institution. And the additional intellectual sources they drew upon to supplement their neo-Ricardianism also varied, from Locke, in the case of Hodgskin, to Utilitarianism, which allowed William Thompson (1775–1833) to support his argument for Owenite mutual cooperation with an appeal to the principle of 'the greatest happiness of the greatest number'.

The Ricardian Socialists were, nevertheless, united in the belief that labour was not merely the measure of value but the source of all wealth, and both Hodgskin and Gray almost transmuted this into a general philosophy of labour:

> The necessity for man to labour . . . is a law of the universe, like the principle of gravity . . . It is a law of our being, that we must eat bread by the sweat of our brow; but it is reciprocally a law of the external world, that it shall give bread for our labour, and give it only for labour.[119]

The conclusions that those who did not work were unproductive, parasitic and a drain on national wealth was easy to draw from this premise. On the basis of calculations derived from Patrick Colquhoun's *Treatise on the Wealth of the British Empire* (1814) Gray triumphantly announced that the productive labourers of Britain, estimated by him to constitute only a third of the population, received a bare fifth of the national income even allowing for the expenses of a number of workers engaged in 'government, direction and superintendence' who, though unproductive, were 'useful' and would be necessary in any society. To eradicate poverty it was only necessary to redistribute income in accordance with contributions to production.[120] Hodgskin agreed: 'The capitalist being the mere *owner* of the instruments, is not, as such, a labourer.' The real workers must therefore share their product with 'unproductive idlers'.[121]

Ricardo is hardly ever cited in these texts and Hodgskin, especially in his *Popular Political Economy*, seemed more concerned to secure respectability and scientificity by establishing a direct line of continuity with Smith's *Wealth of Nations*. Indeed, the division of labour is singled out by Hodgskin as the fundamental cause of increased productivity, although many of Smith's propositions are skilfully reversed. If labour is the source of all wealth then the division of labour and the development of complex skills must have *preceded* the accumulation of stock, while inventions in turn must have preceded the division of labour.[122] Nor was Smith thought to be correct in locating the origins of the division of labour in an inherent human propensity for exchange: although the division of labour necessarily implied exchange, its roots lay according to Hodgskin in differences in natural talent and disposition amongst individuals, and in variations in climate, soil and other 'natural circumstances' which generated and provided an overall organisation of the territorial division of labour as well.[123] Although Smith had correctly identified in the extent of the market a basic limit to the possibilities for the 'appropriation of men to distinct and separate occupations', Hodgskin noted that this limit was synonymous with 'the number of labourers communicating with each other'; unproductive labourers, in this case primarily the owners of the means of production who employed wage labour, thus represented a very significant barrier to an expansion of the market, the further subdivision of work and therefore the productivity of a nation.[124]

The rights of the worker to the whole produce of his labour could thus be said to follow from the science of political economy, although in his *Natural and Artificial Right of Property Contrasted* (1832) Hodgskin felt it necessary to annex Locke's argument that a real right to property could only be established by demonstrating that an individual had 'mixed' his labour with the objects that were in possession. Indeed, in this work Hodgskin's philosophy of labour assumes an almost Hegelian dimension, with property becoming an extension of personality. 'It is as impossible for men not to have a notion of a right to property, as it is for them [not] to want the idea of personal identity. When either is totally absent', Hodgskin concludes, 'man is insane.'[125] But unlike Hegel, Hodgskin remained unimpressed by Smith's critique of the effects of the endless subdivision of tasks on the worker. Manual labour, we are told in *Labour Defended*, 'invigorates' rather than 'enfeebles' the mind; if the labourers 'reap no benefit from division of labour', if their tasks become more burdensome rather than lighter, this can only be, Hodgskin argues in *Popular Political Economy*, because of the 'unjust appropriation' of the product, 'usurpation and plunder in the party enriched, and . . . consenting submission in the party impoverished'.[126]

Not all the Ricardian Socialists agreed with Hodgskin's conclusions. Men like Gray, Thompson and later, Bray, all of whom had been considerably influenced by Owen's attempts to create associations of mutual cooperation, advocated changes which carried a much greater potential threat to the forms of production and political representation typical of early capitalist industrialism. Robert Owen's own socialist credentials are as debatable as those of his

French contemporaries, Fourier and Saint-Simon.[127] But in his *Report to the County of Lanark* (1821) Owen had at the very least paved the way for the Ricardian Socialists, arguing that 'manual labour, properly directed, is the source of all wealth', that 'the natural standard of value is, on principle, human labour', and that the labourer is 'justly entitled to his proportion' of wealth.[128] The existence of generalised competition and the introduction of money, Owen suggested, had made it impossible for the labourer to get a fair reward and had made man 'ignorantly, individually selfish', 'placed him in opposition to his fellows' and had 'engendered fraud and deceit'.[129] In a system dependent on unregulated competition, the need to obtain the cheapest labour possible meant that labourers were deprived of the full value of their product; the consequence was an artificially depressed level of demand which could only be restored by the abolition of money and its replacement, according to Owen, by a form of exchange in which both the price of commodities and the medium of exchange accurately reflected embodied labour.[130]

A precondition for the successful operation of this new system of equitable exchange was, for Owen, the setting up of largely self-sufficient associations or villages of mutual cooperation composed ideally of 800 to 1200 people. Although Owen did not envisage the abolition of private property – 'the landholder and capitalist would be benefited by this arrangement in the same degree with the labourer' – he did propose changes in the division of labour and the allocation of tasks. The 'minute' division of labour was seen to be synonymous with the 'division of interests' and both in turn were 'only other terms for poverty, ignorance, waste of every kind, universal opposition throughout society, crime, misery and great bodily and mental imbecility'.[131] Education in the villages of cooperation, Owen therefore proposed, would be organised in such a way that each child would become capable of performing a variety of mental and manual tasks, and it would eventually be possible to eliminate the 'mere animal machines, who could only follow a plough, or turn a sod, or make some insignificant part of some insignificant manufacture'; instead 'there would spring up a working class full of activity and useful knowledge, with habits, information, manners and dispositions, that would place the lowest in the scale many degrees above the best of any class which has yet been formed'.[132]

Owen's vision of a transformed division of labour, like Fourier's, has served as a constant source of inspiration to socialist movements. In his own time the writings of many of the Ricardian Socialists betray a strong Owenite influence and in some cases the proposed reforms of production and labour go well beyond anything envisaged by Owen in his *Report*. William Thompson in *Labour Rewarded* (1827) cites The London Co-operative Society and its articles of agreement as one of the best examples of an 'efficient mode of attaining this great end, "securing to labour the whole products of its exertions"', while Gray appended a full version of these articles to his *Lecture on Human Happiness*; these principles of mutual cooperation provide an interesting insight into the radicalisation of Owenism and its interpenetration with Ricardian Socialism.[133]

The London Co-operative Society's model rules envisage, for example, a form of self-government which is intensely democratic and guarantees women equal rights with men in all respects.[134] Moreover each member of the association is required to learn skills necessary for both agriculture and manufacturing tasks, while the youth are required to perform all menial and unpleasant domestic tasks which cannot be performed by means of rotation amongst all adult members. Indeed the rules specify that any occupation which remains unpleasant and unhealthy despite mechanisation and rotation between members should 'be altogether banished from the Community'.[135] The rotation of occupations emerges as a central feature of the organisation of the community, so that pleasant and unpleasant tasks are more equitably distributed, although the rules allow those with a larger share capital to escape some of the initial labour necessary to erect the buildings and prepare the land for farming.

The Fourierist, Owenite and Ricardian schemes for the restructuring of the division of labour mark a significant departure from assumptions about the inevitability of occupational specialisation dominant in Greek and Enlightenment theory and practice. This decisive rupture in the early nineteenth century was accompanied by an important discursive transformation: the emergence of 'class' as a distinctive term in political economy.[136] The eighteenth century had been characterised by a rather uneasy coexistence between the feudal residues of 'ranks' and 'orders' on the one hand, and the terms 'labouring poor' and 'workmen' on the other which were used to describe the new groups of dispossessed, especially in the centres of growing urban and industrial concentration. The vocabulary of 'class' developed in response to the need to conceptualise economic and political relations in an emergent social order, which was rapidly obliterating localised communities integrated by legally binding ties of fealty and dependence between employers and employees, and for which the terminology of 'stations', 'estates' and 'ranks' had been more appropriate.

The penetration of capitalist social relations produced the nominally free individual whose only property resided in the capacity to labour and whose only tie with the employer was the 'cash nexus'. In contrast with Smith, therefore, the Ricardian Socialists, for instance, referred to the 'working classes' or 'labouring classes' and located their conditions of existence in a generalised structural opposition between 'capital' and 'labour'. 'Throughout this country at present', Hodgskin said at the beginning of *Labour Defended*, 'there exists a serious contest between capital and labour . . . The capitalists and labourers form the great majority of the nation', he concluded, 'so that there is no third power to intervene betwixt them. They must and will decide the dispute of themselves.'[137]

7
The Deskilling of Labour and the Factory System: Ure and Babbage

The Ricardian Socialists had been fascinated by the mechanical inventions spawned by the industrial revolution and which were reported daily in the contemporary press and discussed at the meetings of the Mechanics' Institutes. But neither they nor Smith before them had grasped the true significance of the introduction of machinery in the context of capitalist relations of production. Their definition of the division of labour remained tied to forms of work organisation based primarily on manufacture rather than factory production: their analyses presumed, that is, that mechanisation and the division of labour consisted largely of the technical rationalisation of manual operations, rather than a fundamental restructuring of patterns of work and the differentiation of skills as part of capitalist strategies for control and regulation of the labour process.[138] A more adequate conceptualisation of the division of labour in the machine-based factories of early industrial capitalism emerges in the writings of Andrew Ure (1778–1857) and Charles Babbage (1792–1871).

Ure was not, nor did he pretend to be, a social theorist of note. But he was a keen observer of the factory system and his *Philosophy of Manufactures* (1835) was intended as a systematic account of the principles underlying 'the applications of mechanical and chemical sciences to the arts' for 'proprietors and managers of factories', as he explained in his preface to the volume.[139] Ure manifests a clear awareness that the development of the factory system had made Smith's famous analysis redundant and now could only mislead 'the public mind as to the right principles of manufacturing industry'.[140] Indeed, he went so far as to suggest that 'the division . . . of labour . . . is little thought of in factory employment'. The whole point of the factory system was the replacement of skills altogether by the machine, a process which thereby overcame a crucial barrier to production: insubordination and indiscipline. As Ure observed:

> wherever a process requires particular dexterity and steadiness of hand, it is withdrawn as soon as possible from the cunning workman, who is prone to irregularities of many kinds, and it is placed in charge of a peculiar mechanism, so self-regulating that a child may superintend it.[141]

The eventual outcome of this process is a system of production in which skilled workers are replaced by 'mere overlookers of machines'; the 'union of capital and science' would reduce skill requirements to a level which could be 'speedily brought to perfection in the young'.[142] The 'automatic factory', Ure argued, had advantages for both workers and capitalists. For the worker, Smith's critique of the division of labour no longer had any relevance because 'the operative needs to call his faculties only into agreeable exercise', being rarely 'harassed by anxiety and fatigue', and indeed Ure thought that the worker could now enjoy many 'leisure moments' for 'amusement and meditation'. For the owner, the 'self-acting machine' not only reduced the bargaining power of workers, but also considerably cheapened the cost of their labour because 'journeymen of long experience' could now be replaced by children. 'This tendency', he concluded, 'shows how the scholastic dogma of the division of labour into degrees of skill has been exploded by our enlightened manufacturers.'[143]

In his discussion of the cheapening of labour power consequent upon deskilling Ure does not refer to Charles Babbage, although in his *Economy of Machinery and Manufactures* of three years earlier (1832) Babbage, Professor of Mathematics at Cambridge, one of the founders of the British Association for the Advancement of Science and of the Statistical Society, and an extraordinary inventor, had devoted a whole chapter to this subject. Babbage opens his discussion of the division of labour by insisting upon a distinction which Smith had found both misleading and irrelevant: the division into 'trades', probably originating 'in a very early stage of society', and the division of labour in the 'workshop' which only develops in societies 'in which there is a great competition between the producers'.[144] This is a crucial discrimination, allowing Babbage to conceptualise a specific dimension of the relations of production in the factory which is impossible to appropriate theoretically if, like Smith, the two types of division of labour are assimilated to one another.

By treating the factory as a separate unit of analysis, Babbage is able to bring to light an important advantage of the division of labour which had hitherto been neglected (except, he says, by Gioja in his *Nuovo Prospetto delle Scienze Economiche* of 1815):

> That the master manufacturer, by dividing the work to be executed into different processes, each requiring different degrees of skill and force, can purchase exactly that precise quantity of both which is necessary for each process; whereas, if the whole work were executed by one workman, that person must possess sufficient skill to perform the most difficult, and sufficient strength to execute the most laborious, of the operations into which the art is divided.[145]

Using examples from contemporary pin manufacture and its wage rates Babbage demonstrates that by using skilled workers only on skilled jobs and unskilled workers only for mechanical tasks, the cost of making pins is nearly four times less than it would be if only skilled workers were employed in the entire process:

> The higher the skill required of the workman in any one process of a manufacture, and the smaller the time during which it is employed, so much the greater will be the advantage of separating that process from the rest, and devoting one person's attention entirely to it.[146]

And in a remarkable chapter, 'On the Division of Mental Labour', Babbage demonstrates that in compiling mathematical tables to facilitate the application of the decimal system, the French had quite explicitly used this system of division of labour so that only a handful of eminent mathematicians had been required to set out the general principles for the new tables, while most of the numerical work was done by men who had no knowledge of mathematics beyond 'simple addition and subtraction'.[147] To this discussion Babbage appended his famous plan for what he called a 'calculating-engine' – what later came to be called the 'computer' – which, he argued, also followed the principles of the division of labour.[148]

Babbage was critical of 'combinations' among both 'workmen' and 'masters': strikes by the former resulted eventually either in higher prices or in the invention of labour-saving devices; when owners came together they either thwarted technological innovation by combining against inventors who might otherwise have demanded a high price for their inventions, or they contrived to enforce monopolies and thus raise prices.[149] But his idiosyncratic politics are not really relevant here; what is significant is that in his analysis – and up to a point in that of Ure – the conceptualisation of division of labour is made appropriate to a social order in which the patterns and rhythms of industrial labour are decisively structured by the requirements of capital accumulation. It is in Marx's work that this connection is systematically elucidated; the long, complex and uneven route that led him to it is the subject of much of the rest of this book.

Part II

Marx and the Division of Labour: the Early Writings

1
The Sources of Marxian Theory

It is commonly argued that much of Marx's greatness lay in his powers of synthesis, in the way he was able to combine some of the best elements of previous social analysis into a powerful and compelling theory of the historical and social process. Lenin, for example, once remarked that the distinctiveness of Marx's work lay in the hitherto unprecedented combination of German philosophy, French socialism and English political economy.[1] This observation contains more than an element of truth, but like all shorthand expressions it oversimplifies. The point is that Marx did not simply confront three *separate* traditions which he then proceeded to weave together in his own work: English political economy, as I have pointed out, had already been appropriated and reworked by German idealist philosophy and had found an important place in Hegel's writings (a fact which certainly did not escape the youthful Marx, who was quick to point out that despite his idealism Hegel's standpoint was firmly rooted in modern political economy).[2] Moses Hess, in turn, had already drawn the attention of the Young Hegelians to socialism as the practical realisation of the Feurbachian humanism which they had so eagerly embraced in the aftermath of the disintegration of the Hegelian system.[3] And English political economy had been deployed even earlier to provide a theoretical foundation for the nascent socialist movement in Britain.

The publication of many of Marx's works that were not available to Lenin, and subsequent Marx scholarship, have also served to underline the uneven nature of Marx's intellectual development. His theory was not born all of one piece and Marx himself was acutely conscious of the unfinished nature of his project. It is equally clear that he did not encounter previous discursive formations as fully fashioned and integrated wholes, ready for consolidation and synthesis. To put it slightly differently, Marx did not encounter these traditions in the neat chronological and taxonomic order set out in the first part of this book. Although it is possible to make too much of individual biographical influences and developments, it is worth remarking in the present context that Marx came to Smith and Ricardo, for example, *after* he had thoroughly studied Hegel, while references to Ure and Babbage appear only after a first 'synthesis' between German philosophy, French socialism and English political economy had already been achieved in the *Economic and Philosophic Manuscripts of 1844*.

Moreover, despite the fact that it is possible to argue, for instance, that the more sophisticated conceptualisation of the division of labour that appears in *The Poverty of Philosophy* (1847) owed something to Marx's reading of Babbage, it cannot be assumed that his understanding and use of Babbage remained the same in *Capital* twenty years later. Marx often reread important texts, reworking their themes and concepts in the light of his own intellectual and political development. In the 1850s Marx once again studied Ricardo's work and found himself compelled to reappraise his significance, and that of Hegel too. The synthesis, if such a term is applicable at all, was much more a process rather than an accomplished fact at any one point in the formation of Marx's thought.

These qualifications to Lenin's canonical judgement are especially helpful in understanding Marx's shifting and complex use of the concept of division of labour. Marx's analysis of the division of labour, as I shall argue later, changed considerably during the course of his career, but this shift can only be properly understood in the context of his uneven and sometimes selective appropriation of the diverse traditions that may be said to constitute his discursive and political heritage.

2
Marx and the Abolition of the Division of Labour: Two Views or One?

Adam Smith's 'two' views on the division of labour have been the subject of a long-standing scholarly controversy; Marx's own views on the division of labour, no less than Smith's, abound in ambiguity and require careful interpretation. To some extent, at least, this is not surprising; indeed, part of the purpose of my earlier discussion of the concept of division of labour was to underline the variability of its usage before Marx and the complexity of its interrelation with a variety of social and political theories, ranging from those of Plato to the early socialists. In other words, it was perhaps to be expected that his own discourse would register some of the conceptual difficulties and incommensurabilities that had already become apparent in analyses of the division of labour. The problems of meaning and interpretation, partly generated by historical transformations in the concept of division of labour and, in turn, reflected in Marx's work, are in addition considerably exacerbated in his texts by the rapidity and complexity of his intellectual development, even after he had fashioned a doctrine that may be broadly recognised as 'Marxist'.

As I have explained earlier, this book attempts to focus on one central aspect of this relationship between the formation of Marx's discourse and the role ascribed to the division of labour: the idea of the *abolition* of the division of labour (and, as we shall see, exchange). The view that the division of labour, however conceptualised, could and should be abolished as a central structural feature of social organisation emerged, as I have pointed out, in the early part of the nineteenth century and was an important theme in Fourierist and Owenite conceptions of an alternative social order. And the early socialists were not alone in regarding the division of labour as a potent force in the process of dehumanisation and fragmentation that accompanied capitalist industrialism: a protest was simultaneously registered in the writings of German romanticism and here presupposed the validity of evaluations stemming mainly from eighteenth-century political economy and moral philosophy.

That the concept of division of labour has a key function in Marx's own work is not in dispute; nor can it be seriously doubted that in his earlier writings Marx believed it to be both necessary and possible to abolish the division of labour, and that he regarded this as a fundamental precondition for the full and proper development of socialist society. For the present it is only necessary to cite a famous passage from *The German Ideology* (1846) to document Marx's belief in this principle:

> in communist society, where nobody has one exclusive sphere of activity but each can become accomplished in any branch he wishes, society regulates the general production and thus makes it possible for me to do one thing today and another tomorrow, to hunt in the morning, fish in the afternoon, rear cattle in the evening, criticise after dinner, just as I have a mind, without ever becoming hunter, fisherman, shepherd or critic.[4]

But did Marx continue to believe in this idyllic picture as a vision of socialism throughout his life? The question is obviously one of more than academic interest; it touches on the very core of a major ideological issue given the importance of Marxism as a key political force in the contemporary period.

The belief that Marx may have altered his views – albeit reluctantly – on the possibilities of completely transcending the division of labour in future society is not unfounded. In the third volume of *Capital*, for example, Marx seems to argue that the day-to-day labour necessary for individual and social survival will always remain unrewarding, the realm of freedom, creativity and fulfilment only being possible outside this sphere of material production:

> In fact, the realm of freedom actually begins only where labour which is determined by necessity and mundane considerations ceases; thus in the very nature of things it lies beyond the sphere of actual material production . . . Freedom in this field can only consist in socialized man, the associated producers, rationally regulating their interchange with Nature . . . and achieving this

> with the least expenditure of energy . . . But it nonetheless still remains a realm of necessity. Beyond it begins that development of human energy which is an end in itself, the true realm of freedom, which, however, can blossom forth only with this realm of necessity as its basis. The shortening of the working day is its basic prerequisite.[5]

The publication of Marx's early works, the recent upsurge of interest in Marxism and the consequent publication of scholarly and critical studies on Marx of a very high order have, between them, failed to resolve this crucial question in any authoritative and decisive manner. Before elaborating my own analysis of Marx's views on the division of labour and its abolition, it is worth setting out the different standpoints on this issue adopted by interpreters of Marx's thought, although it must be pointed out that there does not appear to have been to date a serious and sustained debate about the precise nature of Marx's views on the abolition of the division of labour.

Of those commentators who have had access to both the early and the later writings of Marx, by far the largest number have seen little contradiction in his views on the abolition of the division of labour. Some of these authors explicitly focus on the problem of the division of labour in future society; others remain silent on this *particular* issue, but emphasise the unity of the earlier and later works, especially as expressed through the concept of alienation, and so can be said to implicitly support the interpretation that Marx did not alter his thinking on the abolition of the division of labour in any significant manner. Among the influential representatives of the first tendency one may include Shlomo Avineri, Robert Tucker, Eugene Kamenka, Ernest Mandel, T. Bottomore and K. Axelos.[6] Works by Istvan Mészáros, Roger Garaudy, Raya Dunayevskaya and Bertell Ollman provide notable instances of the second tendency.[7]

Some interpreters of Marx, however, have emphasised the discontinuity that seems apparent between the two passages – and others that I shall cite later – on the nature of labour and the division of labour in socialist society as envisaged by Marx. Important advocates of this interpretation include David McLellan, Alfred Schmidt and Michael Evans.[8] The most sustained attempt to chart the evolution of Marx's shifting pronouncements on the abolition of the division of labour is to be found in McLellan's essay, which presents a threefold periodisation of Marx's views on this subject: first, the early Marx of the *1844 Manuscripts*; second, the Marx of *The German Ideology*, still in the process of formulating historical materialism; and third, the mature Marx of the *Grundrisse* and *Capital*.[9]

McLellan assimilates the problem of 'division of labour' to the broader question of Marx's views on human nature and his conception of 'the whole man', arguing that in the *1844 Manuscripts* Marx holds an *artistic* model of properly human work, a conception that obviously makes no distinction between work time and leisure time. A similar ideal pervades Marx's picture of man and work in *The German Ideology*, except that he now makes a distinction between 'constant desires' which are inextricably linked to man's generic nature and 'relative desires' which originate in and are moulded by particular forms of social and economic organisation. The abolition of the division of labour in communist society would make possible the realisation of all those desires and needs which were not limited and deformed by 'particular conditions of production and exchange'.

The *Grundrisse* of 1857, according to McLellan, marks a radical shift in Marx's perspective on work and the division of labour and he suggests that a major reason for this transformation lies in the mature Marx's understanding of the possibilities opened up by the development of advanced machinery and, especially, automation. That is, Marx realised that technological advances would soon make it possible for people to work for only a fraction of the time that they spent on it now in order to satisfy their needs 'and could not be said to be impoverished even if they were doing the same job during those few hours'.[10] At the same time, McLellan argues, Marx's emphasis changes from a conception of fully human work as one which unites theory and practice to a view which stresses much more exclusively its intellectual aspects. Taken together, these two modifications in Marx's position are said to lead to the very different perspective on the abolition of the division of labour advanced in his mature work, from which McLellan cites a passage very similar to the one I have already cited from *Capital*: 'Free time, the time one has at one's disposal, that is the true wealth; and this time is not, like labour, regulated by an external aim whose realisation is either a natural necessity or a social duty.'[11]

McLellan's discussion, although interesting and suggestive, is open to some serious objections and does not bear up to examination especially from the alternative standpoint that is adopted and elaborated later in this book. However, before examining the weaknesses in McLellan's interpretation, one major point of agreement with it needs to be stated at the outset: *the major contention of this and subsequent parts of the volume is that Marx did, indeed, change his views on the abolition of the division of labour in future society*, but not in the form nor for the reasons advanced by McLellan.

There are three major difficulties in McLellan's account. First, the view that the mature Marx came to value the more intellectual aspects of work is inadequately substantiated. McLellan cites in support a passage from the *Grundrisse* where Marx sets out the conditions under which productive labour can be characterised as 'free labour'; but nothing in this passage upholds the contention that Marx's emphasis had changed decisively towards the more intellectual elements: 'The labour concerned with material production can only have this [i.e. 'free'] character if (1) it is of a social nature, (2) it has a scientific character and at the same time is general work, i.e. if it ceases to be human effort as a definite, trained natural force, gives up its purely natural primitive aspects and becomes the activity of a subject controlling all the forces of nature in the production process.' The second condition outlined by Marx, especially, embodies the same distinctive combination of theory, practice and control that is visualised in the *1844 Manuscripts*.

Second, it is important to note that McLellan makes no attempt to investigate the relationship between the changes in Marx's views on the abolition of the division of labour and other equally decisive developments that also took place in his theory; especially important in this context is Marx's adoption of the labour theory of value, his elaboration of the theory of surplus value and the consequent displacement of exchange relations and the market as the methodological and substantive starting point for his analysis of classes and exploitation. As I shall argue later, the clues to Marx's changing views on the division of labour are to be found primarily in this theoretical rupture, which was accompanied at the same time by a serious transformation in his conceptualisation of classes and their structural basis in the relations of production.

In McLellan's account one of the main obstacles to a recognition of the significance of the discursive changes in Marx's work outlined above lies in his failure to problematise the role of 'human nature' in the mature writings. By presuming the continuing centrality of the concept of human nature, McLellan necessarily distorts and misunderstands its displacement by the relations of production as the basic starting point and primary object of analysis from which, in turn, a new conceptualisation of the division of labour is derived in the later works. In this context, it is very striking that in McLellan's 'reading' historical materialism is only significant in so far as it historicises Marx's conception of human nature, rather than in producing *new* concepts which effectively begin to displace 'human nature' from discursive centrality.

Finally, McLellan fails to notice that one of the most significant contrasts between the early and mature writings can be found in the treatment accorded the division between mental and manual labour: while the early texts demand the abolition of the division of labour *tout court*, the later writings are concerned much more with a form of social reorganisation which would emancipate society from the crippling effects of the differentiation between mental and manual tasks.

The main purpose of the pages that follow, then, is to rectify a remarkable absence in the contemporary literature on Marx: a satisfactory explanation for the modification in his views on the abolition of the division of labour. Such an account can only be based on close textual examination and a rigorous understanding of the links and discontinuities between the conceptual structure of his earlier and later work. The discussion that follows is unavoidably long and complex; in view of this it is probably helpful to present at the outset a brief summary of my overall interpretation.

I shall argue that in his earlier writings Marx did believe in the possibility of the abolition of the division of labour *tout court* because at this stage of his formation he consistently conflated, and assimilated to one another, the concepts of 'class' and 'division of labour'. The failure to separate out these two elements in his theory meant that the abolition of *classes* became synonymous with the abolition of the *division of labour*. As *one* aspect of this conceptual assimilation Marx conflated class with occupation such that the disappearance of classes automatically entailed the abolition of occupational specialisation. To avoid possible misunderstanding, however, it must immediately be noted that Marx did not think of occupations *as* classes, or *vice versa*, in the manner of some varieties of academic sociology; Marx's assimilation concerned class and the division of labour, as part of a quite different theorisation in which classes are defined in relation to ownership and non-ownership of the means of production.

The absence of conceptual specification in his theory was powerfully conditioned by two factors: first, conflation between 'class' or ownership and various aspects of the division of labour had been endemic in social theory before Marx and to some extent Marx simply took over and reproduced this in his own early work; second, and largely because of the tenacious hold of Young Hegelian notions – especially the concept of alienation – on his thought, Marx at this time firmly believed in the possibility of *total* human emancipation through social reorganisation. The division of labour was seen by Marx as an impediment to this emancipation, and its complete abolition was therefore already presupposed in his vision of liberation and 'disalienation'. The importance of this lies in the fact that it considerably reinforced his propensity for assimilating the division of labour to the phenomenon of class society. That is, in so far as the abolition of classes was seen as the key to human emancipation, the existence of *all* other social phenomena that were subsequently seen as symptoms of the absence of this realisation were regarded as indissolubly linked with class society. This applies as much to the division of labour as to another closely related phenomenon: relations of exchange and commodity production.

In his later writings, however, Marx's theory displays the *beginnings* of a conceptual separation between class and division of labour. One implication of this is that the disappearance of classes with the emergence of a new mode of production does not automatically entail the complete abolition of occupational specialisation. But only the beginnings – the implications of this theoretical transformation are not fully worked out by Marx and nowhere coherently assimilated into his theorisation of historical materialism or his conception of socialism. The modification in Marx's views on the relationship between class and the division of labour, I shall suggest, were chiefly produced by two closely related developments in his thought. First, a theoretical and methodological shift from market relations to 'production' as a basic starting point in his analysis; this led Marx to a recognition of organisational exigencies imposed by processes of material production *as such*, that is, independent of deformations imposed by the existence of classes. Second, and inextricably bound up with this, his espousal of the labour theory of value and development of the theory of surplus value. Together, these discursive transformations led Marx to revise his previously held belief in the possibility of the abolition of the division of labour. He now came to believe that many aspects of the division of labour were unavoidable given the exigencies of labour processes involved, especially in large-scale industrial production, and his main focus shifted to a concern with breaking down the barrier between one key dimension of the division of labour: the division between mental and manual labour. This whole theoretical transformation is also related, as I shall demonstrate, to Marx's more general attempt to break with a class-reductionist theorisation of historical materialism and to grasp, in addition, the significance of possible 'natural' limits to social reorganisation.

3
A Periodisation of Marx's Views on the Division of Labour

While any attempt to divide Marx's discourse into developmental stages is bound to encounter difficulties, a threefold scheme probably constitutes the most adequate periodisation of his changing views on the division of labour: (1) the early writings, from the *1844 Manuscripts* to *The German Ideology* – at this stage Marx has a vision of total emancipation and completely assimilates 'division of labour' to 'class'; (2) a transitional stage, chiefly represented by *The Poverty of Philosophy* (1847), in which Marx separates 'social division of labour' from the division of labour in manufacture – this period also contains some important political writings which register an attempt to detach the analysis of the state from a reduction to 'division of labour' *tout court*; (3) the mature writings, beginning with the *Grundrisse* (1856–7), in which Marx develops the theory of surplus value and begins to separate 'class' from the 'division of labour' in his analysis. I shall examine each period in turn.

It is first necessary, however, to enter a caveat concerning this periodisation. It must be emphasised that the proposed segmentation relates specifically to Marx's views on the division of labour and cannot necessarily function by itself as a representation of Marx's intellectual development in some more general sense although, in so far as any overall interpretation of this development must make reference to his views on class and the division of labour, the periodisation suggested here necessarily carries implications for it. At the same time my account cannot be completely abstracted from a specific conception of Marx's general intellectual formation. Instead of setting out this interpretation separately at this stage, however, I have integrated it into the discussion that follows.

4
Marx's Early Writings: The Prelude to 1844

It is in the *Economic and Philosophic Manuscripts of 1844*, composed after Marx's first serious encounter with classical political economy, that the concept of division of labour makes its appearance in his writings. The use to which Marx puts this concept in the *Manuscripts* and later in *The German Ideology* has a distinctiveness that should not be overlooked: while it is the case that preceding discursive formations had constantly obscured the conceptual dividing line between ownership, 'class' and 'division of labour', Marx managed to produce a degree of conflation between them which was unparalleled. Although this conceptual outcome is obviously partly attributable to underlying forms of taxonomic assimilation already crystallised in the past usage of the concept, it is also necessary to look elsewhere in order to explain the peculiarity of Marx's own theorisation: we have to examine, that is, certain features of the intellectual and political position that Marx had already adopted *before* he composed the *1844 Manuscripts*. Two interrelated standpoints are of key importance in this context: Marx's belief in total, 'universalistic' emancipation, and the theory of class which made the proletariat the supreme instrument of this liberation. Both these strands in his formation crucially mediated his reading of classical political economy and must be regarded as vitally important elements in the development of the distinctive Marxian conflation of class and the division of labour in the early writings.

Thus Marx's views in the *1844 Manuscripts* were a product of the fusion between the two strands outlined above *and* the specific theorisation of class, exchange and the division of labour that he borrowed from political economy. But this was no simple, unilinear, mechanical superimposition: for the theory of class and proletarian revolution which filtered his reading of classical political economy already presupposed some of the insights of this political economy and which Marx had absorbed from Hegel, and to some extent from the early socialists. Hence the importance of my earlier remarks about Lenin's rather mechanical conception of the sources of Marx's thought.

Some of Marx's pre-1844 writings provide excellent illustrations of the extent to which he had already begun to assimilate into his own thinking the results of previous conceptualisations of the relationship between class, exchange and the division of labour. The concept of division of labour, however, is not mentioned at this stage by Marx: it is simply subsumed and presupposed in the broader dialectic of class, exchange, alienation and emancipation that emerges in the course of Marx's critique of Hegel and of bourgeois society. It is not surprising that when Marx does introduce the notion of division of labour, its role is more or less predetermined by the structure of his discourse as it had developed during this critique.

In *The Philosophy of Right*, as I have argued earlier, Hegel had already made some tight conceptual connections between property, exchange, division of labour and 'alienation' in modern society. Marx, after an early period of infatuation with Hegel as a student, subjected parts of the *Philosophy of Right* to a devastating analysis in his *Critique of Hegel's Philosophy of Right* (1843). Another Young Hegelian, Ludwig Feuerbach, had by then exposed Hegel's basic error and in his *The Essence of Christianity* and especially *The Theses for the Reform of Philosophy*, Feuerbach had attempted to put Hegelian analysis back onto its feet as it were by transforming the subject, thought, into a predicate, and the usual Hegelian predicate, man, into the subject.[12] Marx used the new humanist standpoint with great effect to expose the mystifications which shrouded Hegel's theorisation of the state. Whereas Hegel had seen the family and civil society as elements subordinate to the universal spirit of the state, Marx pointed out that the family and civil society were actually 'the presuppositions of the state'; thus 'it is not the constitution that creates the people, but the people which create the constitution'.[13]

Moreover, while Marx agreed that in modern society there existed a bifurcation between two independent spheres, civil society and the state, he pointed out that the egoism of civil society, dominated by commerce, exchange and private property, could not be abolished by conceiving of the bureaucracy in Hegelian fashion as a 'universal class' which could transcend all particular interests. The bureaucracy itself was one particular interest among others in civil society, although by protecting property rights it served to maintain the economic and political power of the landed Junker aristocracy.[14] Any form of parliamentary representation would simply lead to a politicisation of the war of each against all. 'True democracy' could only be realised if private property and private interests ceased to be the basis of political organisation, although it must be pointed out that Marx does not actually advocate the abolition of private property.[15]

The *Critique*, fragmentary and incomplete though it is, provides a powerful indication of the extent to which Marx had already taken over some contemporary propositions on private property, exchange and alienation, many of them deriving in fact from Hegel's own work. The close links established between these different elements in Marx's pre-1844 discourse become even more apparent in an immediately subsequent work: *On the Jewish Question*. Here Marx reiterates the argument that formal political freedom cannot be regarded as synonymous with human emancipation, for the latter requires the abolition of *alienation*, which in turn presupposes that neither private property nor exchange dominate and deform the character of social relationships. The right of property, Marx points out, is simply 'the right of self-interest', the right to dispose of possessions 'without regard for other men and independently of society'. To defend the right of individual property is thus tantamount to defending a social form in which the individual and society remain separate and opposed to each other, although in fact society is no more than man's 'species-being, his species-life itself'.[16] Symptomatic of this alienation of the individual from society, for Marx, is the dominance of exchange and commerce over properly human relationships: 'Selling', Marx says, 'is the practice of externalisation.' And the overriding importance of self-interest and property is reflected in the significance of money: 'Money is the alienated essence of man's labour and life, and this alien essence dominates him as he worships it.'[17]

The next step in Marx's intellectual itinerary coincided with another kind of journey: he travelled to Paris in October 1843 to join Ruge and to establish the *Deutsch-Französische Jahrbücher*, in which *On the Jewish Question* was published in February 1844, on a firmer footing. The same issue of the journal carried another piece by Marx: *Introduction to the Critique of Hegel's Philosophy of Right*, written in Paris. This article marks a decisive transformation in Marx's views. It is the first piece of writing by him which can unambiguously be regarded as socialist; it is also the first time that the decisive role of the proletariat in the transition to socialism is announced. Another important element in his discourse is also clearly represented: the belief in the possibility of total emancipation (although little substantive content is given to this commitment). The doctrine of emancipation is clearly enunciated in Marx's exhortation to be 'radical', 'to grasp things by the root': 'The criticism of religion ends with the doctrine that man is the highest being for man, hence with the categorical imperative to overthrow all conditions in which man is a degraded, enslaved, neglected, contemptible being.' Marx's hopes here derive particularly from the situation in Germany where all major classes – except the embryonic proletariat – lacked political will and effectiveness: 'Radical revolution, universal human emancipation, is not a utopian dream for Germany.'[18]

Marx assigns to the proletariat the key role in bringing about this 'universal human emancipation'; the 'positive possibility' of emancipation, Marx says, is to be found:

> in the formation of a class with radical chains, a class in civil society that is not of civil society, a class that is the dissolution of all classes, a sphere of society having a universal character because of its universal suffering and claiming no particular right because no particular wrong but unqualified wrong is perpetrated on it; a sphere that can invoke no traditional title but only a human title, which does not particularly oppose the consequences but totally opposes the premises of the German political system; a sphere, finally, that cannot emancipate itself without emancipating itself from all the other spheres of society, thereby emancipating them; a sphere, in short, that is the complete loss of humanity and can only redeem itself through the total redemption of humanity. This dissolution of society as a particular class is the proletariat.[19]

The appearance of the proletariat as a central figure in Marx's discourse has provoked considerable debate. Avineri, for instance, has suggested that Marx 'arrives at his idea of the proletariat not through an economic study or an historical analysis, but through a series of arguments and confrontations all of which are within the Hegelian tradition and relate to the Hegelian idea of a universal class'.[20] But this is to ignore the influence on Marx of his reading of the history of the French Revolution which had begun to heighten his sensitivity to the role of classes in social transformations – an understanding that is occasionally and partially evident in the *Critique*; more importantly, it underrates the impact that socialist ideas must have had on Marx as he began to establish contact with radical French and German intellectuals in Paris. 'From October 1843', McLellan notes, 'Marx was breathing a socialist atmosphere and even living in the same house as Germain Mäurer, one of the leaders of the League of the Just whose meetings Marx frequented.'[21]

Nevertheless, if Avineri's remarks are detached from his overall argument and instead connected up with the perspective I am advocating, they yield an important insight: the relationship between the language of 'universality' and the doctrine of total emancipation. In *The Philosophy of Right* Hegel had suggested that the bureaucracy completely eliminated the antinomy between civil society and the state, hence its designation as a universal class. The fact that Marx retains this vocabulary of 'universality' is important as an indication of his search for total solutions and this is clearly evident in the role Marx attributes to the proletariat in the passage cited above, where it is said in fact to be capable of achieving 'the total redemption of humanity'.[22] The theoretical basis for the language of universality and the doctrine of total emancipation is provided, of course, by the concept of alienation and its presupposition of a human essence, a 'species-being', denied in the contemporary epoch but to be fully realised in future society. The particular conception of alienation that informs Marx's thinking – and of the Young Hegelians – at this time clearly bears the imprint of Feuerbach and is especially evident in *On the Jewish Question*: man is seen as essentially a communal being whose essence however is denied by the domination of social relations by competition, private property and self-interest.

The key role assigned to the proletariat, taken together with Marx's espousal of a view which postulated tight links between private property, exchange relations and estrangement, makes it possible to understand why, when Marx did finally incorporate the concept of division of labour into his analysis, he was able to assimilate it so closely to the concept of class: if complete emancipation was only possible through the emancipation of the proletariat (or propertyless) as a class; if 'unqualified wrong' and the absence of emancipation were therefore directly attributable to the existence of private property; and if – this being the crucial element that Marx added *after* his reading of political economy – as a dimension of its 'universal suffering' the proletariat was subjected to the degradation of the division of labour in the factory, it logically followed that division of labour was indissolubly tied to class (or private property) and must necessarily disappear completely with the total abolition of classes and private property.

It is my contention that it was the sort of complex chain of rationalisation outlined above which resulted in Marx's fateful conflation between class and the division of labour. In so far as Marx had already identified *exchange relations* as an endemic dimension of the contradictions and alienation of bourgeois society, certain aspects of the concept of division of labour and its assimilation with the notion of class were implicit in the analysis that Marx had begun to fashion out of a curious amalgam of Hegelian, Young Hegelian and early socialist ideas. Given the double relationship of the concept of division of labour – that is, to exchange and to the differentiation of tasks – it reinforced the tendency to fuse occupational specialisation with the phenomenon of class, a tendency already contained in the reduction of all aspects of the proletariat's degradation and exploitation to its lack of property, and which derived from the combination of the ethic of total emancipation with the putative emancipatory role of the proletariat. As Marx was to put it later:

> the emancipation of the workers contains universal human emancipation – and it contains this, because the whole of human servitude is involved in the relation of the worker to production, and every relation of servitude is but a modification and consequence of this relation.[23]

The actual dramatic emergence of the concept of division of labour into the open from its subterranean existence in Marx's discourse owed much to the reading of classical political economy that he embarked upon during his sojourn in Paris. The young Engels was instrumental in impressing upon Marx the importance of studying economics. They had met in Cologne in 1842 but at the time Marx had remained unfriendly, regarding Engels simply as a member of the Young Hegelian movement from which he had dissociated himself. But meanwhile Engels had been converted to communism by Hess, he had been influenced by the English socialists and had begun to study Smith, Mill, Ricardo and others. His reflections upon them were published in the form of a critique in the pages of the *Deutsch-Französische Jahrbücher*: entitled 'Outlines of a Critique of Political Economy', it made a profound impression on Marx. In it, Engels indicted capitalism and its system of private ownership for producing wanton competition and anarchy in production, endemic crises and impoverishment. And, significantly, he attacked capitalism for its division of labour: referring to the defence of capitalism offered by the economist, Engels asked, 'Is he forgetting that with the division of labour, developed to such a degree by our civilization, a worker can only live if he can be used at this particular machine for this particular detailed operation; that the change-over from one type of employment to another newer type is almost invariably an absolute impossibility for the adult worker?'[24]

Marx immediately began a correspondence with him, thus initiating their long friendship and collaboration which was considerably strengthened by a subsequent meeting in the summer of 1844. Marx began, too, a serious study of economics and in characteristic fashion took copious notes and made extensive comments on about fifteen important authors, including Smith, Ricardo, Say, Skarbek, List, James Mill, Destutt de Tracy, McCulloch, Boisguillebert, Lauderdale, Schultz and others.[25] He began to compose an overall critique of political economy which, however, remained unfinished. The surviving manuscripts were finally published in 1932: the famous *Economic and Philosophic Manuscripts of 1844*. Their content and significance has been the source of well-known controversy, but it is not my purpose to provide a detailed commentary on the text beyond that which is necessary for an understanding of his theorisation of the relationship between class and the division of labour.[26]

5
The Economic and Philosophic Manuscripts of 1844

The central unifying theme in the *Manuscripts* is the alienation of labour under capitalist conditions of private ownership and its transcendence and abolition under communism. The doctrine of total emancipation which, as I have argued, was crucial in enabling Marx to assimilate 'class' and the 'division of labour' in his work is much more clearly articulated here and eloquently expressed. Communism, Marx argues, is 'the positive transcendence of all estrangement'; the abolition of private property, communism:

> is the genuine resolution of the conflict between man and nature – the true resolution of the strife between existence and essence, between objectification and self-confirmation, between freedom and necessity, between the individual and the species. Communism is the riddle of history solved, and knows itself to be this solution.[27]

The vision of communism Marx unfolds in the *Manuscripts* derives much of its force from his remarkable analysis of the alienation of labour and is clearly underpinned by a preconception of truly human, free productive activity. Man's productive interchange with nature is in fact taken as the defining characteristic of the species: 'the productive life is the life of the species'; and Marx is careful to point out that while an animal can also be said to engage in production it 'only produces what it immediately needs for itself or its young'. Man's transformation of nature, on the other hand, is 'free, conscious activity . . . man produces even when he is free from physical need'.[28]

Marx's critique of capitalism, therefore, focuses on the manner in which man and his labour are stripped of their truly human character in a system based on private property and production for exchange and profit. Political economy, he points out, is unable to penetrate the true secret of capitalism: alienated labour. Incapable of visualising any alternative, it simply codifies and legitimises the dominant order: 'political economy has merely formulated the laws of estranged labour'.[29] Economics, like capitalism, dehumanises the worker by seeing him 'only as a working animal – a beast reduced to the strictest bodily needs': 'In political economy *labour* occurs only in the form of *wage-earning activity*.' When the labourer is not working, political economy ignores him and abandons his fate 'to criminal law, to doctors, to religion, to the statistical tables, to politics and to the poorhouse overseer'.[30] The political economist refuses to pass moral judgement on the grounds of a separation between science and ethics, but for Marx this is simply the reflection of alienation and fragmentation in the cultural life of capitalist society: 'It stems from the very nature of estrangement that each sphere applies to me a different and opposite yardstick – ethics one and political economy another.' The separation, Marx argues, is a spurious one for all 'that happens is that political economy expresses moral law in its own way'.[31]

What, then, does the alienation of labour consist of under conditions of capitalist production? Marx identifies at least two central dimensions, the *result* and the *act* of production. Or, as he makes abundantly clear, *class* and the *division of labour*. What Marx does here is to translate and reinterpret the insights gained from his reading of political economy into the language of alienation, and it is through the unification provided by his use of 'alienation' that Marx weaves a tight web between class and the division of labour. The concept of alienation in the *Manuscripts* is expressed in two different terms: *Entäusserung* (vb. *Entäussern*) and *Entfremdung* (vb. *Entfremden*). The first has strong associations with property, in the sense of either selling or renouncing it; the second emphasises a sense of distance in interpersonal relations and, more importantly in the present context, a state of mind, a feeling of something being strange and alien. In the translation used here *Entäusserung* is translated as 'alienation' while *Entfremdung* is rendered 'estrangement'. Marx uses the two terms almost interchangeably, but this is hardly accidental for the two terms are admirably suited to the substantive propositions that Marx links together in his theory: alienation as class relations, as propertylessness, and alienation as a feeling of painful strangeness imposed by the division of labour in capitalist factory production.

The first aspect of alienation manifests itself in the result of production, in the fact that the worker's product is appropriated by another who grows ever more powerful through this process: 'the object which labour produces – labour's product – confronts it as something alien, as a power independent of the producer . . . the more the worker spends himself, the more powerful becomes the alien world of objects which he creates over and against himself'.[32] The fact that Marx is referring here to class and its basis in private property becomes quite clear when the same idea is expressed a number of times elsewhere in the *Manuscripts*, not in the language of alienation but of political economy. What is the source of a country's wealth, Marx asks rhetorically at one point; the exploitation of the worker by the capitalist, he answers, developing the critical potential of Smith and classical political economy. Thus a society's wealth is:

> the result of the accumulation of much labour, capital being accumulated labour; as the result, therefore, of the fact that more and more of his products are being taken away from the worker, that to an increasing extent his own labour confronts him as another man's property and that the means of his existence and his activity are increasingly concentrated in the hands of the capitalist.[33]

Marx postulates an indissoluble link between the loss of the product, the result of production, and the estrangement the worker experiences in the *act* of production in which 'he does not affirm himself but denies himself . . . does not develop freely his physical and mental energy but mortifies his body and ruins his mind'. 'Its alien character emerges clearly', Marx indicates, 'in the fact that as soon as no physical or other compulsion exists, labour is shunned like the plague.'[34] But if for the worker his activity is 'torment' this is only because it is a 'delight', 'life's joy' for someone else: 'If his own activity is to him related as an unfree activity, then he is related to it as an activity performed in the service, under the dominion, the coercion, and the yoke of another man.'[35]

Or, in the language of political economy, class and the division of labour are two sides of the same coin, feeding on each other, enriching the capitalist but 'mortifying' the worker's body and 'ruining' his mind, turning him into a mere machine:

> The accumulation of capital increases the division of labour . . . just as the division of labour increases the accumulation of capital. With this division of labour on the one hand and the accumulation of capital on the other, the worker becomes ever more exclusively dependent on labour, and on a particular, one-sided, machine-like labour at that . . . he is thus depressed spiritually and physically to the condition of a machine and from being a man becomes an abstract activity and a belly.[36]

Marx's economic propositions here derive from Smith, of course, but it would be a mistake to see in the conflation between class and the division of labour in this passage simply a reproduction of the analysis in *The Wealth of Nations*, for Marx's argument carries an implication absent in Smith's: that the abolition of capital entailed the abolition of the division of labour, a view strongly conditioned by and closely interrelated with the ethic of total emancipation and the concept of alienation.

Nevertheless, like Smith's great work, Marx's *Manuscripts* are also centrally concerned with the phenomenon of exchange and if a third dimension of alienation is to be sought in Marx's thought at this time, then the exchange relationship is a much better contender than the idea of 'self-alienation' which, given Marx's characterisation of the species, is already presupposed in the analysis of class and the division of labour. Indeed, in the manuscript entitled 'The Meaning of Human Requirements' Marx himself makes this explicit. 'The examination of division of labour and exchange is of extreme interest', he notes, 'because these are perceptibly alienated expressions of human activity and of essential human power as a species of activity and power.'[37]

Marx's indictment of exchange relations is evident in his critique of the status of the labourer in a society where market forces convert all human relations into relations between commodities. The worker, too, is converted into a commodity and his fate like that of other commodities depends on the capricious movement of supply and demand: 'The demand for men necessarily governs the production of men, as of every other commodity. Should supply greatly exceed demand, a section of the workers sinks into beggary or starvation . . . The worker has become a commodity, and it is a bit of luck for him if he can find a buyer.'[38] This is alienation as *Entäusserung,* a renunciation of man's essential powers to the inhuman forces of the market; as with all other aspects of alienation, for the young Marx the market dehumanises man. 'Estrangement is manifested not only in the fact that my means of life belong to someone else', Marx says, 'but also in the fact that . . . (and this applies also to the capitalist), all is under the sway of inhuman power.'[39]

Marx has little to say about the origins of exchange and the division of labour and it seems fairly clear from his comments on Smith and others that he finds the relationship puzzling and in need of further examination. But he seems quite sure that division of labour, private property and exchange are closely interlinked and that in the abolition of private property lies the key to a transcendence of all these dehumanising social forms:

> To assert that division of labour and exchange rest on private property is nothing but asserting that labour is the essence of private property . . . Precisely in the fact that division of labour and exchange are embodiments of private property lies the twofold proof, on the one hand that human life required private property for its realisation, and on the other hand that it now requires the supersession of private property.[40]

And the extreme form of reductionism which characterises Marx's argument throughout the *Manuscripts* is aptly illustrated by his assertion that private property and exchange are actually the results rather than the cause or foundation of alienated labour: 'though private property appears to be the source, the cause of alienated labour, it is rather its consequence'.[41]

6
The Emergence of Historical Materialism, 1845–6: A New Problematic?

Marx's obvious curiosity about the origins and development of private property, division of labour and exchange soon culminated in a massive work in which he and Engels also attempted to provide an overall assessment of German idealist philosophy and historiography: *The German Ideology*, written between November 1845 and October 1846, but never published in their lifetime for want of a publisher. Meanwhile they had already collaborated in a savage polemic against the Young Hegelians, *The Holy Family* (1845), in which they had attempted to provide a philosophical foundation for socialism by combining Feuerbach's humanism with the materialism of the Enlightenment.[42] But, in the final analysis, *The Holy Family* failed to progress much beyond the themes already worked out in the 1844 *Manuscripts*.

The German Ideology, on the other hand, marked a decisive theoretical advance over the viewpoint of 1844 and this in two interconnected respects. To begin with, this work was the first to contain the theory that later came to be called 'historical materialism'; second, and equally significant, Marx dropped the terms 'species-being', 'essence of man' and the generic concept of 'man' from his discourse. Even the term 'alienation', so central to the *Manuscripts* and *The Holy Family*, recedes from view to lead a subterranean existence for the rest of Marx's intellectual career.

Historical materialism is discussed later; for the present it is worth commenting on the changes in Marx's view symbolised by his aversion to Feuerbachian terminology, a change that had already been prefigured in the famous 'Theses on Feuerbach', one of which condemned Feuerbach for reducing human activity to 'human essence'. The essence of man, Marx argued, 'is no abstraction inhering in each single individual. In its actuality it is the ensemble of social relationships.' Feuerbach, Marx pointed out, presupposes 'an abstract-isolated-human individual' and views 'the essence of man merely as "species", as the inner, dumb generality which unites the many individuals naturally'.[43] Marx's remarks are aimed not only at Feuerbach but implicitly at the very foundation of his own views in the *1844 Manuscripts*; otherwise it is impossible to account for the disappearance of terms like 'essence of man' and the closely related 'species-being' from his own subsequent work. In dropping these terms Marx relinquishes the notion, implicit in his earlier work, that capitalism denied – and socialism would realise – a set of known and fixed needs which remained more or less constant throughout history.[44] It is partly because Marx wished to distance himself from such an anthropology that the concept of alienation, too, loses its centrality in his discourse. But the displacement of 'alienation' also results, as I shall argue, from the emergence of historical materialism. My interpretation here implies neither that Marx's pre-*German Ideology* writings are entirely unhistorical nor that the *concept* of alienation entirely disappears from his work. Nor, indeed, that some view of man's essential nature does not survive into his later writings. The concept of alienation survives and, as Mandel points out, is henceforth much more thoroughly historicised; forms of alienation are now seen to derive from historically specific structures of production and domination.[45]

However, to insist that a historicised concept of alienation survives to some extent in all of Marx's mature writings does not help to resolve one of the basic issues posed by the emergence of historical materialism in *The German Ideology* and subsequent texts: the theoretical compatibility between the concept of alienation and the basic concepts of historical materialism, and their relative importance in the earlier and later writings. It is above all Althusser who has posed this problem most sharply, and whose interpretation has provoked most controversy.[46] Although it is neither possible nor necessary here to provide a comprehensive overall assessment of his commentaries on Marx, it is essential to grasp the significance of some of his basic theses before proceeding to a more detailed explication of Marx's conceptualisation of the division of labour in *The German Ideology*.

Althusser has argued that texts like the *Economic and Philosophic Manuscripts* cannot be discursively identified with *The*

German Ideology and subsequent writings because the emergence of historical materialism marks a theoretical rupture, the development of a new 'problematic', displacing the problematic of alienation. The latter continues to coexist, in a modified form, as an element subordinate to historical materialism, but only because new problematics do not usually detach themselves from previous ones immediately, without an immense theoretical labour, which Marx was not able to carry out. 'Problematic' refers to the specificity of a discursive structure, the organisation of concepts into a definite framework, which determines the kinds of questions a theory or text is able to pose. Thus its significance lies as much in the identification of 'absences' and 'silences' as in the specification of a surface and literal discourse. What a text, for example, is not able to 'say' is often more important, as an indication of the structure of concepts which organises it, than what it actually 'says'.[47]

The emergence of historical materialism, Althusser points out, is marked by the appearances of a set of new concepts in Marx's texts, beginning with *The German Ideology*: the concepts of social formation, productive forces, relations of production, superstructure, ideologies, determination in the last instance by the economy, and so on. This is accompanied, as I have already indicated, by a critique of the philosophical humanism and essentialist anthropology which had characterised his own early works.[48] Historical materialism is thus based on a 'theoretical anti-humanism' in so far as concepts such as 'man', 'human needs', 'human nature' and 'human essence' are replaced, as theoretical starting points, by a rigorous conceptualisation of the relations of production.[49] This disengagement is never complete in Marx's texts, although it does make decisive progress in the discourse of *Capital* where 'men' only appear as 'bearers' of the relations of production, thus establishing the primacy of a structural analysis.[50] This retheorisation, Althusser argues, is an essential element in the production of the concept of surplus value. Moreover, the displacement of 'man' from the centre of the stage also necessarily implies a break with empiricist epistemologies which take the 'subject' as their starting point, and for this reason theoretical anti-humanism also forms one of the preconditions for the development of a non-reductionist conception of the relation between the economy and the superstructures.[51]

Some of these formulations are adapted and developed later in this book, especially in relation to Marx's conceptualisation of the division of labour. For the present it is only necessary to register a very broad agreement with Althusser's characterisation of the break between the problematics of alienation and historical materialism, first evident in *The German Ideology*. That is, it cannot seriously be disputed that the emergence of historical materialism leads to the posing of entirely new kinds of questions which are outside the field of the alienation problematic, for example those concerning contradictions between forces and relations of production, determination by the economy in the last instance, and the relative autonomy of superstructures.[52] At the same time, the general field of application of Marx's discourse is also transformed: the alienation problematic is very closely tied, as I have indicated earlier, to forms of production involving the selling of labour and the dominance of relations of exchange. These features are part of the very meaning of the term 'alienation' in Marx's early writings, a meaning which, however, prevents its full applicability to modes of production in which 'free' labour and relations of exchange exist only peripherally. The problematic of alienation is only fully applicable in the capitalist mode of production although here too, of course, it poses different questions from those arising out of historical materialism; it is hardly accidental that those who work within the alienation problematic often end up either denying the full applicability of Marxism to pre-capitalist modes of production, or denying altogether the validity of the base-superstructure schema.[53]

Several disclaimers are necessary, however, to avoid possible misconceptions arising from the above discussion. First, it should be noted that Althusser underplays the extent of the survival of 'alienation' in the mature texts and, as Geras has pointed out, Althusser also misinterprets the character of the concept that survives into these writings.[54] Second, Althusser gives little attention to what I have called the transitional period in Marx's formation and therefore fails to explicate properly the significance of Marx's break with the centrality of exchange relations as a precondition for the emergence of the new theorisation of the relations of production in *Capital*. Third, the notion of problematic in Althusser's works is subject to several limitations both in conceptualisation and application.[55] In addition, as Althusser has himself now come to recognise, the distinction between ideology and science which had organised his discussion of the relation between Marx's earlier and later writings is in need of considerable revision.[56] Finally, as I shall now document, in understanding Marx's views on the division of labour it is necessary to recognise that the form of Marx's analysis of the division of labour in *The German Ideology* is close enough to the *Economic and Philosophic Manuscripts* to be included, in this context, within the 'early' writings.

7
The German Ideology

Despite the emergence of historical materialism in *The German Ideology*, several themes broached in the earlier works remain central to this text and none more so than the close identification of class and the division of labour. While the notion of man's 'essence' and alienation – and, correspondingly, the inspiration these had provided for the doctrine of total emancipation – had been crucial in enabling Marx to produce a close theoretical link between class and the division of labour, the transcendence of anthropologism led to no significant adjustment in this respect. The idea of complete liberation remained a strong *motif*, although this time underpinned not by a conception of human nature but by a theoretical structure which left no room for doubt that class and the division of labour both derived from private property and that the abolition of the latter necessarily implied the disappearance of the former. Thus there is a significant continuity in the (reductionist) structure of Marx's discourse between the *1844 Manuscripts* and *The German Ideology*. The assimilation of class to the division of labour now independently performs the discursive function which had previously been accomplished by combining this form of reductionism with an essentialist anthropology. In an important sense the notion of division of labour replaces 'alienation': in the process, as we shall see, Marx expands the concept to the point where it becomes synonymous with almost all divisions of social interest whether in capitalist or pre-capitalist social formations.

The methodological and substantive starting point of the historical materialism that is sketched out in *The German Ideology* is provided by men's activity as producers. Before men can 'make history' they must be able to live: 'The first historical act is thus the production of the means to satisfy these needs'; but the distance between the earlier conception and the one adopted in *The German Ideology* is immediately established, for Marx adds that 'the satisfaction of the first need . . . leads to new needs'.[57] Not only is this activity basic, but it is always a cooperative activity, involving social organisation and social relationships: 'a certain mode of production, or industrial stage, is always combined with a certain mode of co-operation . . . the multitude of productive forces . . . determines the nature of society, hence . . . the "history of humanity" must always be studied and treated in relation to the history of industry and exchange.'[58]

Two other aspects of the materialist conception of history that were later developed much more systematically are also embryonically registered in the text. First, the distinction between base and superstructure, which receives several overlapping formulations: the state, morality, philosophy and all other forms of ideology, it is argued, have no independent existence, but evolve out of 'material intercourse' and class relationships; thus each epoch is dominated by the ideas of its ruling class for 'the class which is the ruling material force of society, is at the same time its ruling intellectual force', while the emergence of revolutionary ideologies in a particular period is dependent upon the existence of a revolutionary class.[59] Second, the notion of the contradiction between forces and relations of production, which is associated with the transition from one epoch to another through the practice of a revolutionary class: the development of productive activity is said to lead to a stage where 'productive forces and means of intercourse are brought into being, which, under the existing relationships only cause mischief, and are no longer productive but destructive forces'.[60]

The division of labour and its development have a crucial place in this dialectical interplay between men and nature, providing an index of the evolution of productive capacity in any human community. 'How far the productive forces of a nation are developed', Marx argues, 'is shown most manifestly by the degree to which the division of labour has been carried. Each new productive force . . . causes a further development of the division of labour.'[61] The conflation between class and the division of labour is a pervasive feature of the entire work and is boldly announced as a guiding principle almost at the beginning of the text:

> The various stages of development in the division of labour are just so many different forms of ownership, i.e. the existing stage in the division of labour determines also the relations of individuals to one another with reference to the material, instrument, and product of labour.[62]

This fusion – or confusion – between class and the division of labour structures all aspects of Marx's delineation of historical development in *The German Ideology* and the two concepts are used almost interchangeably and indiscriminately. The origins of property and the division of labour are located, Marx argues, in the family; in the tribal community both are inextricably related as extensions of the patterns of power given by the structure of kinship:

> With the division of labour, . . . and which in its turn is based on the natural division of labour in the family and the separation of society into individual families opposed to one another, is given simultaneously the distribution, and indeed the unequal distribution, both quantitative and qualitative, of labour and its products, hence property: the nucleus, the first form, of which lies in the family, where wife and children are the slaves of the husband.[63]

The second stage in the development of the division of labour is said to lie in 'the separation of industrial and commercial from agricultural labour' which, Marx argues, is identical to the separation between town and country and leads to an endemic conflict of interest between the two.[64] But the division between town and country is regarded at the same time as a division between mental and 'material' labour: 'The greatest division of material and mental labour is the separation of town and country.'[65] This whole development is an aspect of the transformation 'from barbarism to civilization, from tribe to State' and implies the necessity for more centralised administration and the collection of taxes, a process in which the town exploits the countryside. Marx seems to see in this little more than a direct manifestation of class conflict based on the division between industrial and commercial (or 'mental'), and agricultural (or 'material') labour: 'Here first became manifest the division of the population into two great classes, which is directly based on the division of labour and on the instruments of production.' The division between town and country, Marx argues, can also be understood 'as the separation of capital and landed property', but reserves his sharpest comments for the way in which the process reflects the division of labour, and he precedes a case for its abolition and of private property with the following acid remark: 'It is the most crass expression of the subjection of the individual under the division of labour . . . which makes one man into a restricted town-animal, the other into a restricted country-animal, and creates anew the conflict between their interests.'[66]

It is possible to observe in these passages a quite remarkable extension in Marx's usage of 'division of labour' and he places upon the notion a heavy explanatory and descriptive burden which threatens to strip it of any distinctive meaning. Almost any and every structural division, institutional separation and conflict of social or individual interest is either reduced to or seen as an aspect of the 'division of labour'. The central underlying principle here is, of course, the conflation between *class* and the division of labour – a direct legacy from the *1844 Manuscripts* – but Marx's polymorphous usage is indicative of even greater conceptual extension and moreover enables him to gloss over a whole variety of issues which surely require greater discussion. For instance, Marx was well aware that both the town and the countryside were themselves internally stratified: he pointed to the guild-system as an example of the hierarchical division of labour within the feudal town and often referred to the exploitation of the serfs in the countryside; indeed, he even commented upon the way in which the serfs escaped in droves into the towns to escape persecution by feudal lords only to find themselves a powerless 'rabble' against the might of the urban guild-masters.[67] How, then, could the conflict between town and country be seen as a simple class conflict or indeed simply as the separation between 'mental' and 'material' labour? The question is obviously begged and Marx is only able to do so without any conscious sense of anomaly because of the remarkable number of phenomena that he nonchalantly assimilates to the concept of 'division of labour'.

Division of labour between and within the urban guilds, to follow Marx's narrative, was limited by the level of exchange between towns and the overall size of population. The medieval craftsman was thus 'proficient in the whole of his craft'; not surprisingly, given the commitment to total emancipation, Marx remained highly critical of the craftsman's conditions of work: the craftsman's proficiency, he argued, was capable of rising only 'to a narrow artistic sense' and the craftsman's absorption in his work was seen merely as a 'slavish' contentment which bound him that much closer to work when compared with 'the modern worker, whose work is a matter of indifference to him'.[68] It seems evident that whatever his criticisms of the nature of work under capitalism, Marx certainly did not see in the medieval craftsman a model to be emulated under socialism.

The gradual erosion of feudal relationships, especially in the urban centres, is again conceptualised by Marx in terms of the development of the division of labour: 'The next extension of the division of labour', Marx informs us, 'was the separation of production and commerce, the formation of a special class of merchants' which, he argues, soon led to the breakdown of localised self-sufficiency and inaugurated a period in which productive forces expanded rapidly.[69] The central dynamic of this process lay in the 'new division of production between the individual towns' the immediate consequence of which was 'the rise of manufactures, branches of production which had outgrown the guild system', chief among them being weaving, the demand for which grew quickly with increasing population and the accumulation of capital.[70]

The eventual result of this burgeoning process, of course, was the development of capitalism, that is, a system in which property in the means of production came to be in the hands of a small minority who produced only for exchange and profit; or, alternatively, a system in which wage labour became for the first time the key principle for the organisation of production. It is not my intention to pursue Marx's historical account of the rise of western capitalism in any detail as several reliable accounts already exist to which little can be usefully added here.[71] In the present context it is more important to deepen our understanding of Marx's use of 'division of labour' by examining further the more theoretical aspects of his discussion.

One important dimension of Marx's analysis is the rise of the state and it is worth underlining that – as with almost every other fundamental social institution examined by Marx in *The German Ideology* – its particular morphology is seen as a direct outcome of the evolution of the division of labour, for the division of labour is seen as the true source of the 'contradiction between the interest of the individual and that of the community' which allows the state to appropriate an illusory communal and unifying role; illusory, because in reality the state is always based on classes 'already determined by the division of labour, which in every such mass of men separate out, and of which one dominates all the others'.[72]

An equally important feature of Marx's theorisation is the place accorded to exchange relations and market forces; the latter play a crucial mediating role in enabling Marx to weave a tight web between 'division of labour' and 'class', and it is necessary at this stage to integrate Marx's reasoning on exchange into his account of the evolution of property forms and the organisation of labour. From its origins in sexual divisions and domestic slavery within the tribal family, Marx argues, the development of differentiated labour and private property have gone hand in hand. Private property (and, *ipso facto*, the division of labour) inherently counterposed the interests of the owner of those of others; it is synonymous, therefore, with the 'contradiction between the interest of the individual and the community'. This contradiction, for Marx, is institutionalised and exacerbated by the development of exchange. At this point it is again possible to see an important line of continuity between the *1844 Manuscripts* and *The German Ideology*: that is, exchange acquires its centrality partly because it had already been assimilated to the generic concept of alienation and it is interesting to note that while Marx is rather circumspect about using the term 'alienation' in *The German Ideology* it is in the context of *exchange* relations that the term reappears most frequently:

> In history up to the present it is certainly an empirical fact that separate individuals have, with the broadening of their activity into world-historical activity, become more and more enslaved under a power alien to them, . . . a power which has become more and more enormous and, in the last instance, turns out to be the world market.

And the phenomenon of exchange is similarly assimilated to private property, for Marx adds: 'But it is just as empirically established that, by the overthrow of the existing state of society by the communist revolution . . . and the abolition of private property which is identical with it, this power . . . will be dissolved.'[73]

In *The German Ideology* and in subsequent texts the concept of alienation becomes almost synonymous with overall loss of control over production; the notion of exchange fits snugly into this scheme in so far as it concerns an 'invisible hand' that 'allots fortune and misfortune to men, sets up empires and overthrows empires, causes nations to rise and to disappear'.[74] It is only by recognising that Marx assimilates division of labour, exchange relations and private property that propositions of the following kind, which recur in *The German Ideology*, can be understood:

> The social power, i.e. the multiplied productive force, which arises through the co-operation of different individuals as it is determined by the division of labour, appears to these individuals, since their co-operation is not voluntary but has come about naturally, not as their own united power, but as an *alien* force existing outside them, of the origin and goal of which they are ignorant, which they thus cannot control, which on the contrary passes through a peculiar series of phases and stages independent of the will of man, nay even being the prime governor of these [my emphasis].[75]

Thus, despite the fact that Marx abandons the language of Feurbachian humanism, *The German Ideology* continues and deepens the central theme of the *1844 Manuscripts*: the conflation between class and the division of labour, mediated by exchange. While this theme initially resulted from a critical encounter between Marx's Feurbachian communism and his reading of classical political economy, it survived the partial disappearance of its 'humanistic' foundations because of the reductionist structure of Marx's discourse – itself partly a legacy of the concept of alienation – and was reinforced by Marx's reading of history. That is, this theme survived partly because Marx at this stage primarily concentrated on the rise of western capitalism, in other words on a part of the globe in which the historical evolution of differentiated labour, exchange and private property was not merely intertwined but culminated in a system in which production became geared centrally to exchange and profit, in which the majority of the population found itself progressively without any property in the means of production, and in which this same propertyless group was subjected to the worst features of the subdivision of tasks and machine-minding in the factories. An appreciation of these sorts of factors in Marx's intellectual formation goes a long way towards explaining the conflation between 'class' and the 'division of labour' in his early works and enables us to understand, too, how Marx was able to telescope vast historical transformations in passages like the following:

> The division of labour implies from the outset the division of the conditions of labour, of tools and materials, and thus the splitting-up of accumulated capital among different owners, and thus, also, the division between capital and labour.[76]

And, of course, it is passages like the one above which contain the clue to Marx's belief in the possibility of the complete abolition of the division of labour in a society without private property and social classes, expressed eloquently in the passage with which this discussion began:

> in communist society, where nobody has one exclusive sphere of activity but each can become accomplished in any branch he wishes, society regulates the general production and thus makes it possible for me to do one thing today and another tomorrow, to hunt in the morning, fish in the afternoon, rear cattle in the evening, criticise after dinner, just as I have a mind, without ever becoming hunter, fisherman, shepherd or critic.[77]

Elsewhere in *The German Ideology* Marx even speaks of 'the abolition of labour'.[78] But is it legitimate to regard such passages as a manifesto for 'total emancipation', and what are the implications of such a conception for the organisation of labour in future society? Although the early texts are less than helpful on both counts, the apocalyptic tone of these writings is very striking and moreover corresponds to their discursive structure, determined initially by an essentialist concept of alienation and subsequently by a form of reductionism in which class and the division of labour are assimilated to one another. And *The German Ideology* passage contains another important clue, for in it Marx asserts that in future society it would be possible to engage in different activities, even during the course of a single day, 'just as I have a mind'. That is, *no* limitations rooted in the structural arrangements necessary for material production and reproduction are posited; individual inclination is the only limiting principle. The rural imagery that appears in this context also shows how little thought Marx had given to the specific exigencies that large-scale industrial production might impose upon any blueprint for social transformation. But it must be emphasised that this lacuna cannot simply be attributed to the influence on Marx of Fourier's brand of socialism, based on small agricultural communities, as McLellan seems to imply.[79] It is in the first place a consequence of the reductionist structure of Marx's discourse.

At another point in *The German Ideology* when Marx confronts the issue again in response to Stirner's remarks on the uniqueness of Raphael and Mozart, he points out that 'it was not Mozart himself, but someone else who composed the *Requiem* and finished it, and that Raphael himself "completed" only an insignifcant part of his own frescoes'.[80] Thus Marx does not really qualify his earlier propositions and indeed he adds:

> The exclusive concentration of artistic talent in particular individuals, and its suppression in the broad mass which is bound up with this, is a consequence of division of labour. If, even in certain social conditions, everyone was an excellent painter, that would not at all exclude the possibility of them being also an original painter, so that here too the difference between 'human' and 'unique' labour amounts to sheer nonsense . . . In a communist society there are no painters but at most people who engage in painting among other activities.[81]

Interpreted *in the context of Marx's discourse as a whole at this stage* the implication of this and other passages is clearly that there are no limits to the transformation of the division of labour in future society; in more concrete terms this is the meaning of the notion of complete emancipation in *The German Ideology*. A more qualified but no less inspiring vision unfolds in the later works, accompanied by a series of discursive transformations of great significance for the whole of Marx's mature work.

Part III

Marx and the Division of Labour: the Period of Transition

1
A Marxian Eschatology?

Marx's early writings have a distinctly apocalyptical character and it is not difficult to understand why some critics have seen in his discourse a sort of disguised and secularised eschatology, an interpretation made much easier if his earlier and later writings are indiscriminately conflated to yield a unified doctrine. Tucker, for instance, has quite bluntly referred to Marx's views as 'through and through a moralistic myth' in which 'the historical world of capital and labour becomes, in the end, a world that knows neither capital nor labour, a world of "full and free development of every individual"'.[1] Marx's belief in the possibility of some kind of total emancipation obviously provides interpretations of this *genre* with much sustenance, and it is in this element of his thought that Avineri locates a central weakness. 'Turning the possibility of human redemption into an historical phenomenon about to be realised here and now', he argues, 'secularises the Hegelian synthesis that saw the dialectical tensions resolving themselves in the present generation and finding their *Aufhebung* in an apotheosis through which the historical process would achieve its ultimate height.'[2] It is thus irrelevant that whereas Hegel regarded this act as the culmination of history, Marx saw it as the beginning of 'true' history.

Had Marx's theoretical and political position failed to progress much beyond the point reached in *The German Ideology*, such interpretations could perhaps be sustained. Marx's voracious appetite for reading and his progressive involvement in the social and political conflicts of the day, however, ensured that his thinking never remained at the same point for very long. *The German Ideology* had been written in Brussels – Marx having been expelled from Paris – and, in preparation, Marx had consulted works in

French on economics and history. Marx and Engels had also visited Manchester in the summer of 1845 and there Marx had once again immersed himself in the study of political economy, the fruits of which were evident not so much in *The German Ideology* as in *The Poverty of Philosophy*, a text which displays significant theoretical advances over the earlier work and, as I shall argue, paved the way for some far-reaching modifications in Marx's overall views on the relationship between class and the division of labour.[3]

2
The Poverty of Philosophy (1847)

The immediate occasion for the composition of this work was the publication of Proudhon's *The Philosophy of Poverty*. Pierre-Joseph Proudhon, a self-taught intellectual from Besançon who had started life as a printer, was at this time an important figure in the radical movement and he had met Marx in Paris in the winter of 1844–5.[4] Proudhon may have had some influence on Marx's views at that point, but by the time he published *System of Economic Contradictions or The Philosophy of Poverty* it seems clear that he and Marx had decisively parted company on theoretical and political grounds. Nearly twenty years later Marx recalled that just before Proudhon published *The Philosophy of Poverty* he wrote to Marx announcing this 'in a very detailed letter in which he said, among other things: "I await the lash of your criticism". This soon fell upon him in my *Misere de la Philosophie*', Marx continued, 'in a fashion which ended our friendship for ever.'[5]

Proudhon was older than Marx by nine years and had begun to immerse himself in economics in the late 1830s, developing his own idiosyncratic concept of exploitation. There was, he argued, a miscalculation (*erreur de compte*) in the economic relationship between the capitalist and the workmen he employed, for the latter were paid individually and therefore deprived of any payment for the increased productivity that resulted from their organisation as a collective force under one roof in modern factories.[6] In his earlier work Proudhon was not particularly critical of the division of labour, arguing that it is 'harmful neither to society nor to the individual if it is capably managed and coordinated'. Indeed, it brought with it considerable advantages:

> When a man has reached his full potential in youth, has thoroughly explored his specialised sphere of activity, and has been in a position to command and instruct others, he likes, when the time comes, to withdraw into himself and have time to reflect. Then, providing he is assured a daily wage, content that he has proved himself, he leaves it to others to carry out great plans and fill dazzling posts, and gives himself up to the musings of his heart, which the regularity of the subdivision of labour serves only to encourage.[7]

In *The Philosophy of Poverty*, however, Proudhon appears much more hostile to the effects of the division of labour; moreover, he attempts to deepen his analysis of capitalist exploitation. Marx, in turn, polemicises against both aspects of Proudhon's thought and *The Poverty of Philosophy* thus provides an excellent illustration of developments in Marx's own views on both subjects.

'All that M. Proudhon says about the division of labour', Marx noted in a letter to Annenkov prior to working on his book, 'is only a summary, and moreover a very superficial and incomplete summary, of what Adam Smith and a thousand others have said before him.'[8] Indeed, at one point in the book Marx quotes from Ferguson's *Essay on the History of Civil Society* and (mistakenly) refers to Smith himself as a student of Ferguson.[9] Too much should not be made of this error, for what is important is that Marx had obviously read Ferguson and that Marx's remarks on the division of labour in *The Poverty of Philosophy*, insofar as they apply to Proudhon, are also implicitly meant to apply to those from whom the latter had borrowed his ideas. Proudhon's discussion, especially on the origins of division of labour, reads like a parody of Smith's views and Marx reserves some of his sharpest criticisms for this aspect of *The Philosophy of Poverty*.

Proudhon, Marx argues, inverts the real historical relastionship between human needs, division of labour, exchange and material production. Instead of beginning with production, and recognising that human needs expand as a result of production and thus lead to the necessity for division of labour to fulfil these new needs, Proudhon begins by postulating both the existence of division of labour and of needs which cannot be met by an existing set of productive arrangements; a solitary individual then inaugurates a new historical phase by turning to his fellow men and proposing that they exchange the products deriving from their different functions.[10] 'But,' Marx points out, 'he [Proudhon] has still to explain to us the "genesis" of this proposal, to tell us finally how this single individual, this Robinson, suddenly had the idea of making "to his collaborators" a proposal of the type *known* and how those collaborators accepted it without the slightest protest.'[11] Marx adds that Proudhon is totally unable to explain why the division of labour and exchange have a history, why they have actually passed through different stages, culminating in a phase 'when everything, moral or physical, having become a marketable value, is brought to the market to be assessed at its truest value'.[12] To the extent that Marx emphasises the primacy of production in the generation of division of labour and exchange, his critique of Proudhon is equally applicable to Smith who had suggested in *The Wealth of Nations* that the origins of exchange lay in an innate human tendency to 'truck' or 'barter'.

It is in Marx's own analysis of the genesis and evolution of the division of labour that one finds a completely new development in his thought on the subject, a development that formed the prelude to important changes in his conceptualisation of the connections between class, division of labour and exchange: in *The Poverty of Philosophy*, probably influenced by Babbage and Ure, Marx distinguishes between *division of labour in society* and *division of labour in the workshop* in a passage that is worth reproducing in some detail:

> Society as a whole has this in common with the interior of a workshop, that it too has its division of labour. If one took as a model the division of labour in a modern workshop, in order to apply it to a whole society, the society best organised for the production of wealth would undoubtedly be that which had a single chief employer, distributing tasks to the different members of the community according to a previously fixed rule. But this is by no means the case. While inside the modern workshop the division of labour is meticulously regulated by the authority of the employer, modern society has no other rule, no other authority for the distribution of labour than free competition . . . It can even be laid down as a general rule that the less authority presides over the division of labour inside society, the more the division of labour develops inside the workshop, and the more it

> is subjected there to the authority of a single person. Thus authority in the workshop and authority in society, in relation to the division of labour, are in reverse ratio to each other.[13]

Marx uses this distinction not to examine the origins of exchange – he still fails to provide any coherent explanation for this himself, despite taxing Proudhon for the same omission – but to analyse the development of the factory system (in Britain) prior to the industrial revolution and the consequent emergence of what he called 'modern industry', that is, production based on machinery. In insisting upon this discrimination and reflecting upon its implications, however, Marx begins to set in motion a discursive transformation that was ultimately to distance himself decisively from Smith. Thus, although Marx grants due weight to the size of the market, he nevertheless points out that 'the extent of the market, its physiognomy, gives to the division of labour at different periods a physiognomy, a character, which it would be difficult to deduce from the single word *divide*' [my emphasis].[14] This conceptual specification allows him to develop Babbage's analysis, for Marx now argues that while there was obviously division of labour in society in the caste system, or under feudalism, the division of labour in the workshop 'was very little developed in all these forms of society'.[15] The greatest impetus to the further development of the workshop, Marx pointed out, came from the increase in trade subsequent to the discovery of America and the growth of profits in the hands of owners of industry who were thus able to bring together 'many workers and many crafts in one place, in one room under the command of one capital'.[16] This process was considerably assisted by the penetration of trade into the East Indies, on the one hand, and the availability of dispossessed peasants and vagrants driven to the urban centres by the enclosure movement and the disbanding of feudal retinues on the other.

It was this accumulation of capital and the concentration of instruments which accompanied it that provided in turn the necessary preconditions for the progressive subdivision of tasks in the workshop, a process which spiralled with the invention of machinery. 'We need not recall the fact', Marx said, 'that the great progress of the division of labour began in England after the invention of machinery.' And Marx was quick to note that all the transformations he had been describing were powerfully interrelated:

> The invention of machinery brought about the separation of manufacturing industry from agricultural industry. The weaver and spinner, united but lately in a single family, were separated by the machine. Thanks to the machine, the spinner can live in England while the weaver resides in the East Indies . . . Thanks to the application of machinery and of steam, the division of labour was able to assume such dimensions that large-scale industry, detached from the national soil, depends entirely on the world market, on international exchange, on an international division of labour. In short – the machine has so great an influence on the division of labour, that when, in the manufacture of some object, a means has been found to produce parts of it mechanically, the manufacture splits up immediately into two works independent of each other.[17]

Marx was well aware that his analysis here was considerably superior to Smith's in *The Wealth of Nations* because the latter obviously had no knowledge of the gigantic transformation that was to overwhelm the division of labour in the factory through machine-based production.[18]

In *The Poverty of Philosophy* Marx is as critical of the effects of subdivided labour as he had been in earlier writings, but he now uses the distinction between the two forms of division of labour to differentiate between interrelated but separate, conflicting tendencies generated by the division of labour: the division of labour in society 'engenders specialised functions, specialists, and with them craft-idiocy'. On the other hand, the machine-based division of labour in the modern factory, he now argues, leads to a form of work which negates specialisation: 'The automatic workshop wipes out specialists and craft-idiocy'; this process is seen to have revolutionary potential, for 'the moment every special development stops, the need for universality, the tendency towards an integral development of the individual begins to be felt'.[19]

Much of this discussion is based on a French edition of Andrew Ure's *Philosophy of Manufacture* and it is interesting to note that the passages from this work that Marx cites include a proposition that is much more fully developed in the *Grundrisse* and has by now become very well known, that 'on the automatic plan, skilled labour gets progressively superseded, and will, eventually, be replaced by mere overlookers of machines'.[20] Later in *The Poverty of Philo-*

sophy Marx also uses insights derived in part from Ure to develop a much clearer view of the emergence of class consciousness, as a process consequent upon the massing of workers in cities and factories.[21] Indeed, throughout this work Marx displays an understanding of the capitalist labour process and its effects which is vastly superior to the analysis contained in his earlier writings where the influence of Smith is much more pronounced, and thus foreshadows many of the themes that finally became evident in *Capital* twenty years later.

However, despite the centrality of the division of labour to Marx's discussion in *The Poverty of Philosophy*, this work contains no clear argument about the *abolition* of the division of labour. The need for such transcendence is implicit throughout the book, of course, but it is not at first sight obvious to what extent Marx continued to believe in the possibility of the complete abolition of the division of labour – a position that he had articulated only a year before, in *The German Ideology*. But insofar as this belief had been predicated upon the conflation between class and the division of labour, it is possible to identify Marx's position on the subject in 1847 by examining the extent to which he continued to assimilate the various forms of division of labour to the phenomenon of class (given, of course, that he continued to believe in the possibility and necessity of abolishing private property and classes). Once the problem is posed in this form, the answer becomes a little easier to find.

Let us note, in the first place, that despite his distinction between two different forms of the division of labour, Marx continues to associate exchange relations and commodity production in the closest possible fashion with both these forms of divided labour; to reiterate a point made earlier, Marx postulates a strong link between the development of the market and competition, on the one hand, and the subdivision of tasks in the factory on the other. Indeed, Marx goes so far as to assert a 'general rule' that the two institutions vary in 'inverse ratio' to each other: the more unregulated the division of labour in society, and hence the greater the freedom given to market forces and competition, 'the more the division of labour develops inside the workshop'.[22] Moreover, Marx asserts an indissoluble connection between exchange, the division of labour and the authority of the employer in the factory, a point superbly illustrated in the law of inverse proportions and well worth citing again: 'It can even be laid down as a general rule that the less authority presides over the division of labour in society, the more the division of labour develops inside the workshop, and the more it is subjected there to the authority of a single person. Thus authority in the workshop and authority in society, in relation to the division of labour, are in inverse ratio to each other.' The implication here is obviously that these diverse phenomena are woven together tightly enough to form a seamless web such that the destruction of one must inevitably lead to the dissolution of the others, an interpretation considerably strengthened by the links that Marx posits between the accumulation of capital, the subdivision of tasks in the factory and the form of ownership.

The interpretation advanced here of Marx's position at this stage is considerably reinforced by many other general remarks in the same work on systems of ownership and associated forms of the division of labour which systematically conflate these two phenomena. Compare, for example, the following two formulations which both express one of the more notorious propositions to be found in *The Poverty of Philosophy*:

> The handmill gives you society with the feudal lord; the steam-mill, society with the industrial capitalist.[23]

> Labour is organised, is divided differently according to the instruments it disposes over. The handmill presupposes a different division of labour from the steam-mill.[24]

Or, as Marx rhetorically asked in his letter to Annenkov, 'Is the whole inner organisation of nations, are all their international relations anything else than the expression of a particular division of labour?'[25] What Proudhon had failed to grasp, Marx added, was that 'the division of labour and *all* M. Proudhon's categories are social relations forming in their entirety what is today known as property . . . The property of a different epoch, feudal property, develops in a series of *entirely* different social relations' [my emphasis].[26] The same point is made in *The Poverty of Philosophy*, for Marx argues here that 'to define bourgeois property is nothing else than to give an exposition of *all* the social relations of bourgeois production' [my emphasis].[27]

In short, despite the more sophisticated analysis of the division of labour elaborated in *The Poverty of Philosophy*, Marx continues to conflate class and the division of labour, and one must draw the conclusion that this discursive structure strongly implies on his part a belief in the possibility of complete emancipation from the division of labour with the dissolution of class society.

3
Economic and Political Writings 1848–56

The period from the writing of *The Poverty of Philosophy* (1847) to the drafting of the famous 'Introduction' to the *Grundrisse* (1857), I have argued earlier, should be treated as a 'transitional' phase in Marx's intellectual development as regards the conceptualisation of the division of labour. In other words, during this period there are both discursive continuities and dislocations, in relation to the earlier writings, which coexist in tension and contradiction within individual texts without finding any decisive resolution towards one standpoint or another. Thus, as indicated in the preceding pages, in *The Poverty of Philosophy* Marx provides a much more sophisticated analysis of the structure and evolution of the capitalist labour process and its associated forms of the division of labour, without breaking free from a discursive formation in which property, or class, and the division of labour remain in the final analysis conceptually undifferentiated from one another. In the same year Marx wrote a polemic against Karl Heinzen where a similar tension is evident. Thus, although Marx emphasises that 'the division of labour brings about very different modes of work within the same class', a formulation which might suggest a more subtle analysis than that provided in earlier works, in general the text continues to assimilate class with division of labour in much the same way as before.[28]

In the economic and political writings of the late 1840s, and primarily in *The Communist Manifesto* (1848) and *Wage Labour and Capital* (published in 1849 on the basis of lectures given in December 1847), Marx systematises some of the propositions already formulated in *The Poverty of Philosophy* relating to the impact of machinery on the division of labour in the capitalist factory system. In doing so he prefigures some of the characteristic emphases of his analysis of the labour process in *Capital*. For example, the deskilling inherent in the introduction of machinery, Marx points out, not only lowers wages but makes it much easier to replace men with women and adults with children.[29] Moreover, discipline within the factory is maintained by placing the labourers like 'privates of the industrial army . . . under the command of a perfect hierarchy of officers and sergeants'.[30]

Nevertheless, the 'transitional' nature of these writings is evidenced by the rather simple form in which the deskilling thesis is employed by Marx to analyse the typical structure and evolution of the labour force under conditions of capitalist production. Little is said about the way in which the process of deskilling necessarily creates a technical hierarchy within the labour force, with the creation of a scientific and technical intelligentsia which designs and monitors the labour process for capital and generally monopolises the skills necessary for understanding and operating the process of production as a whole.[31] Nor is anything implied at this stage about the possible emergence of other categories of workers, better educated and better paid, to cope with the massive amount of calculation and accounting involved in monitoring and realising the surplus generated within the capitalist enterprise. In other words, Marx operates in these writings with a rather unsophisticated conception of the impact of capitalist relations of production on differentiation *within* the category of labour, thus reinforcing the pattern of conceptual assimilation between 'class' and 'division of labour'.

Four other features of Marx's analysis in the late 1840s should be noted. First, the 'polarisation' thesis: it appears that with capitalist development Marx expected a fairly rapid demise of intermediate classes such as the peasantry and petty bourgeoisie, leaving only the bourgeoisie and proletariat in direct, unmediated conflict with each other.[32] Second, Marx seems to discern few obstacles to the development of revolutionary socialist consciousness and the emergence of a mass revolutionary movement within the working class: the massing together of deskilled workers in factories and their concentration in large urban centres are seen by Marx as conditions which, in combination with the experience of periodic capitalist crises, would lead this already homogeneous proletariat to recognise its common interests and unite under a common political programme.[33] Third, forms of politics and ideology are given little autonomy and are seen as merely expressive of economic conditions and class relations: continuing a line of thought first advanced in *The German Ideology*, the state is said to be little more than 'a committee for managing the common affairs of the whole bourgeoisie', while phases in the development of economic theory and in the evolution of socialist movements are reduced to forms of class relations in simple unilinear terms.[34] Finally, despite the commitment to a labour theory of value, already evident in *The Poverty of Philosophy*, Marx's analysis at this stage is theoretically located at the level of exchange relations: capitalism is indicted for transforming labour into a commodity like any other, to be bought and sold at the mercy of market forces, while competition is identified as the central dynamic of capitalist development and as the greatest divisive force within the working class itself.[35]

The Communist Manifesto, in which all four emphases are particularly pronounced, unfortunately contains little of significance concerning the transformation of the division of labour in future society; the various reforms contained in part II of the pamphlet were seen only as an interim programme and were quite possibly influenced by the desire to secure alliances with radical sections of the bourgeoisie.[36] The *Manifesto*, it now appears, was almost entirely written by Marx. But he drew extensively upon a draft prepared by Engels, one of two that Engels produced in an attempt to undermine the influence of 'artisanal communism' within the Communist League which, however, was eventually persuaded to authorise Marx and Engels to write *The Communist Manifesto* as a statement of the principles and programme of the League.[37] Entitled 'Principles of Communism', Engels's draft took the form of a catechism of twenty-five questions and answers and *inter alia* contains the most detailed statement on the abolition of the division of labour that either of them made during this period. As such, it is worth exhibiting in detail:

> Classes came into existence through the division of labour and the division of labour in its *hitherto existing form* will *entirely* disappear . . . The joint management of production cannot be carried on by people as they are today, when each individual is assigned to a single branch of production, is shackled to it, exploited by it, of whom each has developed only one of his abilities at the expense of all others, knows only one branch, or only a branch of a branch of production as a whole . . . Industry which is

> carried on jointly and according to plan by the whole of society wholly presupposes people whose abilities have been developed all round, who are capable of surveying the *entire* system of production. Consequently, the division of labour . . . which makes one man a peasant, another a shoe-maker, a third a factory worker, a fourth a stockjobber, will thus *completely* disappear. Education will enable young people quickly to acquaint themselves with the *whole* system of production, it will enable them to pass in turn from one branch of industry to another *according to social needs* or *the bidding of their own inclinations* . . . Thus, a communistically organised society will be able to provide its members with the opportunity to utilise their comprehensively developed abilities in a comprehensive way. Concomitantly, the various classes will vanish of necessity [my emphasis].[38]

In writing to Marx immediately afterwards Engels warned that the document was 'miserably worded, in fearful haste', and it is of course necessary to bear in mind this qualification when analysing passages from it.[39] Nevertheless, something may be said about a fundamental tension that systematically disorganises the text: on the one hand Engels reiterates an earlier Marxian commitment to the *complete* abolition of the division of labour, to the creation of individuals who can understand the *entire* system of production; but on the other hand it is the total elimination of the *hitherto existing form* of the division of labour that is at issue, therefore leaving open the possibility of a different form of the division of labour in a classless society. The appearance of this latter proposition, in so far as it is not merely a rhetorical flourish on Engels's part, is symptomatic of a rethinking of the relationship between class and the division of labour away from the type of conceptual conflation characteristic of the earlier texts.[40] But in the overall process of intellectual transformation between the earlier and later writings, 'The Principles of Communism' represents only a transitional phase. Not only does the vocabulary of complete elimination survive, but the text also registers the absence of an argument that was later to become very prominent: that the exigencies of large-scale industrial production set limits to opportunities for the transformation of the division of labour in a society without classes. 'Principles of Communism', not unlike *The German Ideology*, refers only to 'social needs' and individual 'inclinations' in this context.

The 1848 revolutions actually broke out before *The Communist Manifesto* was published. Marx, expelled from Brussels, went first to Paris and then to Cologne where he and Engels set up the *Neue Rheinische Zeitung* as an organ of the German strand of a movement that was sweeping over Europe.[41] In keeping with the line of analysis advanced in the *Manifesto,* Marx argued that the major strategic objective of the German working class had to be a bourgeois revolution brought about by an alliance with the more radical and militant factions of the bourgeoisie. The *Neue Rheinische Zeitung* achieved a circulation of 5000, helped in part by Marx's active involvement in local political campaigns, especially in the setting up of the Committee of Cologne Democratic Unions which brought together the Workers' Association, Marx's Democratic Society and the Union of Employees and Employers.[42] But both the paper and the revolutionary movement soon ran into difficulties; the one because of chronic financial shortfalls, the other mainly because of a series of disastrous retreats by the political representatives of the German bourgeoisie and petty bourgeoisie, and the failure of local uprisings to fuse into an unified movement. Marx himself came under attack, from a Left faction within the Workers' Association, for not being radical enough. By the beginning of May 1849 the military and civil authorities felt confident enough to serve Marx with an expulsion order and to issue him with a passport valid only for Paris. After hastily winding up the paper, Marx and Engels made one final effort to rekindle the forces of revolution: they travelled first to Frankfurt and then to Baden in an attempt to unite the Left in the Frankfurt Assembly with the revolutionary leaders who had set up a provisional government in Baden, but to no avail. In June Marx arrived in Paris, only to witness the end of the French Revolution as well and to find himself forced to leave for England.

In exile in London Marx remained optimistic, expecting a fresh round of European revolutions as the unstable coalitions which had defeated the progressive forces disintegrated under the mounting weight of their own internal contradictions. An economic crisis, he believed, was a fundamental precondition for any new revolutionary upsurge; but in contrast with his earlier writings he began now to emphasise the importance of *political* preconditions as well. This is a line of thought that had already begun to emerge in Marx's articles in the *Neue Rheinische Zeitung* in the wake of the counter-revolution; the renewal of the revolutionary movement in

Germany, he had suggested, was dependent upon social upheavals in France and Britain, but the success of the British working class and its main representative, the Chartists, was in turn only possible if a French uprising resulted in a European war.[43]

The form of analysis Marx had begun to develop in relation to the German experience of 1848–9 has significant theoretical implications: transformations at the level of the economic can only provide *one* of the elements of a revolutionary conjuncture, while mutations at the political level have both an independent effectivity and a relative autonomy *vis-à-vis* the economic without, in the final analysis, displacing the determinant role of the latter.[44] But Marx himself very rarely *theorised* this new and more complex form of articulation between the economy and other levels which the experiences of 1848–9 forced him to recognise. Instead, apart from some passages in the *Grundrisse* and *Capital*, this new discourse is registered in his texts in a 'practical' state and coexists with the earlier more reductionist view so clearly evident in *The Poverty of Philosophy* and *The Communist Manifesto*. Above all it is in Marx's political writings, and especially his magnificent analyses of the events in France between 1848 and 1851, that the new discourse is most clearly apparent although always in complex coexistence with what Johnson has referred to appropriately as 'Manifesto Marxism'.[45] It is not necessary here to provide as detailed an explication of these writings as they deserve although, as we shall see, the problem of theorising complex articulations between different levels of the social formation has considerable relevance for appropriating and developing the mature Marx's insights into the division of labour in different modes of production.[46] The political writings of the 1850s thus have a relevance extending well beyond their character as occasional pieces; this is especially true of *The Eighteenth Brumaire of Louis Bonaparte* from which a number of themes may be regarded as symptomatic of the new standpoint.

In the first place, although Marx makes it very clear that the coexistence of different modes of production and the relative underdevelopment of capitalist relations of production within the French social formation provide the objective limits to possible political solutions, *classes* rarely appear in the text as 'whole' actors in the manner of the earlier writings. There is much greater sensitivity to internal differentiations, particularly within capital; Marx is always careful to distinguish its dominant fractions – industrial bourgeoisie, financial bourgeoisie, big landed property – and to analyse the genuine conflicts of interest between them.[47]

Partly because of the great number of classes on stage – itself a consequence of the coexistence of different modes of production – and partly because of fragmentation within classes, the most characteristic configuration identified at the political level is the *alliance* rather than simple, unmediated rule by a class, although the implication of Marx's remarks is that within every ruling bloc it is possible to identify a dominant class or faction and which in the French case often turned out to be the financial bourgeoisie. However, the significance of alliances is itself predicated upon the irreducibility of politics to the economy: the same economic infrastructure threw up a bewildering variety of political forms, ranging from monarchy to bourgeois parliamentary republic and even a form of dictatorship, depending upon the forms of alliance that were effective.[48] Thus in no sense could the character of the political level be 'read off' from the structure of the economic base, a conclusion reinforced by the significance Marx attaches to the types of ideology that were brought into play during the period. Thus, although he emphasises that what divided the supporters of the House of Orleans and the House of Bourbon was, in the final analysis, a conflict between the industrial and financial factions of the bourgeoisie on the one hand and 'big landed property' on the other, the form of the struggle, he argues, was itself affected by their ideological differences, by 'prejudices and illusions, sympathies and antipathies, convictions, articles of faith and principles' which provided the different groups with a source of political motivation, solidarity and action.[49]

However, Marx's *18th Brumaire* is probably best known for the view, derived from his dissection of Bonaparte's *coup d'état* of December 1851, that in a situation where the major classes are equally matched and politically exhausted, the executive arm of the state can obtain a considerable measure of autonomy by playing off one class against another, although not without rooting itself in one of the groups on stage, in this case the conservative faction of the small-holding peasantry, which harboured the illusion that the second Napoleon would halt and overturn the capitalist transformation of the countryside – a transformation reflected in the savage exploitation of the peasantry by urban merchants and moneylenders – which was rapidly undermining the material conditions of their existence.[50] But the text is equally important for being the first of Marx's writings to explicitly introduce the idea of completely dismantling or 'smashing' the state and for containing some of his most extended remarks on bureaucracy since the early *Critique of Hegel's Philosophy of Right*.[51]

In underlining the systematic interconnections between the French bureaucracy and the French bourgeoisie – 'it is precisely with the maintenance of that extensive state machine in its numerous ramifications that the material interests of the French bourgeoisie are interwoven in the closest fashion' – Marx may perhaps be said to be continuing a line of argument implicit in the instrumentalist conception of the state as a tool in the hands of the dominant classes contained in the earlier works, but he now points out that in perfecting the state machine the bourgeoisie actually strengthened an instrument that was to be used against them politically, and his suggestion that small-holding property provides a particularly fertile basis 'for an all-powerful and innumerable bureaucracy' also adds a new dimension.[52]

The idea of 'smashing' the state is also new, although at this stage little content is given to this notion. Nevertheless, in the present context it is important to take the opportunity to emphasise that although throughout the 'early' and 'transitional' periods Marx posited a very close relation between the division of labour and authority relations, the emergence of the conception of 'smashing' the state represents a significant departure. Certainly, during both periods, the division of labour for Marx always implied relations of subordination and superordination. The idea of the abolition of the division of labour thus went hand in hand with the dissolution of specialisation in administration, whether in productive or political institutions. In the early writings the existence of the state, too, is simply reduced either to alienation or, as in *The German Ideology*, to the division of labour and allied in the latter work to a rather crude form of class instrumentalism. In either case the specificity and independent effectivity of the bureaucracy as an aspect of the state's authoritative function could not properly be posed as a problem to be resolved: the abolition of the state and all its organs was automatically subsumed within an overall discourse which posited the dissolution of class and the division of labour by way of conceptual assimilation between the two.

As I have argued earlier, this discursive structure was not fundamentally undermined during the 'transitional' period; Marx continued to assimilate authority relations in productive institutions with every other relation of subordination and superordination in society including the state, a point superbly illustrated by the proposition, from *The Poverty of Philosophy*, that 'the concentration of the instruments of production and the division of labour are as inseparable one from the other as are, in the political sphere, the concentration of public authority and the division of private interests'.[53] But it is possible to discern during this stage the emergence of elements that were to form part of a new discourse; the idea of the necessity of 'smashing' the state is one such element, symptomatic of a more general direction that Marx was beginning to take away from class reductionism, in this particular case during his attempt to analyse the course of events in France. The abolition of the state could no longer be conceptually swept under the carpet; it posed instead a political problem requiring a genuine resolution at *that* level. Thus an explication of Marx's attempt to conceptualise the relative autonomy of the superstructures, and especially of political bureaucracy, is by no means irrelevant to an understanding of the transformation in his views on the division of labour and indeed forms one of its integral elements.

Engels informs us that the resumption of his economic studies that Marx undertook on his return to England eventually convinced him that 'the state of economic development on the Continent at that time was not, by a long way, ripe for the elimination of capitalist production'.[54] The period between spring and autumn 1850 obviously proved to be a crucial watershed in this respect: while the March 'Address of the Central Committee to the Communist League' still proclaimed the battle cry of 'The Revolution in Permanence' – echoed many years later by Trotsky in the aftermath of 1905 in Russia – the September 15 minutes of the Central Committee meeting document a serious reappraisal of revolutionary prospects. Arguing against those in the Communist League who still upheld the previous strategy, Marx now said: 'What we say to the workers is: You have 15, 20, 50 years of civil war to go through in order to change society and to train yourselves for the exercise of power, whereas they say, we must take over at once, or else we may as well take to our beds.'[55]

Throughout the 1850s Marx continued his economic studies despite extreme personal hardship and the constant interruptions forced upon him by the journalism which, together with generous assistance from Engels and other friends, just managed to keep his family from starving.[56] It was during this period, in the winter of 1857–8, that he composed the draft for *Capital*: the massive *Grundrisse*, first published in German in 1953. Both the *Grundrisse* and *Capital* register a profound discursive rupture in Marx's economic views and one which is bound up in the closest fashion with the conceptual separation between class and the division of labour which marks his mature work. The theoretical and methodological starting point of *Capital*, especially, differs significantly from that of previous writings and it is to an examination of the transformation that led from one to the other that we must now turn.

4
The Young and the Mature Marx: The Transition from 'Market' to 'Production'

It has been one of the major preoccupations of recent Marx scholarship to establish the precise relationship between the early and later writings, though it is unlikely that consensus will ever prevail, partly because competing interpretations of Marx always carry – wittingly or unwittingly – conflicting political and ideological ramifications which extend well beyond the world of textual exegesis and scholarship, and partly because his texts contain enough ambiguity to sustain a variety of readings. It is not my intention, however, to provide an overall review of the debate surrounding the relationship between the young and the mature Marx.[57] The major contentious issue in this context has concerned the relevance of the concept of alienation to the later works, a matter on which I have commented earlier. Interestingly enough though, one of the most perceptive contributions to the whole subject, and one which has considerable bearing on my own discussion, has remained relatively uninfluential: I refer to Martin Nicolaus's essay, 'The Unknown Marx', which first alerted English readers to the importance of the *Grundrisse* and clearly set out some of the theoretical elements which separate the mature from the earlier writings.[58] Two qualifications concerning Nicolaus's piece are, however, immediately in order. First, as Tribe has pointed out, Nicolaus tends to exaggerate the actual significance of the *Grundrisse* and fails to notice its status as a *transitional* text in which Marx is still struggling to break out of the discourse of the earlier economic writings; as a consequence Nicolaus is also unable to recognise the distance that separates *Capital* from the *Grundrisse*.[59] Second, and closely related to this, a proper explication of the discontinuity between Marx's earlier and later periods requires close attention to subsequent theoretical work, especially that undertaken by Althusser and Therborn, which in effect amplifies and recasts some of the propositions advanced by Nicolaus.

The chief merit of Nicolaus's article lies in posing very clearly the difference between relations of 'exchange' and 'production' as the basic theoretical starting points for Marx's earlier and later writings respectively. Marx's pre-*Capital* economics centre essentially around a theorisation and critique of the *market* as the fundamental institution of capitalist society: free competition and the untrammelled play of market forces are viewed as the unifying dynamic, the underlying cause of all other structural features of capitalism. As Nicolaus quite rightly observes, 'His polemic against Proudhon (*The Poverty of Philosophy*) reveals him in sharp disagreement with that self-declared luminary on almost every point of economics and philosophy, including especially every issue relating to the institutions of exchange and competition, except one: that competition is basic.'[60]

Marx's emphasis on the market is particularly evident in the concept of exploitation that is implicit in his critique of capitalism. Capitalist society is indicted for the fact that, along with all other phenomena that come under its sway, even the labourer is turned into a commodity. This theme pervades all of Marx's writings surveyed earlier, from *The Economic and Philosophic Manuscripts* onwards; in all of them wage labour under capitalism is seen as a commodity like any other. Indeed, this is precisely what Marx objects to, locating in this and the division of labour the dehumanisation of the worker. The focus on competition and the market is also reflected in the theory of wages. All of Marx's earlier writings contain a 'subsistence' theory of wages based around the conception that in a society dominated by exchange, competition between workers – reinforced by labour-saving innovations and periodic unemployment – ensures that employers need to pay little above the minimum to keep workers alive.[61]

In *Capital* these elements in Marx's analysis and critique undergo a serious transformation and displacement. Most fundamentally, Marx breaks with the view that the basic mechanism of capitalism is located in its system of exchange and circulation. In *Capital* the market is regarded as a superficial and necessarily illusory representation of a much more essential underlying process which contains the real clue to the operation of capitalism: its system of pumping out surplus value from labourers in the process of *production*. The market under conditions of capitalist production represents the contract between capitalist and worker as an exchange of equivalents, thus masking the systematic asymmetry in the relationship. Marx himself expresses this contrast between exchange and production in a revealing passage in *Capital*:

> The consumption of labour power is completed, as in the case of every other commodity, *outside the limits of the market* . . . Accompanied by Mr Moneybags and by the possessor of labour power, we therefore take leave of this noisy sphere, where everything takes place on the surface . . . and follow them both into the hidden abode of *production* . . . there we shall see, not only how capital produces, but how capital is produced. We shall at last force the secret of profit-making [my emphasis].[62]

The conceptual precondition for the emergence of the theory of surplus value in Marx's work lies in the recognition – only partially evident in the *Grundrisse* – that labour is not in fact a commodity like any other, for it has the unique ability to add more value than is required in its own production, and that what the worker offers for sale is not labour but a certain elastic capacity, *labour power*.[63] In turn, the theory of surplus value leads to modifications in Marx's theory of wages, which now rests on the proposition that the workers' impoverishment is of a relative rather than an absolute kind. And, as we shall see, the theorisation of the division of labour typical of the early writings is also displaced.

In the mature writings, then, the concept of exploitation is based not on the dehumanisation inherent in labour-as-commodity but on the extraction and appropriation of surplus value from the working class in the process of capitalist production. However, this implies in turn the emergence in Marx's discourse of a new conception of 'relations of production'. This term, as I have already pointed out, actually makes its appearance in *The Poverty of Philosophy*, but the discursive hegemony of exchange in the works of that period determines a radically different meaning for it when set against its place in *Capital*. The discontinuity between the earlier and mature theorisations of the relations of production lies primarily in the centrality of *forms of the extraction and appropriation of surplus labour* to the latter.[64] Although it is apparent that by the time he came to compose *The Poverty of Philosophy* Marx had accepted the basic theorems of the labour theory of value and that he was aware of the existence of a surplus, it is also clear, as Nicolaus remarks, that 'he is clearly not conscious of the enormous implications for economic theory of this fact'.[65]

The new theorisation evident in *Capital* is expressed most clearly in two passages, which also justify treating the concept of surplus labour as central to historical materialism more generally, rather than restricting it to capitalist relations of production: 'The essential difference between the various economic forms of society, between, for instance, a society based on slave labour, and one based on wage labour, lies only in the mode in which this surplus labour is in each case extracted from the actual producer, the labourer.'[66] In the third volume of *Capital* we find a much fuller exposition which also points to the determination of political forms by the mode of extraction of surplus labour:

> The specific economic form, in which unpaid surplus labour is pumped out of direct producers, determines the relationship of rulers and ruled, as it grows directly out of production itself and, in turn, reacts upon it as a determining element. Upon this, however, is founded the entire formation of the economic community which grows up out of the production relations themselves, thereby its specific political form. It is always the direct relationship of the owners of the conditions of production to the direct producers – a relation always naturally corresponding to a definite stage in the development of the methods of labour and thereby its social productivity – which reveals the innermost secret, the hidden basis of the entire social structure, and with it the political form of the relation of sovereignty and dependence, in short, the corresponding specific form of the state.[67]

It is only with this reconceptualisation of the relations of production that Marx begins to elaborate some of the principles by which the relative autonomy of the capitalist state can be theorised, while at the same time hinting at a new form of determination of the superstructures by the economy.

It may be remembered that in *The Eighteenth Brumaire* Marx had been struggling to reconcile the principle of determination by the economy with the independent effectivity of politics and ideology. But that text is marked by a genuine tension that finds no real resolution. That is, on the one hand Marx's analysis registers the relative autonomy of political and ideological forces, but on the other implies very strongly that Bonaparte's independence from the major classes was the product of an exceptional conjuncture in which the French state could temporarily play off one class against another. In *Capital*, however, the analysis based on the concept of surplus labour suggests that it is only in pre-capitalist modes of production that there is a direct intertwining of economy and polity, and thus between the dominant classes and the instruments of political and military control, because the conditions of the ownership of the means of production are such that the extraction and appropriation of surplus labour is not possible without extra-economic – and thus political, legal and military – sanctions: 'It is . . . evident that in all forms of production in which the direct labourer remains the "possessor" of the means of production and labour conditions necessary for the production of his own means of subsistence . . . the surplus labour for the nominal owner . . . can only be extorted . . . by other than economic pressure, whatever the form assumed may be.'[68]

Under conditions of capitalist relations of production, in contrast, the direct producers are divorced from ownership of the means of production and the owners can thus extract surplus labour without the direct intervention of coercive agencies. In turn this means that state apparatuses in general are separate from the relations of production and thus separate also from the *classes* which grow out of these relations of production. It is precisely this double separation which creates the necessary structural conditions for the relative autonomy of the state in capitalist social formations, allowing it, *inter alia*, to make concessions to the working class against the overt wishes of many fractions of capital, and to present itself as an agent of the national rather than class interest. Marx himself does not develop these insights in any systematic way, but they represent genuine developments opened up and made possible by the reconceptualisation of the relations of production by way of the notion of surplus labour. It is above all in the writings of Nicos Poulantzas that these implications of Marx's mature theorisation have been most fruitfully developed; they have thus laid the basis for a conception of the state in capitalism radically different from the *impasse* of crude class-instrumentalist views which operate essentially within a pre-*Capital* discourse.[69]

Marx's new theorisation based on the concept of surplus labour also contains hints for a more general reconceptualisation of the principle of determination by the economy in a non-reductionist direction. It implies, that is, a distinction between the *determinant* and the *dominant* levels of a social formation: in this reformulation the economy is said to be determinant in the sense that its structure determines which of the levels of a social formation is to be the dominant one.[70] Thus, to take the example discussed earlier, it is the character of the economy – defined by the forms of ownership and possession of the means of production – which determines that in all pre-capitalist social formations a level other than the economic will be dominant. Expressed in this manner, the thesis of the primacy of the economic level is freed from implications of 'necessary correspondence' between the economy and superstructures. The economy merely sets limits to possibilities at the political and ideological levels, by determining an overall pattern of articulation between the different levels within which each level has to operate, and by determining the structure of classes at the economic level.

Again, it cannot be emphasised too strongly that this type of retheorisation is only implicit in Marx's remarks in *Capital*, representing one possible line of discursive development, and that throughout the mature period it coexists with a much more reductionist framework which is often more dominant at the surface level of his texts. It is Althusser, in the first place, who has attempted to rescue this new, submerged discourse from obscurity and to systematise its propositions with some rigour. At the same time, it is necessary to recognise that this process of developing the discursive possibilities inherent in *Capital* is still in its infancy and many difficulties still remain, for example in rigorously formulating a viable concept of mode of production, in the delineation of different pre-capitalist modes of production and in securing for the concept of relative autonomy an adequate specification.[71] Moreover, it has not been generally appreciated that the emergence of the discourse of surplus labour introduces ambiguities and difficulties in Marx's theorisation of class, in so far as the existence of surplus appropriation can now appear as a partially *competing* axis for the definition of classes, alongside the traditional index of private ownership of the means of production. The effects of this source of incoherence are evident, not so much in Marx's own work, as in the researches of contemporary Marxist anthropologists who, armed with the concept of surplus labour, threaten to find classes in all primitive social formations whether characterised by private ownership or not.[72] These issues cannot, however, be pursued here. My basic purpose has been to demonstrate that within the general problematic of historical materialism it is possible to discern in Marx's work a new discourse based on the concept of surplus labour, that this therefore transforms the meaning of the concept of 'relations of production' in the mature texts, and that this new discourse contains *some* of the elements of a fruitful reconceptualisation of the base-superstructure theorem in non-reductionist directions. In what follows I shall show the complex but systematic connection between this new discourse and the development of a non-class-reductionist conception of the division of labour in Marx's mature writings as well, although, before presenting a detailed discussion of Marx's analysis of the division of labour in *Capital*, two brief detours are necessary.

5
The 1857 *Introduction*: The Problem of Production in General

One very important contribution made by the new theorisation of the relations of production to the emergence of a non-reductionist conception of the division of labour lay precisely in displacing exchange relations and installing production, in the sense already indicated, as the fundamental level of analysis. The shift signalled by this new starting point in production was a crucial stage in the disengagement of the division of labour from class, in my view, because it compelled Marx to rethink and to reconstitute the category of production itself which, in one sense, had after all always been his point of departure. Especially, it led Marx to conclude that certain features of production were generic to it as a process and, however unacceptable they might be on other grounds, it was to all intents and purposes futile to postulate their disappearance with changing social formations. This is not to suggest that Marx's views became crudely ahistorical; it is the contention here that Marx became especially sensitive to the exigencies of *large-scale industrial* production and that this made him much less sanguine about the possibility of completely dissolving the division of labour even in post-capitalist society. In the process, as I shall document later, Marx also found himself compelled to take account of limitations imposed by 'nature' in this context.

This new perspective is fully apparent only in *Capital* – although here too this particular discourse is overshadowed by others – but the foundations were laid in a set of reflections contained in the *Introduction* which Marx composed just before writing the *Grundrisse*. Here we find some of the first fruits of Marx's resumed interest in 'production' as a category and the first attempt to think through the exigencies of the production process abstracted from its conditions of existence in particular social formations:

> Whenever we speak of production, then, what is meant is always production at a definite stage of social development . . . However, all epochs of production have certain common traits, common characteristics. Production in general is an abstraction, but a rational abstraction in so far as it really brings out and fixes the common element . . . the elements which are not general and common, must be separated out from the determinations valid for production as such.[73]

Marx makes it perfectly clear in the *Introduction* that his object is not to produce a form of meta-historical analysis. The general category of production, 'this common element sifted out by comparison, is itself segmented many times over and splits into different determinations'.[74] In any particular instance, he points out, production is always carried out in the form of a specific branch of production, for example agriculture, cattle-raising or manufacture, and it is necessary to bear in mind that some natural conditions are 'more advantageous to production than others'.[75] On the other hand, Marx warns against the dangers of a straightforward technicism: 'But political economy is not technology.' The real task is to explore the 'relation of the general characteristics of production at a given stage of social development to the particular forms of production' which, he indicates he intends to undertake later.[76]

In these and other passages it is possible to discern on Marx's part an attempt to give adequate expression to a new element in his discourse: the necessarily complicated articulation between the exigencies of particular branches and techiques of production, the process of production in general, and the impact of specific social relations in organising the whole mode of production into a complex totality, and which therefore includes at the same time distribution, exchange and consumption. 'The conclusion we reach', he says, 'is not that production, distribution, exchange and consumption are identical, but that they all form the members of a totality, distinctions within a unity.'[77] The type of production, which necessarily includes as *one* of its 'moments' the distribution of the agents of production, and therefore classes, 'predominates' over the distribution of products and the processes of exchange and consumption, determines the forms they take, without excluding the possibility of secondary determinations by which exchange (for example in the form of the size of the market), distribution (for instance, the different distribution of the population into town and country), and consumption in turn affect production.[78]

There is, however, scant agreement about the general significance of the *Introduction* for an interpretation of Marx's work; indeed, there is some doubt surrounding Marx's own subsequent appraisal of it.[79] Nevertheless, although the methodological prescriptions of the *Introduction* are by no means unequivocal, the *leitmotive* seems very strongly to be the injunction to begin with simple, abstract, general relations such as labour, division of labour, value and exchange and only then to focus on the more concrete determinations, while recognising the fact that, especially in pre-capitalist societies, the development of these forms and their interrelationship is uneven and historically variable. However, in his famous *Preface* to *A Contribution to the Critique of Political Economy* (1859), Marx apparently changed his mind about this whole procedure, for he now writes: 'I am omitting a general introduction which I had jotted down because on closer reflection any anticipation of results still to be proved appears to me to be disturbing, and the reader who on the whole desires to follow me must be resolved to ascend from the particular to the general.'[80]

On the basis of this remark, Nicolaus concludes in his *Foreword* to the English edition of the *Grundrisse* that Marx had obviously decided that the 1857 *Introduction* had represented a false start; henceforth, Nicolaus argues, Marx's starting point, as in *Capital*, lies in an analysis of the commodity, 'a compound, determinate, delimited and concrete whole'.[81] But this is only partially correct, for it seriously underestimates the extent to which, beginning with the *Introduction*, Marx continues to reflect on the problem of production in general, the structural consequences of particular types of production processes, and their articulation with the social relations of production. Discursively this form of analysis necessarily plays a secondary role in *Capital*, for the explicit object of that work is the step by step demonstration of the theory of surplus value and thus the hidden mechanism of capitalist production. Nevertheless, as we shall see, at several stages of the argument in *Capital* Marx's exposition proceeds by way of general remarks on various aspects of production *per se*, and includes a theorisation, usually in explicit terms, of the structural necessities imposed by particular processes of production on forms of social organisation including the division of labour. Hence my argument that the reconceptualisation of the articulation between class and the division of labour that is apparent in *Capital* is only properly intelligible when viewed against the backdrop of the remarks on production in the 1857 *Introduction*.

6
Division of Labour and the Theory of Surplus Value

The fact that the theory of surplus value necessarily entailed a shift away from the market as the primary level of analysis and thus compelled Marx to reconceptualise 'production' is only one sense in which it contributed to the separation of 'class' from 'division of labour' in *Capital*. Another source of this retheorisation resides in the distinction between *use value* and *exchange value*, a fundamental discrimination within the theory of surplus value and, more broadly, a longstanding one in the history of economic thought. The significance of this distinction in the present context lies in the discursive space it opened up for Marx to reflect on the nature of production processes as such, simply for use, abstracted from the forms they might assume in social formations based on exchange, thus reinforcing a methodology already inscribed in the more general move to 'production'. Indeed, both features may be regarded as 'moments' of the same discursive transformation, an articulation that is particularly evident in one of Marx's letters to Kugelmann written in 1868, the year after the publication of *Capital*. Marx writes:

> Every child knows that a nation which ceased to work . . . even for a few weeks would perish. Every child knows, too, that the masses of products corresponding to the different needs require different and quantitatively determined masses of the total labour of society. That this *necessity* of the *distribution* of social labour in definite proportions cannot possibly be done away with by a particular *form* of social production but can only change the *mode* of its *appearance*, is self-evident. No natural laws can be done away with. What can change in historically different cir-

> cumstances is only the *form* in which these laws assert themselves. And the form in which the proportional distribution of labour asserts itself, in a state or society where the interconnection of social labour is manifested in the *private exchange* of the individual products of labour, is precisely the *exchange value* of these products [Marx's emphasis].[82]

This passage illustrates superbly Marx's conceptualisation of what he referred to as the 'dual' nature of the labour process: the necessarily intricate relation between the exigencies of production as such, in this case even abstracted from particular types of production processes, and their form of appearance in a society dominated by the production of commodities. It demonstrates, too, the distance Marx had travelled from *The German Ideology* and *The Poverty of Philosophy*; in both works this kind of theorisation is only conspicuous by its absence.

The basic propositions of the theory of surplus value are, of course, too well known to require detailed elaboration here.[83] It is sufficient to point out that for Marx the origins of surplus value – and hence profit – lie in the particular ability of labour power to add more value in the course of production than is required for its own reproduction. By virtue of his command over the means of production, the capitalist owner is able to compel the worker to labour for a longer period than is necessary to cover wages and, therefore, the cost of the reproduction of labour power. The capitalist thus commands and appropriates surplus labour which, in conditions of generalised commodity production, takes the form of surplus value.

Part IV

Marx and the Division of Labour: the Analysis in *Capital*

1
Production in General, the Labour Process and the Division of Labour

It has been my argument that in transforming his theoretical starting point from exchange to production in the 1850s and 1860s, Marx found himself compelled to reflect afresh upon the conditions of existence of human production as such and its relation to the exigencies of what he referred to as 'large-scale' production, abstracted from their concrete realisation in social formations, characterised by forms of commodity production and class relations, and that the first fruits of this retheorisation are evident in the *Introduction* to the *Grundrisse*. It is also the contention here that this led Marx, in turn, to revise his earlier belief in the possibility of a complete emancipation from the division of labour in a future classless society and that in *Capital* and subsequent writings Marx's remarks on the transformation of the division of labour in future society should *primarily* be understood as referring to one fundamental aspect of the differentiation of productive tasks: the division between intellectual and manual labour.

The lines of continuity between some of the reflections on production as a category in the 1857 *Introduction* and the discourse of *Capital* are not immediately apparent. Marx's attempts to conceptualise the fundamental elements of the process of production are not to be found at the beginning of the text, which starts with an analysis of the commodity, but are set out separately at several other points in *Capital*. The same is true of his remarks on the exigencies of production on a large scale, for they are scattered throughout the different volumes of *Capital*. The links between these various pieces of analysis only become apparent when they are detached from the rest of his argument and, as it were, made to run together as a single discourse. *In this sense* the starting point can be seen to reside in chapter VII on 'The Labour-Process and the Process of Producing Surplus-Value'. Characteristically, and entirely in keeping with my interpretation concerning the importance of 'production' as a theoretical category in *Capital*, Marx begins this chapter by attempting to identify the nature of the labour process as such, abstracted from its realisation in different modes of production: 'The fact that the production of use-values, or goods, is carried on under the control of a capitalist and on his behalf, does not alter the general character of that production. We shall, therefore, in the first place, have to consider the labour-process independently of the particular form it assumes under given social conditions.'[1]

The labour process, Marx argues, 'is human action with a view to the production of use-values, appropriation of natural substances to human requirements'. Thus it is not only the necessary means for effecting a productive exchange with nature but, Marx adds, 'it is the *everlasting* Nature-imposed condition of human existence, and therefore is independent of every social phase of that existence, or rather, is common to every such phase [my emphasis].'[2] At the same time Marx is careful to point out that an identification of this basic process cannot by itself reveal the social conditions under which it is taking place.[3] Both these steps in the analysis and argument follow closely the tentative conclusions of the 1857 *Introduction* on the discursive rationality of production as a general category.

The basic elements of the labour process are identified as '1, the personal activity of man, *i.e.*, work itself, 2, the subject of that work, and 3, its instruments'.[4] The second includes natural resources and raw materials, while the third is said to be 'a thing, or complex of things, which the labourer interposes between himself and the subject of his labour, and which serves as the conductor of his activity'.[5] Marx's interest in providing the most elementary specifications is allied to an attempt to penetrate the basic distinctiveness of *human* production. Thus he points out that while spiders and bees engage in highly complex operations, 'what distinguishes the worst architect from the best of bees is this, that the architect raises his structure in imagination before he erects it in reality. At the end of every labour-process, we get a result that already existed in the imagination of the labourer at its commencement.'[6] The production and use of instruments of labour, moreover, is also said to be 'specifically characteristic of the human labour-process'.[7]

It is hardly fortuitous that in the process of identifying the basic constituents of the human labour process, Marx at the same time refers to the social and organisational exigencies imposed by particular *instruments* of production. As I have suggested earlier, Marx's interest in specifying the nature of production in general was systematically related to an attempt to grasp the specific limits and determinations stemming from particular forms of production and processes of labour. Although similar remarks also occur, of course, in earlier writings and elsewhere in *Capital*, the existence of the following passage in the present context – overly technicist though it may seem – is illustrative of the basic discursive procedure which the reading of *Capital* offered here is aiming to underline:

> It is not the articles made, but how they are made, and by what instruments, that enable us to distinguish different economic epochs. Instruments of labour not only supply a standard of the degree of development to which human labour has attained, *but they are also indicators of the social conditions under which that labour is carried on* [my emphasis].[8]

The only reason that particular instruments of labour can provide 'indications' of the social conditions of production in which they are involved is, as we shall see, that specific forms of production are seen by Marx to set limits to the variability of social organisations for which they form a 'material' infrastructure. Nevertheless, it is worth pointing out that throughout Marx's analysis in *Capital* there is some uncertainty and ambiguity surrounding the precise scope of determination attributable to the nature and level of productive technique. In the present context, this manifests itself in the tension between the claim that instruments of labour provide no more than indications of the social conditions of production, and the explicit approval of the 'materialist' classification of pre-historic epochs 'into the stone, the bronze, and the iron ages'.[9]

In the light of the interpretation of Marx's method in *Capital* advanced above, it should also come as no surprise that very early in his chapter on 'Co-operation' as well – and this is the second point at which the discourse on production in general manifests itself – Marx provides an abstract and formal definition of this form of social production: 'When numerous labourers work together side by side, whether in one and the same process, or in different but connected processes, they are said to co-operate, or to work in co-operation.'[10]

Moreover, he immediately proceeds to analyse its general advantages regardless of the overall mode of production – for example, slave, feudal or capitalist – in which it is concretely realised. Cooperation, Marx argues, represents 'the creation of a new power, namely, the collective power of masses'. It not only allows greater possibilities than individual labour (for instance, in raising heavy weights), but reduces costs because 'a portion of the same means of production are now consumed in common': 'A room where twenty weavers work at twenty looms must be larger than the room of a single weaver with two assistants.' 'But,' Marx adds, 'it costs less labour to build one workshop for twenty persons than to build ten to accommodate two weavers each.'[11] He also points out that in a variety of productive tasks cooperation is a vital *technical* necessity either because it allows a greater spatial field of activity – as in draining, irrigation works, construction of roads, and so on – or because there are exigencies of time, as in harvesting where 'the quantity and quality of the product depends on the work being begun and ended within a certain time'.[12]

This new discourse in *Capital* on production and its general forms is allied to a more considered conceptualisation and specification of the division of labour and *its* general forms; together they raise Marx's theorisation to a level of sophistication unmatched in earlier texts like *The German Ideology* and *The Poverty of Philosophy* although, as we shall see, several conceptual issues still remain unresolved even in *Capital*. One of the most striking features of Marx's general analysis of the division of labour in *Capital* is that the distinction between the 'social' and the 'manufacturing' division of labour – first announced in *The Poverty of Philosophy* without carrying the same labels and subsequently absent altogether in Marx's writings – appears in the very first chapter, but this time combined with an analytical separation between *the existence of the social division of labour* and *the production of commodities* (that is, goods and services for exchange):

> division of labour is a necessary condition for the production of commodities, but it does not follow, conversely, that the production of commodities is a necessary condition for the division of labour. In the primitive Indian community there is social division of labour, without production of commodities. Or, to take an example nearer home, in every factory the labour is divided

> according to a system, but this division is not brought about by the operatives mutually exchanging their individual products. Only such products can become commodities with regard to each other, as result from different kinds of labour, each kind being carried on independently and for the account of private individuals.[13]

The conceptual discrimination evident in this passage immediately announces the qualitatively different level of analysis to be found in *Capital* when compared with earlier works. And in this context it is worth noting that in reintroducing the distinction between division of labour in society and division of labour in the workshop, Marx has a much clearer and surer grasp of the discursive break between his analysis and that of Smith than he had had in *The Poverty of Philosophy*. While Smith imagined that the distinction between the two forms of division of labour was 'merely subjective', Marx insists that despite 'numerous analogies and links' between them, 'division of labour in the interior of a society, and that in the interior of a workshop, differ not only in degree, but also in kind'.[14] The social division of labour involves the dispersion of the means of production among independent producers of commodities in different sectors of industry, hegemonised by wanton competition and economic anarchy. Division of labour in the workshop, in contrast, derives from the concentration of the means of production in the hands of the individual capitalist under whose despotic authority and supervision the work of individual labourers is organised and subdivided for production, only the combined product of the labourers producing a commodity.[15]

The role of the distinction between division of labour in society and division of labour in the workshop in the discursive structure of *Capital* is now widely recognised, as is its general significance in the analysis of capitalist production. But it is not so well known that this is not the only relevant discrimination that Marx introduces into his analysis, for in the same context he distinguishes between 'division of labour in general', 'division of labour in particular' and 'division of labour in detail':

> If we keep labour alone in view, we may designate the separation of social production into its main divisions of *genera* – viz., agriculture, industries, &c., as division of labour in general, and the

> splitting up of these families into species and sub-species, as division of labour in particular, and the division of labour within the workshop as division of labour in singular or in detail.[16]

It is, of course, entirely consistent with my interpretation that the parameters of theorisation here are set by the category of labour in general, as Marx underlines at the beginning of the passage. On the other hand, the point of these discriminations and their relation to the central distinction between the social and the workshop division of labour are not immediately apparent. As we shall see, this is an important conceptual issue, but it is discussed later in the context of a more general interrogation of the coherence and analytical clarity of Marx's usage of 'division of labour' in *Capital*. For the present it is more appropriate to point to a further conceptual refinement that Marx incorporates into his discussion of the division of labour in *Capital*.

It may be remembered that in *The German Ideology* and other earlier writings the separation of 'commerce' from industry and agriculture is regarded by Marx as yet another dimension of the division of labour. Indeed, in *The German Ideology* this is assimilated to the schism between town and country and mental and manual labour. Moreover, Marx makes no systematic discrimination between separation in relation to distinct branches of production like industry and agriculture, and the specific process of differentiation of capitals (for example, industrial and commercial capital) and further subdivisions internal to these. It is thus interesting to note that in the second volume of *Capital* Marx produces a new term – 'division of social labour' – in an attempt to conceptualise this particular form of articulation within capitalist production:

> When production by means of wage labour becomes universal, commodity production is bound to be the general form of production. This mode of production, once it is assumed to be general, carries in its wake an ever increasing *division of social labour*, that is to say an ever growing differentiation of the articles which are produced in the form of commodities by a definite capitalist, ever greater division of complementary processes of production into independent processes [my emphasis].[17]

In this passage Marx refers specifically to 'processes of production', but the analysis is meant to apply more generally to the constant tendency within capitalism for production functions, including those of commerce and surplus realisation, to be seized upon by separate, more specialised entrepreneurial units. The new term signals the intention to treat this emergent process of segmentation as analytically distinct from other forms of the division of labour. It represents an attempt to theorise the distinct shape that capitalism, as a specific type of commodity production, imposes on the contours of social production.

The much greater rigour that is evident in the conceptual discriminations referred to above, also characterises Marx's albeit brief discussions (more in the nature of digressions) of the origins of division of labour and exchange in *Capital*. At this point it is instructive to refer back to *The Poverty of Philosophy*: one of the ironies of this polemic against Proudhon, penned twenty years before the writing of *Capital*, is that while Marx rightly pours scorn on Proudhon for totally mystifying the origins of the division of labour and exchange, his own analysis of the subject at the time is rather poorly developed and, in addition, is compromised by a systematic conflation between division of labour and forms of ownership, and a grossly over-extended usage of the term 'division of labour' itself. One discursive consequence of this is that the origins of exchange still remain obscure. *Capital* replaces this undifferentiated analysis with the closely and succinctly set out argument that the social division of labour on the one hand, and the 'tying down of individuals to a particular calling' on the other, actually develop from *opposite* starting points in relation to exchange, which derives from the first and serves only to accentuate the second form of the division of labour. Different communities, finding themselves in distinct environments, develop different means of subsistence and different products; thus evolves a spontaneous social division of labour which later leads to production for exchange when these communities come into contact and regularise social interaction between themselves. In turn, this encourages a subdivision of productive tasks within each community, only present initially in rudimentary form on the basis of differences in sex and age. At this point Smith's proposition concerning the extent of the market becomes significant, for it is only if the sphere of exchange is extensive enough that it becomes possible for each community to introduce a division of tasks for the production of individual commodities; hence, ultimately, the origins of division of labour in manufacture.[18]

Nevertheless, while the conceptual sophistication of Marx's usage of 'division of labour' in *Capital* – when set against earlier texts – should not now be in doubt, several difficulties remain. Any systematic interrogation of Marx's conceptual vocabulary must first confront the relation between the notions of 'social division of labour' (and the 'division of labour in manufacture') and the concepts of 'division of labour in general', 'in particular' and 'in detail'. The latter, it may be remembered, are referred to by Marx as the main divisions within 'social production'. The only example that Marx himself cites under division of labour 'in general' is the differentiation between agriculture and industry. He fails to provide any illustrations for the division of labour 'in particular', although by referring to the latter as an aspect of the splitting up of industry and agriculture into 'species and sub-species' it may be inferred that Marx had in mind what he elsewhere refers to as 'branches of trade' and 'crafts' such as shoemaking and tailoring, that is, the production of distinct types of goods which could, with the development of exchange relations, become commodities. Division of labour in 'detail' is referred to as division of labour 'within the workshop'.[19]

It is not immediately clear whether or not these two sets of concepts are situated at the same theoretical level. The concepts of division of labour 'in general', 'in particular' and 'in detail' seem to refer to differentiations within production as such, that is, abstracted from the social distribution of tasks between specialised individuals and groups. However, 'social division of labour' sometimes also appears to be used in this form in *Capital*: 'To all the different varieties of values in use there correspond as many different kinds of useful labour, classified according to the order, genus, species and variety to which they belong in the social division of labour.'[20] While it is not possible to resolve this issue beyond doubt, a close textual examination suggests that the term 'social', when it appears in this context, almost invariably carries with it the implication of specialisation at the level of individuals and groups and therefore represents theorisation at a level distinct from division of labour 'in general', 'in particular' and 'in detail'. Thus, in the projected fourth volume of *Capital, Theories of Surplus Value* (1862–3), Marx refers to the social division of labour as a 'separation of occupations' and distinguishes it, at this stage, from 'coexisting labour':

> Division of labour is, in one sense, nothing but coexisting labour, that is, the coexistence of different kinds of labour which are represented in different kinds of products or rather commodities. The division of labour in the capitalist sense, as the breaking down of the particular labour which produces a definite commodity into a series of simple and co-ordinated operations divided up amongst different workers, presupposes the division of labour within society outside the workshop, as separation of occupations.[21]

In so far as the concept of 'coexisting labour' prefigures and serves as a shorthand expression for division of labour 'in general', 'in particular' and 'in detail', it is possible to reinforce the conclusion that this set of concepts theorises the division of labour at the level of *positions*, while the concept of 'social division of labour' theorises it at the level of *agents* who occupy these positions. The fact that this distinction is implicit in much of Marx's discussion in earlier texts should not be allowed to obscure the theoretical advance marked by the more explicit acknowledgement and specification it receives in *Capital*. As I shall argue later, this discrimination is systematically related to changes in Marx's views on the abolition of the division of labour. And it is hardly necessary to labour the point that there is an obvious connection between the emergence of this conceptual refinement in *Capital* and the continuing influence of the methodological prescriptions of the 1857 *Introduction*.

The social division of labour (or the division of labour in society) is also distinguished from the division of labour in the workshop (or in manufacture). Indeed, Marx insists that the difference between the two is not merely one of degree but of kind. Note, however, that in terms of the distinction between the level of positions and the level of agents, both 'social division of labour' and 'division of labour in the workshop' are conceptually located at the level of agents (the concept of division of labour 'in detail' corresponding, at the level of positions, to the concept of division of labour in the workshop). Although this discursive identity does not undermine *Marx's* rationale for a strict analytical separation between the social division of labour and the division of labour in the workshop, it does make it more difficult to incorporate other forms of differentiation, also referred to in *Capital*, into his overall conceptual schema. This is particularly true of the sexual division of labour: located at the level of agents, it manifests itself both 'in society' and 'in the workshop'. While there is only a limited amount of material on sexual differences in *Capital*, it is not surprising that it appears in discussions of both forms of division of labour; without further refinement the concept of sexual division of labour inevitably blurs what was for Marx a fundamental analytical discrimination between the social and workshop division of labour. Marx's remarks on the employment of female labour in the capitalist factory are examined later. For the present it is only necessary to note that as far as sexual division of labour 'in society' is concerned he confined himself to a view that he had formed much earlier, that in the course of social development 'there springs up naturally a division of labour, caused by differences of sex and age, a division that is consequently based on a purely physiological foundation'.[22]

The distinction between intellectual and manual labour encounters even greater theoretical difficulties, even if the problem of rigorously differentiating between its two constituent elements is set aside. At the level of agents its presence, like that of the sexual division of labour, is registered both 'in society' and 'in the workshop'. But the distinction can also be located at the level of *positions*, thus introducing an additional element of ambiguity into Marx's conceptual vocabulary.

In *Capital* Marx also refers to the 'territorial division of labour', which 'confines special branches of production to special districts of a country', and to the differentiation between town and country: 'The foundation of every division of labour that is well developed, and brought about by the exchange of commodities, is the separation between town and country.'[23] Although these forms of segmentation are easily distinguished from the division of labour in the workshop, they may be located both at the level of positions and at the level of agents, thereby leading to the same type of indeterminacy of meaning identified above in connection with the distinction between intellectual and manual labour.

There is, finally, a further difficulty embedded in Marx's discussion of forms of the division of labour in *Capital* which must be considered. While he does introduce a distinction between the existence of a social division of labour and the existence of commodity production, he fails to keep commodity production and exchange relations sufficiently distinct from private ownership of the means of production. Thus, whenever Marx refers in *Capital* to the relationship between the social division of labour and exchange, this is invariably mediated by private ownership such that the possibilities for coexistence between a social division of labour and exchange relations under conditions of common ownership of the means of production are written out of the discussion.[24] This lacuna underlies some of the limitations in his understanding of forms of exchange necessary and possible under socialism, an issue that is explored in greater depth later in this book. The conflation between the social division of labour and forms of private ownership of the means of production is one important sense in which the concept of division of labour is *not* sufficiently detached from that of class or mode of production in *Capital*. As I have already argued, although some fundamental propositions from the early writings on the relation between class and the division of labour are modified in the later works, the implications of these revisions are not systematically thought through and integrated into Marx's mature discourse. It should also be noticed that the failure to separate private ownership from the social division of labour compounds the difficulties, already indicated, of integrating the sexual division of labour and the differentiation between mental and manual labour into Marx's conceptual framework.

2
Large-Scale Production and the Duality of the Capitalist Production Process

The theorisation of production in general in *Capital*, documented above, is systematically related to Marx's frequent attempts in the text to abstract the organisational necessities inherent in large-scale production from the specific social forms created by the *capitalist* organisation of large-scale industry. As a type of abstraction the latter has the same discursive structure as the theorisation of production in general and may be seen as an extension of this form of analysis to a more concrete and historically specific level. Its emergence in *Capital*, like that of the discussion of production in general, is inexplicable except as the outcome of the general reflections contained in the 1857 *Introduction* on forms of production and their interrelationship. And both may thus be said to derive from the discursive transformation from 'exchange' to 'production' signalled by the *Grundrisse*.

The analytical differentiation between organisational forms rooted in large-scale production and their 'deformed' structure within the capitalist mode of production finds its conceptual basis in the notion of the duality of the capitalist production process, expounded at some length in *Results of the Immediate Process of Production* (written between 1863 and 1866 and originally planned as part seven of the first volume of *Capital*). 'The capitalist process of production', Marx points out here, 'is the unity of labour process and valorisation process.'[25] This duality mirrors the product of the capitalist process, the commodity, which is 'the immediate unity of use-value and exchange-value'.[26] The defining feature of the valorisation process is that 'it is essentially the production of surplus-value', which is the 'determining, dominating and overriding purpose of the capitalist'.[27] The labour process, on the other hand, is 'a process which creates new use-values by performing useful labour with existing use-values' and forms the 'material substratum' of capitalist production.[28] That this conception of duality derives from a theorisation of production in general is emphasised by Marx himself: the elements of the capitalist labour process, he argues, 'are those of the labour process itself, of any labour process, irrespective of the mode of production or the stage of economic development in which they find themselves'.[29]

Marx's analysis of the twofold nature of the capitalist production process in the *Results* relies on an assertion of the 'materiality' of the labour process and the relative independence of this process from the social relations of production which organise it. It is precisely by conflating these two forms, Marx points out, that many bourgeois economists 'demonstrate' the eternal validity of capitalism and manage to establish capital 'as an immutable natural element in human production as such': 'By confusing the appropriation of the labour process by capital with the labour process itself, the economists transform the material elements of the labour process into capital simply because capital itself changes into the material elements of the labour process among other things.'[30] 'But the fact that capital has taken over the labour process and the worker therefore works for the capitalist instead of himself', Marx argues elsewhere in the *Results*, 'does not mean any change in the general nature of the labour process itself.'[31]

Much of Marx's discussion in this context is concerned with the *physical* elements of production, for example raw materials and instruments of production, which enter into *every* labour-process and which by conceptual fiat are assimilated into the economists' category of 'capital'. But in a proposition which foreshadows a crucial element of the argument later incorporated into the final version of *Capital*, Marx extends the analysis of the *Results* to include organisational forms, and also shifts the level of abstraction from production in general to large-scale production, by arguing that in so far as the capitalist process of production is a 'real labour process', 'the capitalist has a definite function to perform within it as supervisor and director'.[32] The significance of this proposition and its discursive location at the level of what Marx variously termed 'large-scale co-operation', 'combined labour on a large scale', 'combined social labour', and so on, become clear not in the *Results* but in *Capital* where it is repeated several times and in a more explicit and developed form:

> All combined labour on a large scale requires, more or less, a directing authority, in order to secure the harmonious working of the individual activities, and to perform the general functions that have their origin in the action of the combined organism, as distinguished from the action of its separate organs. A single violin player is his own conductor; an orchestra requires a separate one. The work of directing, superintending, and adjusting, becomes one of the functions of capital, from the moment that the labour under the control of capital, becomes co-operative. *Once a function of capital, it acquires special characteristics* [my emphasis].[33]

This crucial passage illustrates several interconnected aspects of the interpretation of Marx's mature work that is being advanced in this book. First, it clearly demonstrates Marx's attempts to separate out what for the present may be referred to as 'technical' requisites implicit in a particular form of production ('combined labour on a large scale') from specific deformations imposed by *capitalist* relations of production. Second, and especially when understood in the context of the remarks in the *Results*, it reveals the continuing influence of the 1857 *Introduction* and its relevance to an elucidation of the methodology of *Capital*. Third, in so far as the labour of coordination and authoritative regulation had always been included in the concept of division of labour, Marx here is obviously detaching this important element of the concept from the concept of class within which it had previously been completely submerged. Fourth, and by the same token, the passage exemplifies the transformation in Marx's views on the *abolition* of the division of labour, for there is now a clear acknowledgement of the *limits* to this form of dissolution. Other aspects of Marx's earlier belief in the abolition of the division of labour are also modified in *Capital*, but these are examined later, as are the older Engels's (often controversial) views on the subject. For the present it is worth exploring further Marx's analysis of the duality of the capitalist production process.

Capitalist deformations of the division of labour within the productive enterprise are a direct outcome of the fact that the 'directing motive' of the capitalist is the greatest possible exploitation of labour power. But Marx never loses sight of the dual nature of the capitalist production process, on the one hand as a technical mode of cooperation with its own dynamic and on the other as a form of systematic exploitation which imposes a distinct physiognomy on the division of labour:

> The control exercised by the capitalist is not only a special function, due to the nature of the social labour-process, and peculiar to that process, but it is, at the same time, a function of the exploitation of a social labour-process, and is consequently rooted in the unavoidable antagonism between the exploiter and the living and labouring raw material he exploits.[34]

Those who justify these peculiarly capitalist forms of authoritarianism as a matter of simple technical necessity – political economists like Cairnes and Steuart as well as 'Auguste Comte and his school' – come under particularly severe criticism from Marx because they treat '*the work of control made necessary by the co-operative process* as identical with the *different work of control, necessitated by the capitalist character of that process* and the antagonism of interests between capitalist and labourer' [my emphasis].[35]

The duality of the capitalist production process, especially in relation to the exigencies of large-scale production, also emerges as an important element in Marx's discussion of productive and unproductive labour, although it is not necessary here to consider in any detail the well-known difficulties associated with Marx's attempts to develop a coherent distinction between these two forms of labour, except in so far as they are relevant to an understanding of the duality of the capitalist production process. Several different versions of the differentiation between productive and unproductive labour are available in Marx's texts and contemporary Marxists appear to be hopelessly divided as to the real meaning of the distinction or its analytical value.[36]

The most consistent definition of productive labour in Marx's writings identifies such work with the production of surplus value: 'That labourer alone is productive, who produces surplus value for the capitalist, and thus works for the self-expansion of capital.'[37] Marx notes at the same time that as the labour process becomes more cooperative it becomes increasingly necessary to conceptualise this relation in terms of the 'collective labourer' *and explicitly refers to the fact that this theorisation results from an extension of the analysis of production in general and its integration with an analysis of the capitalist production process*:

> In considering the labour-process, we began . . . by treating it in the abstract, apart from its historical forms, as a process between man and Nature . . . We now proceed to a further development of this subject . . . As the co-operative character of the labour-process becomes more and more marked, so, as a necessary consequence, does our notion of productive labour, and its agent the productive labourer, become extended. In order to labour productively, it is no longer necessary for you to do manual work yourself; enough if you are an agent of the collective labourer, and perform one of its subordinate functions.[38]

Elsewhere Marx reiterates that managers and engineers are integral productive elements of the collective labourer within the capitalist mode of production.[39]

The idea of organisational exigencies inherent in 'cooperative' production is, of course, implicit in the role played by the concept of collective labourer in the definition of productive labour discussed above. But Marx does offer at least one other definition of productive labour, in which the thesis of the 'technical' necessities of large-scale production is a much more central principle. In the third volume of *Capital* Marx equates productive labour with work which must be performed in any 'combined mode of production', including the labour of supervision and management:

> The labour of supervision and management is naturally required wherever the direct process of production assumes the form of a combined social process . . . all labour in which many individuals co-operate necessarily requires a commanding will to co-ordinate and unify the process, and functions which apply not to partial operations but to the total activity of the workshop, much as that of an orchestra conductor. This is a productive job which must be performed in every combined mode of production.[40]

The greater the antagonism between the direct producer and the owner of the means of production, Marx argues, the greater the role of supervision, which therefore 'reaches its peak in the slave system'. Nevertheless, he continues to detach management and supervision functions necessary in any large-scale form of production from those deriving specifically from the *class* character of such production. Moreover, in linking this proposition with the concept of productive labour again, in the same text, Marx implies that supervision and management in large-scale production would be the tasks of specialised individuals:

> The labour of supervision and management, arising as it does out of an antithesis, out of the supremacy of capital over labour, and being therefore based on class contradictions like the capitalist mode, is directly and inseparably connected, also under the capitalist system, with *productive functions which all combined social labour assigns to individuals as their special tasks* [my emphasis].[41]

In keeping with this form of theorisation Marx also emphasises that even the work of the capitalist contains aspects which result 'from combination and co-operation of many in pursuance of a common result' and is therefore 'just as independent of capital as that form itself as soon as it has burst its capitalist shell'.[42] In a 'co-operative factory', he adds, 'the antagonistic nature of the labour of supervision disappears, because the manager is paid by the labourers instead of representing capital counterposed to them.'[43]

The propositions deriving from Marx's analysis of the duality of the capitalist production process carry profound implications for the meaning of the idea of the abolition of the division of labour in his mature writings; many of the passages cited above are reconsidered during the course of an overall assessment of Marx's views on the subject in the final part of the book. For the present it is necessary to emphasise that these passages exhibit clearly the mature Marx's attempt to analytically differentiate the issue of class domination and exploitation from that of the division of labour, and they also demonstrate the centrality of the notion of organisational exigencies stemming from large-scale production to this form of theoretical abstraction. The form of argument which organises this discourse in Marx's texts also underlines the continuing significance of the 1857 *Introduction* for a proper understanding of the theoretical structure of *Capital*.

Two caveats must now be entered, however, before proceeding to an exposition of Marx's analysis of the capitalist transformation of the division of labour. First, Marx's remarks on the need for the labour of supervision and management under socialism should not be allowed to obscure his belief in the necessity and possibility of a fundamental democratisation of production relations under conditions of common ownership of the means of production and 'co-operation on a large scale'. Second, the variety of concepts that emerges in this context – 'combined social labour', 'combined labour on a large scale', 'large-scale industry', and so on – indicates some degree of theoretical ambiguity. Both sets of issues are discussed in greater depth in Part V.

3
The Capitalist Transformation of the Division of Labour

The development of capitalism brought in its wake a quite unprecedented multiplication of productive forces and a fundamental reorganisation of the labour process and the division of labour. Marx's account of these profound transformations remained unmatched until the recent resurgence of interest in the capitalist labour process. Yet the brilliance of Marx's analysis does not derive merely from the shrewd use of contemporary documents. Its discursive conditions of existence lie in a thorough reworking of the concept of mode of production, in turn deriving from a reconceptualisation of production in general (of which the specification of the labour process is an outstanding example) and the integration of this latter form of analysis with the theory of surplus value. Thus the delineation of the capitalist transformation of the division of labour can only be understood in the context of Marx's more general remarks on the structure of modes of production, while its sophistication is inexplicable except as the result of the theoretical transformation which decisively separates the mature works from earlier texts.

The analysis of the constituent elements and differential forms of the labour process provides the basis for Marx's frequent attempts in *Capital* to develop a more rigorous classification of distinct modes of production or 'economic epochs':

> Whatever the social form of production, labourers and means of production always remain factors of it. But in a state of separation from each other either of these factors can be such only potentially. For production to go on at all they must unite. The specific manner in which this union is accomplished distinguishes

> the different economic epochs of the structure of society from one another.[44]

In class societies the combination of labourers and means of production is accomplished by the intervention of a third element: the owner of the means of production who organises production and appropriates surplus labour. Thus a specification of the form of combination which brings together the labourer, the means of production and the owner is at the same time the identification of a distinct mode of production. 'The specific economic form, in which unpaid surplus-labour is pumped out of direct producers', Marx argues, 'determines the relationship of rulers and ruled, as it grows directly out of production . . . It is always the direct relationship of the owners of the conditions of production to the direct producers . . . which reveals the innermost secret, the hidden basis of the entire social structure.'[45]

The methodological procedure recommended in *Capital* for the identification of distinct modes of production differs from the one adopted in earlier texts in two fundamental respects. The first has been indicated earlier: the ownership relation in *Capital* is discussed with specific reference to the analysis of forms of surplus labour, a discursive feature determined by the theory of surplus value. The second also derives from the development of the theory of surplus value in so far as it necessitated, as part of a more general reconceptualisation of production and its forms, a clearer specification of the elements of the labour process and their material effects on forms of surplus extraction and appropriation. That is, in *Capital* Marx's theorisation posits, in addition to the ownership relation, a relation of 'real' or 'material' appropriation of the means of production by the labourer in the labour process. This relationship refers to the actual control exercised by direct producers in the labour process and is analytically distinct from the ownership relation.

Balibar has pointed out that in much of Marx's discussion of the capitalist mode of produiction in *Capital*, the distinction between the property relation and the relation of 'real' appropriation is not made explicit, because under conditions of capitalist production the labourer is separated from the means of production in terms of both relations; thus Marx uses the single term 'separation' to refer to both forms of disconnection between the labourer and the means of production.[46] However, the distinction does surface more clearly in some formulations: 'The labour-process, turned into the process by which the capitalist consumes labour-power, exhibits two characteristic phenomena. First, the labourer works under the control of the capitalist . . . Secondly, the product is the property of the capitalist and not that of the labourer, its immediate producer.'[47] The discrimination used here also forms the basis of Marx's analysis of surplus appropriation under feudalism, already referred to, in which it is posited that the 'real possession' of the means of labour by the direct producer necessitates the extraction of surplus labour by the landlord 'by other than economic pressure'.[48]

The conceptual differentiation between the ownership relation and the relation of real appropriation, implicit though it often is, is fundamental to an understanding of Marx's discussion of the development of the capitalist mode of production and the capitalist transformation of the division of labour. The ownership relation is, of course, basic: the development of capitalism is predicated upon the expropriation of the direct producers and the concentration of the means of production in the hands of non-producers, a process that Marx called 'primitive accumulation'.[49] The English enclosure movement of the late fifteenth and early sixteenth century, Marx pointed out, was a classic example of primitive accumulation, resulting in the expulsion of peasants from the land, which was then either appropriated by landlords for grazing sheep or leased to capitalist farmers. At the same time, urban craftsmen came increasingly under the control of capitalist owners at the dawn of the era of manufacturing.

The expropriation of the peasantry and the urban craftsmen results in 'the formal subsumption of labour under capital', as Marx puts it.[50] The peasant becomes an agricultural labourer, the guild craftsman finds that his master confronts him not as the master of his craft but simply as the owner of capital, while the journeyman is reduced to a simple 'venor of labour'. The cash nexus shatters the 'patriarchal, political or even religious cloak' that had hitherto mediated the forms of exploitation. The rhythm of labour becomes marked by greater continuity and longer duration: the former because the once-independent craftsman is no longer reliant on individual customers but is under the control of the owner of the means of production, the latter because the primary means available to the owner for raising the level of surplus-value is the extension of the working day. The formal subsumption of labour under capital corresponds, therefore, to the period of the production of absolute rather than relative surplus value, the latter referring to the form of exploitation made possible by rapid technological innovation and consequent increases in the productivity of labour. The formal subsumption of labour under capital and the production of absolute surplus value coincide with the period of manufacture, extending in England from the middle of the sixteenth to the last third of the eighteenth century. Almost throughout this period, although the ownership relation is clearly transformed, the relation of 'real appropriation' is much less affected; the fact that 'capital has taken over the labour process and the worker therefore works for the capitalist instead of himself does not mean any change in the general nature of the labour process.' 'Technologically speaking, the labour process goes on as before, with the proviso that it is now subordinated to capital.'[51]

The system of manufacture – the 'typical' form of cooperation based on the division of labour – arises in two separate ways: either by the bringing together within the capitalist workshop of workers with different skills necessary for the production of a single commodity, or the assemblage of labourers who all perform the same kind of work, such as producing paper or needles.[52] What identifies them as forms of 'manufacture' is that they are both based on manual operations and therefore rely on the strength and skill of the individual worker in employing his tools.[53] And Marx argues that there is, in any case, a tendency for the operations characteristic of the second type of manufacture to be split up and to 'ossify' into a systematic division of labour typical of the first form.

The really distinctive creation of the manufacturing system is the 'detail labourer'. Manufacturing seizes upon 'the naturally developed differentiation of trades' (the social division of labour) and systematically fractionalises it inside the workshop, ensuring that each worker now becomes exclusively tied to a partial function, and converts 'his whole body into the automatic, specialised implement of that operation'.[54] Adopting the logic of Smith's argument, Marx assumes that this fractionalisation leads to increased productivity by improving the individual worker's dexterity and preventing the wastage of time that would have resulted from the transition from one type of work to another.[55] Manufacturing also transforms the rhythms of work and Marx argues that this is at least partly inherent in the technical logic of the system of manufacture and is, therefore, distinct from the forms of compulsion which result from the formal subsumption of labour under capital. The complex interdependence that exists between productive tasks in the manufacturing division of labour compels each worker to spend only a minimum time on his task, leading to 'a continuity, uniformity, regularity, order, and even intensity of labour, of quite a different kind . . . than is to be found in an independent handicraft or even in simple co-operation'. 'In Manufacture,' Marx continues, 'the turning out of a given quantum of product in a given time is a technical law of the process of production itself.'[56]

The progressive development of specialisation in manufacture means that it is the 'collective labourer' that now possesses the skills that were in the beginning distributed among individuals. The increase in productivity that results from individual specialisation ensures that the collective labourer is now richer, but only at the expense of individual workers whose range of skills is systematically squeezed into a narrow and partial competence.[57] Deskilling is the strategy *par excellence* by which the labour process is first fragmented and then reconstructed in the form of a new hierarchy of competences among the workers. It is in this context that Marx introduces Babbage's remarkably astute analysis of the fractionalisation of labour and the benefits it confers on capital in its never-ending search for surplus value:

> Since the collective labourer has functions, both simple and complex, both high and low, his members, the individual labour-powers, require different degrees of training, and must therefore have different values. Manufacture, therefore, develops a hierarchy of labour-powers, to which there corresponds a scale of wages . . . Every process of production, however, requires certain simple manipulations, which every man is capable of doing. They too are now severed from their connection with the more pregnant moments of activity, and ossified into exclusive functions of specially appointed labourers . . . Alongside of the hierarchic gradation there steps the simple separation of the labourers into skilled and unskilled. For the latter, the cost of apprenticeship vanishes; for the former, it diminishes, compared with that of artificers, in consequence of the functions being simplified. In both cases the value of labour-power falls. The fall in the value of labour-power . . . implies a direct increase of

> surplus-value . . . for everything that shortens the necessary labour-time required for the reproduction of labour-power, extends the domain of surplus-labour.[58]

Notice here that in contrast with *The Poverty of Philosophy*, in *Capital* Babbage's work is employed to underline the intricate hierarchy of divisions into which the category of labour is fractionalised in the period of manufacturing and leads also to the production of a new concept, 'collective labourer', to theorise the complexity of the labour process.[59] As we shall see, this is also allied to a more sophisticated understanding of the impact of machinery and large-scale industry on the structure of labour when set against the earlier analyses.

The strategy of deskilling does not go unchallenged by the workers. Citing Ure, Marx argues that skilled workers, who constituted the largest fraction of labour during the manufacturing period, continually resisted attempts by individual capitalists to shorten apprenticeships and incorporate women and children into the labour force. The deskilling strategy, in England especially, came to grief 'on the habits and resistance of the male labourers': for the entire period between the sixteenth and eighteenth century 'capital failed to become the master of the whole disposable working-time of manufacturing labourers' and the owners of capital were forced to relocate their plants continually in search of compliant labour.[60]

It was just as well that the workers resisted, for wherever manufacturing processes managed to establish themselves they emasculated the worker and turned him into a 'crippled monstrosity'. The manufacturing division of labour 'attacks the individual at the very roots of his life' and consequently, Marx observes, 'is the first to afford the materials for, and give a start to, industrial pathology'.[61] The manufacturing system displays the beginnings of an endemic tendency within capitalism to deprive workers of their knowledge of the production process and their control over it. 'What is lost by the detail labourers', Marx says, 'is concentrated in the capital that employs them.' 'It is a result of the division of labour in manufacture,' he continues, 'that the labourer is brought face to face with the intellectual potencies of the material process of production, as the property of another, and as a ruling power.' Thus it is above all the widening gulf between intellectual and manual labour that converts the manufacturing worker into a mere appendage of the capitalist labour process; the gulf is driven to a perverse extreme in the era of large-scale industry.[62]

The invention and increasing use of machinery, Marx argues, revolutionises the conditions of production and ushers in the period of large-scale industry.[63] Initially production by machinery coexists with the framework established by manufacture but at a certain level of development becomes 'technologically incompatible' with its handicraft basis; manufacture had always ultimately relied on the individual strength and skill of workers and thus could not provide an adequate basis for the production of machines to make machinery, nor for the development of such machines as the hydraulic press, the power loom and the carding engine.[64] Once established in any branch of industry, machine production sets in motion a process that again has a powerful technical logic: related branches are formed to introduce mechanisation, and the applied mechanical and chemical sciences are forced to innovate rapidly as bottlenecks quickly emerge in the process of production and as it becomes necessary to make machinery by machines.[65] The social division of labour is also profoundly transformed: machine production engenders 'entirely new branches of production, creating new fields of labour' and 'carries the social division of labour immeasurably further than does manufacture'.[66] Soon the means of communication and transport – 'the general conditions of the social process of production' – have to expand to cope with the 'feverish haste' and international markets of large-scale industry.[67] A new international division of labour rapidly emerges, converting 'one part of the globe into a chiefly argicultural field of production, for supplying the other part which remains a chiefly industrial field'.[68]

Machinery can only be operated by 'associated labour'; hence 'the co-operative character of the labour-process', Marx suggests, is 'a technical necessity dictated by the instrument of labour itself'.[69] But in the context of the capitalist mode of production and its typical form of associated labour for the employment of machinery, the factory, the historical significance of production by machinery lies in its consequences for the extension of capitalist power in terms of the relation of real appropriation. The introduction of machinery allows a thorough integration of science into the production process and also revolutionises the labour process, thus providing the conditions for the 'real' – as opposed to the 'formal' – subsumption of labour under capital.[70] The real subsumption of labour under capital constitutes for Marx 'the specific mode of capitalist production', for it completes the process by which 'production for production's sake', irrespective of needs, is institutionalised as an overriding imperative.[71] In the history of capitalist development it corresponds to the period of 'relative', rather than the earlier 'absolute' production of surplus value, relying primarily on rapid and continuous technological innovation to increase the rate of exploitation and not on the intensification of labour or the extension of the working day (although both of these latter forms of exploitation continue and indeed are given fresh impetus).[72]

Capitalist hegemony in the labour process is secured, above all, by a new form of deskilling. Machinery appropriates both the tool and the skill in wielding it that had formerly belonged to the worker. The 'technical foundation' of the division of labour in the manufacturing workshop had created a 'hierarchy of specialised workmen', but in the 'automatic factory', Marx says, there is a tendency to 'equalise and to reduce to one and the same level every kind of work that has to be done by the minders of the machines'.[73] One important consequence is that manual work now has a 'light character' and thus allows the incorporation of women and children into the labour force; combined with the creation of an industrial reserve army – itself partly the product of machine based production – it considerably undermines the capacity of the workers to resist the attempts of capitalists to expand the rate of exploitation by lengthening the working day, increasing the intensity of labour and dispensing with essential safety and health measures.[74]

While in the manufacturing system the worker had been chained to a 'life-long speciality of handling one and the same tool' he now finds himself 'serving one and the same machine', reducing the costs of his reproduction and rendering him even more dependent on the capitalist. Scientific knowledge is appropriated by capital and the 'intellectual powers of production' confront the worker as the property of the owner of the means of production.[75] The worker is thus systematically and brutally transformed into 'the living appendage' of a 'lifeless mechanism', a process whose effects on the worker Marx describes in a powerful, haunting passage:

> At the same time that factory work exhausts the nervous system to the uttermost, it does away with the many-sided play of the

> muscles, and confiscates every atom of freedom, both in bodily and intellectual activity. The lightening of the labour, even, becomes a sort of torture, since the machine does not free the labourer from work, but deprives it of all interest . . . By means of its conversion into an automaton, the instrument of labour confronts the labourer, during the labour-process, in the shape of capital, of dead labour, that dominates and pumps dry, living labour-power . . . The special skill of each individual insignificant factory operative vanishes as an infinitesimal quantity before the science, the gigantic physical form, and the mass of labour that are embodied in the factory mechanism and, together with that mechanism, constitute the power of the 'master'.[76]

There are some striking similarities between the description of the conditions of work in the capitalist factory in *Capital*, and the moral outrage that accompanies it, and the passages on the alienation of the worker in some of the earlier texts, especially the *Economic and Philosophic Manuscripts* and *The Communist Manifesto*. But to focus exclusively on the resemblances – a common tendency this, amongst those who see Marx's writings as a seamless web – would be to obscure the real differences that distance the analysis of the labour process in *Capital* from that of earlier writings. The differences represent genuine advances in Marx's understanding of the structure of labour and capital under conditions of large-scale industry and a more developed stage of the capitalist mode of production, a form which Marx in fact considered to be the *specific* mode of capitalist production. While the earlier texts, as I have indicated before, were premissed on the twin theses of the polarisation between capital and labour and the homogenisation of the proletariat, *Capital* and the mature writings posit instead a series of complex, contradictory and uneven processes which generate new forms of fractionalisation and differentiation within both labour and capital. This new discourse deserves wider recognition. Although it is not possible here to do full justice to its richness and complexity, some attempt must be made to elucidate its outstanding features; it is high time that the polarisation–simplication couple *simpliciter* is seen for what it is, a youthful prognostication that is thoroughly reworked and transformed in *Capital*. This is *not* to argue that both theses are completely overthrown, nor to contend that they do not sometimes reappear in their original form, and nor even to suggest that Marx's new analysis is adequate to the real complexity of capitalist development, but to point out that any account which presents the polarisation–simplification couple as Marxism *tout court* does a grave injustice to Marx.

Note, first, that although the introduction of machinery has a technical logic, that is, a tendency to compel mechanisation and factory production in related processes, this is not seen as a linear effect: in some cases, Marx argues, mechanisation gives fresh impetus to 'domestic industry', whether located in individual houses or workshops, although the form of labour in domestic industry has necessarily to be modified to integrate with mechanised processes in related branches of production.[77] A torturous intensification of labour, the brunt of which is more often than not borne by women and children, is the usual consequence if domestic industry survives the invasion of mechanisation in a connected sector of production, or partial mechanisation in its own midst. Manufacturing, too, is seen by Marx to coexist in a variety of forms with mechanised production.[78] Thus although it is now increasingly clear that Marx (in common with contemporary observers and recent historians) considerably underestimated the extent to which domestic industry and the manufacturing system survived and indeed were essential to nineteenth-century British capitalism,[79] a careful reading of *Capital* also establishes that he did not postulate a factory proletariat as the only and immediate outcome of capitalist industrialisation, or as the sole condition of existence of the working class. While mechanisation homogenised the class in some respects, at another level, and simultaneously, it created within it new structural divisions. The whole process, moreover, is marked by an endemic *unevenness* as between the production-goods and consumer-goods departments of the economy, between industries within each department, and between branches within each industry, while superimposed upon it are important regional variations which defy any simple logic of development. This generic unevenness is best captured by Marx's remarks on the processes of capital accumulation that are intrinsically connected with it:

> Considering the social capital in its totality, the movement of its accumulation now causes periodical changes, affecting it more or less as a whole, now distributes its various phases simultaneously over the different spheres of production. In some spheres a

> change in the composition of capital occurs without increase of its absolute magnitude, as a consequence of simple centralisation; in others the absolute growth of capital is connected with absolute diminution of its variable constituent, or of the labour-power absorbed by it; in others again, capital continues growing for a time on its given technical basis, and attracts additional labour-power in proportion to its increase, while at other times it undergoes organic change, and lessens its variable constituent.[80]

Despite appearances to the contrary – and in contrast with his earlier conceptions – the deskilling process set in motion by mechanisation is also seen by Marx as a powerful source of differentiation within the category of labour, although the forms of fragmentation obviously differ from those that prevail under manufacture. The basic elements of the structure of division of labour inside the modern factory are set out by Marx in an important passage:

> The essential division is, into workmen who are actually employed on the machines (among whom are included a few who look after the engine), and into mere attendants (almost exclusively children) of these workmen. Among the attendants are reckoned more or less all 'Feeders' who supply the machines with the material to be worked. In addition to these two principal classes, there is a numerically unimportant class of persons, whose occupation it is to look after the whole of the machinery and repair it from time to time; such as engineers, mechanics, joiners, etc. This is a superior class of workmen, some of them scientifically educated, others brought up to a trade; it is distinct from the factory operative class and merely aggregated to it. This division of labour is purely technical.[81]

Marx presents here not just the single process of deskilling, which produces the 'mere attendants', but two other tendencies which obviously coexist with it: the continuation of older skills, represented by the 'joiners, etc.', and the development of *new* skills – a process therefore of *re*skilling – which brings into being the engineer. Like deskilling, both these latter tendencies are consistent with Marx's overall conceptualisation of the forms of development of the capitalist labour process in the era of large-scale industry: the presence of older skills derives from the generic unevenness of these forms of development, the rise of new skills from the increasing application of science and the revolutions in technique which result from it. With hindsight it is possible to assert that Marx seriously underestimated the strength and variety of reskilling pressures both in nineteenth-century British capitalism and in the capitalist economy in general.[82] But the argument that he posited a simple process of deskilling, leading to the emergence of a homogeneous, undifferentiated proletariat can only be sustained by ignoring *Capital*. And it is worth mentioning here that *Capital* replaces the earlier notion of a subsistence wage as the general condition of the working class with the concept of *relative* immiseration, a modification that finds much of its theoretical basis in the theory of surplus value.[83]

At least three other persistent forms of division and differentiation within the working class are identified in *Capital*. First, the continuing problem of maintaining a 'barrack discipline' in the capitalist factory leads to a division of the workforce into operatives and 'overlookers', 'into private soldiers and sergeants of an industrial army'; as soon as he is able to, the capitalist delegates the work of direct and constant control to 'a special kind of wage-labourer', the foreman.[84] Second, the 'lightening' of labour consequent upon mechanisation leads to the incorporation of women and children into the labour force; differences of sex and age fractionalise the workers and, by introducing competition, weaken the resistance to new types of superexploitation, although it must be said that the torturous forms assumed by female labour call into question the naturalistic assumption about female strength that underlies Marx's analysis.[85] However, the incorporation of women into the labour force, Marx argues, also has other advantages for capital and these generate further pressures for their continuing employment: amongst other things, it spreads the cost of reproducing labour power over the whole family, thus allowing lower wages to be paid to both male and female workers and it also generates a demand for ready-made articles, which might otherwise have been made by women in the home.[86] Finally, the industrial reserve army may be identified as the third form of fragmentation intrinsic to the structure of the working class under conditions of capitalist industrial production as theorised in *Capital*. The industrial reserve army varies in size, depending upon the forms assumed by the processes of capital accumulation from which its existence derives. In so far as capital accumulation leads to labour-saving technological improvements, crises of profitability and the displacement of the agricultural population, it swells the size of the reserve army; to the extent that it creates new branches of production, exploits new markets and expands the scale of production, capital accumulation diminishes the ranks of the reserve army of labour. For Marx the uneven and contradictory character of capital accumulation ensures that at any one point in time there is always an actual or potential reserve army available for mobilisation by capital to increase the competition for jobs, depress the level of wages and raise the levels of exploitation and profitability.[87]

Elsewhere Marx points to 'the forced immigration of poor Irish', arguing that this constitutes an additional pool of reserve labour and a crippling source of division within the English working class:

> the English bourgeoisie has not only exploited Irish destitution to worsen the condition of the working class in England by the forced immigration of poor Irish, but it has also divided the proletariat into two hostile camps . . . The ordinary English worker hates the Irish worker as a competitor who causes a drop in wages and the standard of life. He feels national and religious antipathy towards him . . . This antagonism between the proletarians of England itself, is artificially nourished and maintained by the bourgeoisie. It knows that the true secret of the preservation of its power lies in this split.[88]

The liberation of Ireland from English domination, Marx adds, 'is a preliminary condition of the emancipation of the English working class'. In other words, the complex economic and political relations *between* social formations is itself a source of fragmentation *within* the working classes of individual social formations, reinforcing divisions stemming from the process of capital accumulation. Notice also, in this context, Engels's point that 'during the period of England's industrial monopoly' an 'aristocracy of the working class' – engineers, carpenters, bricklayers – had succeeded both in resisting mechanisation and negotiating for itself 'a relatively comfortable portion'. Its privileges, he concluded, would only end with the demise of English industrial supremacy.[89]

If the thesis of the increasing homogenisation of the proletariat cannot survive in its original form once the analysis in *Capital* and other mature texts is taken into account, nor can the proposition of growing polarisation between labour and capital, and partly for the same reason. However, before discussing this issue in more detail, two sets of qualifications must be made: first, the polarisation thesis is not so much *rejected* as *modified* in *Capital*; second, Marx's analysis at this point is both fragmentary and incomplete, providing little more than indications for a more elaborate and coherent discussion which might have ensued had Marx lived to rework the drafts which, eventually, were revised and published first by Engels (the second and third volumes of *Capital*) and then, in part, by Kautsky (*Theories of Surplus Value*).

The polarisation thesis, as originally formulated, survives in *Capital* in so far as Marx continues to hold that with the development of capitalism, the *petty bourgeoisie* and small independent producers of all kinds have a tendency to diminish in number, forced by the twin pressures of accumulation and competition either to expand and join the ranks of capital or to sink into the proletariat. But polarisation at this level is countered by the emergence of *new* intermediate groupings in the social division of labour; criticising Ricardo's analysis of the consequences of a rising surplus, Marx says:

> What he forgets to emphasise is the constantly growing number of the middle classes, those who stand between the workman on the one hand and the capitalist and landlord on the other. The middle classes maintain themselves to an ever increasing extent directly out of revenue, they are a burden weighing heavily on the working base and increase the social security and power of the upper ten thousand.[90]

Elsewhere in *Theories of Surplus Value*, this time in a discussion of Malthus, Marx restates the point:

> His supreme hope, which he himself describes as more or less utopian, is that the mass of the middle class should grow and that the proletariat (those who work) should constitute a constantly declining proportion (even though it increases absolutely) of the total population. *This in fact is the course taken by bourgeoisie society* [my emphasis].[91]

The prognosis of a growing 'middle class' does not constitute an *ad hoc* empirical modification to the polarisation thesis in the light of contemporary developments; it derives in the first place from Marx's theorisation of capital accumulation and the circuit of capital in a developed system of capitalist production and thus finds its discursive basis in the theory of surplus-value. Marx's analysis operates at several different levels; for present purposes each strand in the argument can be set out briefly, although without glossing over the difficulties internal to Marx's account.[92]

Much of Marx's analysis of the growth of a 'new' middle class rests on the tendency for the *total* volume or mass of surplus and profit to rise, a form of development within the capitalist economy unaffected by the tendency for the *rate* of profit to fall. The growing volume of surplus value, Marx suggests, encourages, allows and, in some respects, requires the creation of new types of employment by capital: forms of 'unproductive' labour which do not directly produce surplus value but are paid out of revenue and thus consume surplus value. At least four categories of labour are identified on the bases of this theorisation, although only the last three can be assimilated to the concept of a middle class and, it must be said, not entirely without ambiguity. The first consists of domestic servants, both male and female, increasingly employed by individual capitalists to service their private needs; this group is seen to be part of the working class and further complicates its internal structure.[93] The second group identified comprises of ideological and political functionaries, especially government officials, and soldiers, whose numerical expansion is partly explained by the requirements of social control, as capitalist relations of production establish their hegemony over sectors of the economy hitherto organised around pre-capitalist and transitional forms of production.[94] It is the implication of Marx's analysis that any accentuation of class conflict will lead to an increase in the number of agents called upon to perform the functions of repression and containment, although, given that this type of labour is strictly speaking unproductive, the total volume of surplus available in the economy presumably sets a determinate limit to its expansion.

From the point of view of each individual capital, surplus value can only be realised in the form of profits and money capital by successfully selling the commodities in which surplus value is embodied. Thus the increasing scale of production upon which the rising volume of surplus is predicated requires the enlargement of commercial operations and the growth in number of a third group, commercial workers employed in offices:

> The office is from the outset always infinitesimally small compared to the industrial workshop . . . it is clear that as the scale of production is extended, commercial operations required constantly for the circulation of industrial capital . . . multiply accordingly. Calculation of prices, book-keeping, managing funds, correspondence – all belong under this head. The more developed the scale of production, the greater, even if not proportionately greater, the commercial operations of the industrial capital, and consequently the labour and other costs of circulation involved in realizing value and surplus-value. This necessitates the employment of commercial wage-workers who make up the actual office staff . . . The commercial worker produces no surplus-value directly . . . but adds to the capitalist's income by helping him to reduce the cost of realizing surplus-value, inasmuch as he performs partly unpaid labour.[95]

And the growth of joint-stock companies, deriving from the twin processes of the concentration and centralisation of capital, generates a fourth new group, 'a numerous class of industrial and commercial managers' who take over the supervisory and administrative functions of the capitalist and render the capitalist superfluous. Marx views this form of organisation as 'a necessary transitional phase towards the reconversion of capital into the property of producers', into 'outright social property'; and once the capitalist becomes irrelevant to the actual process of production, his role as a simple appropriator of surplus labour also becomes easier to expose, again facilitating the transition to socialism.[96]

Marx's expectation of a growing number of ideological and political functionaries, commercial workers, and industrial and commercial managers marks a decisive shift away from the sort of simple polarisation thesis advanced in *The Communist Manifesto*. And it should by now be clear that the theory of surplus value is of central importance in generating modifications to the original polarisation thesis. However, before concluding this discussion, several additional remarks are necessary. First, while Marx argues that the development of unproductive forms of labour performs a necessary function for the capitalist economy, in facilitating the consumption of a portion of the surplus which the relative immiseration of the proletariat leaves unabsorbed, his analysis of the causal mechanisms which lead to the development of *particular* types of unproductive labour is poorly developed, except perhaps in the case of commercial workers, although it is worth pointing out here that Nicolaus's seminal discussion of these issues considerably exaggerates the significance of unproductive consumption in Marx's explanation of the rise of the 'new middle class'.[97] Second, note that Marx himself does not use the term 'middle class' for commercial workers, who are usually referred to as 'the better-paid class of wage-workers . . . whose labour is classed as skilled and stands above average labour'.[98] Indeed, Marx predicts for this group a process of partial but rapid proletarianisation with the accentuation of division of labour in the office and the development of public education which, he argues, 'enables capitalists to recruit such labourers from classes that formerly had no access to such trades and were accustomed to a lower standard of living', besides increasing supply and competition. Hence with the development of capitalist production, there is a tendency for the labour of commercial workers to be 'devaluated': 'Their wage falls, while their labour capacity increases.'[99] Third, although it is implicit in Marx's analysis of the capitalist labour process and in his remarks on the growth of public education, that the development of the capitalist mode of production is associated with a rapid rise in the numbers of scientists, engineers, and so on, there is little discussion of the relevance of this for an understanding of the class structure of a developed capitalist social formation, especially in terms of the concept of the middle class; Marx's analysis of scientists and engineers is usually couched in terms of the concept of 'collective labourer'. Finally, it is at least arguable that the absence of the term 'middle class' in *Capital*, in comparison with the usage in *Theories of Surplus Value*, indicates some modification in Marx's position on this issue, although the fragmentary character of Marx's writings on these questions makes any definite judgement difficult if not altogether impossible.[100]

The discussion presented so far has gone some way towards establishing on a more secure foundation two propositions that are central to the interpretation of Marx advanced in this book: first, that it is no longer possible to pretend that Marx's discourse has some essential and simple unity, which can be reconstructed by pulling together extracts from texts written during an intellectual and political biography spanning several decades; second, that what is true of the general structure of Marx's discourse is also valid for his theorisation of the division of labour. Nevertheless, the problem of Marx's mature views on the *abolition* of the division of labour still remains. Some of the evidence suggestive of a modification in Marx's perspective on this issue has already been documented in the analysis of *Capital* presented above and provides the basis for the more thorough re-evaluation that follows.

Part V

The Abolition of the Division of Labour? Marx's Mature View Reappraised

1
The Meaning of the Abolition of the Division of Labour in the Mature Texts

Both Marx and Engels consistently refrained from what they regarded as an ahistorical and essentially utopian exercise: the drawing up of precise and detailed blueprints – 'recipes for the cookshops of the future' – for the reconstruction of society. Almost invariably their conception of the possible or probable structure of socialist economic and political organisation is contained in incidental remarks and has to be reconstructed, often from negative statements, that is, from propositions setting out what they thought socialism could *not* be identified with. The student of Marx has to tread a wary path, moreover, because it is not always easy to separate rhetoric and polemic from considered and genuine reflection. Of course, none of these difficulties have prevented attempts to reassemble and force into coherence Marx's writings on future society – the most recent and comprehensive effort being that of Ollman – and it is arguable that there is sufficient material available to construct a picture that is detailed enough to allow us to determine whether any serious modifications are registered in Marx's perspective over his (socialist) lifetime.[1] That is the premise which necessarily underlies the project undertaken in this book.

The discussion so far has attempted to compile and present, in more or less chronological order, some of Marx's disparate statements about one crucial element of the socialist order: the abolition of the division of labour. In the process it has been necessary to chart in some detail the development of his views on the division of labour more generally, and to set this discursive evolution in the context of his intellectual formation. This laborious task accomplished, it is now possible to present a more systematic assessment of Marx's later standpoint on the abolition of the division of labour, taking into account many mature formulations hitherto ignored in the discussion, but also restating propositions which have until now been introduced in a slightly different context. Before embarking upon this exercise, the basic contention that underlies the interpretation of Marx advanced in this book is worth repeating: in contrast with the earlier writings, the mature texts register an attempt to separate 'class' from 'division of labour' such that the abolition of class society does not imply the complete abolition of divided labour. Put slightly differently, it is possible to discern in Marx's later writings the emergence of a new type of theorisation in which forms of division of labour are not reduced to modes of production or the forms of class relationship to which these modes give rise. The 'break' with a reductionist conception, in this as in other contexts, is never complete: the whole process is uneven and sometimes contradictory. Marx's discourse often lapses into older, more reductionist habits without warning or conscious sense of anomaly. The implications of the new standpoint, moreover, are nowhere systematically thought through, and the new conception is thus never integrated into an overall discourse in which related elements are also re-theorised. The rupture, nevertheless, exists and its main features can be identified by a rigorous reading of the mature texts.

The first important sense in which 'class' becomes detached from 'division of labour' concerns the distinction between the division of labour at the level of *positions* and the division of labour at the level of *agents* which has been identified earlier. It is fair to say that before *Capital* it is difficult to find in Marx's texts any rigorous separation between these two levels of analysis. Hence the implication of Marx's remarks in *The German Ideology*, for example, is that the very category of division of labour is inapplicable and inappropriate to the mode of organisation of production under socialism. In *Capital* and other mature writings, where Marx keeps the two levels of divided labour separate from one another, the implication is that although it is possible to abolish classes, by the abolition of private ownership of the means of production, distribution and exchange, the necessity for a determinate division in productive tasks is rooted in the nature of production itself and regardless of who performs the various tasks. One manifestation of this new standpoint is contained in his letter to Kugelmann where Marx points out that 'the *necessity* of the *distribution* of social labour . . . cannot possibly be done away with by a particular form of social production but can only change the *mode* of its *appearance*' [Marx's emphasis].[2] Marx even points to this as a 'natural law' and reiterates that in 'historically different circumstances' it is only possible to alter the 'form' of this distribution. The distinction between the two levels of the division of labour is also evident in the emergence of the categories of division of labour 'in general', 'in particular' and 'in detail'. As Marx notes, these discriminations are located at the level of 'labour' or 'production' as such and relate to the fundamental, general sectors within 'social production'; it is clear from the context that these categories are relevant to both class-structured and classless modes of production.[3]

The distance that separates *Capital* from *The German Ideology*, the *Economic and Philosophic Manuscripts of 1844* and other early texts is even more clearly indexed in Marx's remarks on the exigencies of large-scale production. Thus, while individual inclination appears as the only constraint on the structure and rhythm of productive activities in the socialist vision that Marx paints in *The German Ideology, Capital* is replete with references to the inherent limitations imposed by large-scale production on the socialist reorganisation of the division of labour at the level of positions. Production by machinery appears as one of the key elements in Marx's conception of large-scale industry and its determinate effects. Machine production is said by Marx to be 'technologically incompatible with the basis furnished for it by handicrafts'; the use of machinery in one sector of production requires a similar method in a related branch and, most fundamentally, machine-based production can only operate on the basis of cooperation, 'of associated labour, or labour in common'.[4] The whole cycle of differentiation begins afresh periodically as 'entirely new branches of production, creating new fields of labour, are also formed, as the direct result either of machinery or of the general industrial changes brought about by it'.[5]

Marx's argument that large-scale industry under *any* mode of production can only be sustained on the basis of a separate 'directing authority', which assumes the functions of coordination, planning and supervision, is perhaps the most obvious manifestation of the separation between 'class' and 'division of labour' which emerges in the mature texts. I have discussed this earlier in some detail and for the present only wish to draw attention to the fact that Marx consistently employs two analogies to make his point. One is organicist:

'All combined labour on a large scale requires . . . a directing authority . . . to perform the general functions that have their origin in the action of the combined organism, as distinguished from the action of its separate organs.'[6] The second draws upon a comparison with the coordinating task necessary to the proper functioning of an orchestra: 'A single violin player is his own conductor; an orchestra requires a separate one.'[7] Now, I will argue later that the forms of argument which underpin Marx's analysis of the need for a 'directing authority' suffer from a number of limitations and thus cannot be accepted without qualification. But these weaknesses should not be allowed to obscure, first, the profound rupture in Marx's discourse inaugurated by the emergence of a type of analysis in which forms of division of labour are not reduced to the mode of production and class character of a social formation and, second, the need for Marxist theory to appropriate and develop this form of analysis.

It would, however, be erroneous to suppose that for Marx the division of labour at the level of positions is entirely independent of the class character of a mode of production. The conceptual distinction between divided labour at the level of positions and at the level of agents actually enables Marx to develop a more sophisticated analysis of the effect of class relations on the structure of production, and allows him to pose much more sharply the question of the reciprocal relationship between the two levels of the division of labour in specific modes of production. One result is the emergence of the category of 'division of social labour' in the second volume of *Capital*; as indicated earlier, it serves to conceptualise the manner in which within capitalism there is an endemic tendency for production functions, including those of commerce, to be seized upon by separate entrepreneurial units, leading to 'an ever greater division of complementary processes into independent processes'.[8] We are left to draw the conclusion that a socialist system would not be characterised by this frantic tendency towards differentiation or that it would assume a different form. And in *Capital* Marx points also to the Factory Acts which, forced upon the capitalist class as a whole by way of working-class pressure on the state, hasten the development of capitalist relations themselves by encouraging labour-saving technical innovations and the conversion of numerous small capitalist firms into larger combined units.[9]

The mature texts also contain the argument that several categories of 'work' – in addition to that allegedly performed by the capitalist – are specific to capitalism or, more generally, to exploitative societies, and are therefore destined to disappear or undergo drastic modification under socialism. This is especially true, of course, for state officials and the armed forces: 'The soldier belongs to the incidental expenses of production, in the same way as a large part of the unproductive labourers who produce nothing themselves, either spiritual or material, but who are needful and necessary only because of the faulty social relations – they owe their existence to social evils.'[10] And the same applies to the vast army of industrial supervisors whose existence is predicated on the need to enforce the capitalist's authority in the factory.[11] On the other hand, some tasks would become necessary on a much larger scale under socialism than in previous modes of production and Marx cites book-keeping as an important instance of this tendency in the socialist division of labour:

> Book-keeping . . . becomes the more necessary the more the process [of production] assumes a social scale and loses its purely individual character. It is therefore more necessary in capitalist production than in the scattered production of handicraft and peasant economy, *more necessary in collective production than in capitalist production* [my emphasis].[12]

We are also invited to draw the conclusion that the advent of socialism will profoundly restructure the *international* division of labour (although it is not clear whether socialism on an international scale is a precondition for this transformation). Industrialisation in the centres of capitalism, as Marx points out, 'converts one part of the globe into a chiefly agricultural field of production, for supplying the other part which remains a chiefly industrial field'.[13]

Now, the persistence of a determinate division of labour at the level of positions does not necessarily imply the existence of a division of labour at the level of agents, or what will henceforth be referred to as the *social division of labour*. And it must be said immediately that there are few *explicit* references to the survival of a social division of labour in socialist society in Marx's later writings. However, it will become evident that such a thesis is strongly implied by the forms of conceptualisation that Marx adopts in the mature texts and that this is, indeed, the only thesis compatible with the dominant thrust of his views in these writings. The proposition that occupational specialisation will be a continuing feature – albeit in form very different from that under class societies – constitutes the second sense in which the concept of division of labour is detached from the notion of class into which it had been totally assimilated in the early texts. There is at least one passage in *Capital* where Marx unambiguously registers the presence of some sort of occupational specialisation under socialism, thus indexing the gulf separating his later views from works such as the *1844 Manuscripts* and *The German Ideology*:

> The labour of supervision and management, arising as it does out of an antithesis, out of the supremacy of capital over labour, and being therefore common to all modes of production based on class contradictions like the capitalist mode, is directly and inseparably connected, also under the capitalist system, with *productive functions which all combined social labour assigns to individuals as their special tasks* [my emphasis].[14]

An underlying and often submerged conceptualisation of the limitations imposed by 'nature' provides perhaps the most significant foundation for the transformation in Marx's belief in the abolition of occupational specialisation under socialism. Note first of all that in *Capital* Marx actually displays a much greater understanding of the geographical and environmental roots of specialisation; it is this understanding which finally allows him to solve the riddle of the origins of the division of labour and exchange: 'It is . . . the differentiation of the soil, the variety of its natural products, the changes of the seasons, which form the physical basis for the social division of labour.'[15] Indeed Marx even goes so far as to argue that the *absence* of fertility is actually vital in promoting economic development: 'Where Nature is too lavish . . . She does not impose upon him any necessity to develop himself. It is not the tropics with their luxuriant vegetation, but the temperate zone, that is the mother-country of capital.'[16] Elsewhere Marx notes the 'special advantages' that accrue from siting different forms of production in geographically appropriate areas (nationally and internationally).[17] The implication here is that there are 'natural' limits to the abolition of occupational specialisation in so far as particular types of occupation are tied to the existence of favourable environmental conditions. While the development of communications may greatly enhance the possibilities for geographical mobility and thus enlarge the opportunities for occupational variation for individuals, it is intrinsic to Marx's mature view that there will continue to be a social division of labour both at a national and, more especially, international level.

The form of argument that underlies Marx's mature views also has important consequences for the abolition of the divisions between town and country, and industry and agriculture, for both these aspects of the social division of labour have a significant residual geographical and environmental basis. While references to both social differentiations only surface occasionally in Marx's later writings, there is little doubt that he continued to believe in the necessity for effecting a social transformation at both levels. In *Capital* we are told that while 'capitalist production completely tears asunder the old bond of union' between 'agriculture and manufacture' it simultaneously 'creates the material conditions for a higher synthesis in the future'. Capitalism, by vastly increasing the population of the urban centres, not only 'disturbs the circulation of matter between man and the soil', but at the same time destroys 'the health of the town labourer and the intellectual life of the rural labourer'. The 'full development of the human race' and the necessity for maintaining the fertility of the soil requires, Marx argues, a restoration of 'the naturally grown conditions for the maintenance of that circulation of matter'.[18]

Although there is nothing in these propositions which explicitly supports the argument that in *Capital* Marx accepted the idea of geographical and environmental limitations to the abolition of the social division of labour between town and country and industry and agriculture, it is possible to suggest that the implication of Marx's general views on the necessities imposed by nature should lead to just that conclusion. There is certainly nothing in these statements to suggest that Marx continued to believe in the possibility of *completely* abolishing these particular social divisions, and indeed the whole discussion is couched in terms of natural necessity. This demonstrates the importance of a conceptualisation of natural necessity in Marx's mature writings and, given its implications, also supports the contention that in contrast to the early texts his later views tend strongly towards the recognition of 'natural' – geographical and environmental – limits to the abolition of occupational specialisation. As Schmidt observes, summarising Marx's mature view: 'Men cannot in the last resort be emancipated from the necessities imposed by nature.'[19]

It has been indicated earlier that beginning with *The German Ideology* the concepts of 'man' and human nature, as ahistorical, anthropological 'essences', disappear from Marx's writings. It is sufficient to note here the following comment from *The Poverty of Philosophy*: 'M. Proudhon does not know that all history is nothing but a continuous transformation of human nature.'[20] Nevertheless, this should not be taken to mean that Marx fails to acknowledge that the fundamental physical constitution of human beings creates a basic, residual limitation to possible variations in the forms of labour and production. For instance, Marx argues that the introduction of machinery has considerable economic advantages because 'man is a very imperfect instrument for producing uniform continued motion'.[21] Elsewhere in *Capital* he uses this same belief to argue that 'constant labour of one uniform kind disturbs the intensity and flow of a man's animal spirits, which find recreation and delight in mere change of activity' and one of his basic criticisms of capitalism was directed at that system's 'longing to reduce to a minimum the resistance offered by that repellant yet elastic natural barrier, man'. Capitalism, for Marx, had an endemic tendency 'for lengthening the working-day beyond all bounds set by human nature'.[22]

These statements establish Marx's belief in the existence of limitations set by the physical characteristics of human beings and in one instance he actually suggests that some sort of change in the existing division of labour is a natural, human necessity. However, if we are to infer from such propositions an argument concerning the limitations set by 'human nature' to the complete abolition of occupational specialisation, we require a clear recognition on Marx's part that because of intrinsic human constitution, *individuals* will necessarily have differing aptitudes and that a future socialist order would thus have to take into account that not every individual (even potentially) is capable of engaging in every type of work. There are at least two points in his later writings where Marx implies such a view. In the first case the inference is rather indirect, but it is worth noting that in locating the origins of the division of labour, in *Capital*, Marx refers not merely to the natural necessity imposed by geographical and environmental circumstances but also to the 'natural endowments' of individuals, a differentiation which he claims forms 'the foundation on which the division of labour is built up' (and which the manufacturing system develops to a perverse extreme).[23] The second instance occurs in the famous 'Critique of the Gotha Programme' (1875) where Marx points out that 'one man is superior to another physically or mentally and so supplies more labour in the same time, or can labour for a longer time', and that the application of the principle of equal remuneration for equal labour is bound to lead to inequality – because of the existence of 'unequal individual endowment and thus productive capacity'.[24] Of course, neither of the passages cited explicitly argue that differences in individual ability will prevent the complete abolition of the division of labour in the sense of occupational specialisation, but – as with the propositions on geographical and environmental limits – this is a point that is intrinsic to the later writings and serves to reinforce the view that there is a definite (if sometimes submerged and implicit) separation between 'class' and 'division of labour' in Marx's mature discourse.

However, if the 'break' between the youthful and the later vision of socialism in Marx's texts is to be properly explicated and understood, one final discursive theme demands attention: the question of 'scarcity'. A certain ambivalence permeates Marx's conceptualisation of scarcity and its social conditions of existence throughout his writings, and more will be said about this issue later. For the present it is sufficient to note that despite various equivocations a definite shift of emphasis can be detected, especially as between *The German Ideology* and *Capital*. The vision of socialism that unfolds in the earlier text appears to rest upon an 'absolute' conception of scarcity, thus presupposing the possibility of the abolition of scarcity as a result of the development of productive forces. This premise is implicit in the form of connection that Marx establishes between scarcity and the emergence and reproduction of class relations in *The German Ideology*:

> All conquests of freedom hitherto, however, have been based on restricted productive forces. The production which these productive forces could provide was insufficient for the whole of society and made development possible only if some persons satisfied their needs at the expense of others and therefore some – the minority – obtained the monopoly of development, while others – the majority – owing to the constant struggle to satisfy their most essential needs, were for the time being (i.e. until the birth

> of new revolutionary productive forces) excluded from any development.[25]

Hence Marx's statement elsewhere in the same text that without the 'universal' development of productive forces 'want is merely made general, and with destitution the struggle for necessities and all the old filthy business would necessarily be reproduced'; hence, too, his belief that 'it is not a matter of freeing labour but of abolishing it'.[26]

The absolute, transhistorical conception of scarcity that is evident in these passages sits uneasily with the idea, also registered in the same work, that the expansion of needs is inherent in productive activity: new forms and levels of production set new parameters for what are to count as the necessaries of life.[27] It is this 'relative' notion of scarcity that achieves prominence in *Capital*. Thus, in the process of establishing a more satisfactory historical perspective on the issue, he writes: 'At the dawn of civilisation the productiveness acquired by labour is small, but so too are the wants which develop with and by the means of satisfying them.'[28] And in a discussion of the determination of the value of labour power Marx remarks that the worker's

> natural wants, such as food, clothing, fuel and housing, vary according to the climactic and other physical conditions of his country. On the other hand, the number and extent of his so-called necessary wants, as also the modes of satisfying them, are themselves the product of historical development, and depend therefore to a great extent on the degree of civilisation of a country, more particularly on the conditions under which, and consequently on the habits and degree of comfort in which, the class of free labourers has been formed.[29]

The premise underlying *this* view is wholly inimical to a belief in the possibility of abolishing labour as such, and Marx himself makes this clear in *Capital*: 'So far therefore as labour is a creator of use-value, is useful labour, it is a necessary condition, independent of *all* forms of society, for the existence of the human race; it is an *eternal* nature-imposed necessity, without which there can be no material exchanges between man and Nature, and therefore no life.' [my emphasis][30] This is not to argue that the mature Marx completely rejects the idea that the development of productive forces provides a necessary precondition for the establishment of socialism. For example, he consistently holds to the view that at least in western Europe a capitalist stage had been fundamentally necessary because the industrial base which provided the precondition for socialism could not historically have come about in any other way.[31] And in the 'Critique of the Gotha Programme' of 1875 he provides a two-stage developmental schema for post-capitalist society, a basic feature of the second, 'higher phase of communist society' being that 'the springs of co-operative wealth flow more abundantly'. It is only on the basis of this relative abundance that 'society can inscribe on its banners: From each according to his ability to each according to his needs!'[32]

But the abundance that Marx refers to here does not imply the complete abolition of scarcity; given also Marx's view – exhaustively documented earlier – that large-scale production and the exigencies of 'nature' set determinate limits to possibilities for the reorganisation of labour, we are now in a position to understand and grasp the significance of the passage on future society in the third volume of *Capital*, cited earlier:

> In fact the realm of freedom actually begins only where labour which is determined by necessity and mundane considerations ceases; thus in the very nature of things it lies beyond the sphere of actual material production . . . Freedom in this field can only consist in socialized man, the associated producers, rationally regulating their interchange with Nature . . . and achieving this with the least expenditure of energy . . . But it nonetheless still remains a realm of necessity. Beyond it begins that development of human energy which is an end in itself, the true realm of freedom which, however, can blossom forth only with this realm of necessity as its basis. The shortening of the working day is its basic prerequisite.[33]

A very similar argument can be found in the first volume of *Capital*, except that the issue of relative scarcity is more clearly underlined here:

> Only by suppressing the capitalist form of production could the length of the working-day be reduced to the necessary labour-

> time. But, even in that case, the latter would extend its limits. On the one hand, because the notion of 'means of subsistence' would considerably expand, and the labourer would lay claim to an altogether different standard of life. On the other hand, because a part of what is now surplus-labour, would then count as necessary labour; I mean the labour of forming a fund for reserve and accumulation . . . The intensity and productiveness of labour being given, the time which society is bound to devote to material production is shorter, and as a consequence, the time at its disposal for the free development, intellectual and social, of the individual is greater, in proportion as the work is more and more evenly divided among all the able-bodied members of society, and as a particular class is more and more deprived of the power to shift the natural burden of labour from its own shoulders to those of another layer of society. In this direction, the shortening of the working-day finds at last a limit in the generalisation of labour.[34]

It should now be clear that these passages do, indeed, index a modification in Marx's vision of socialism when set against the picture of socialism painted in the early texts. And in the light of the discursive transformations documented earlier, the reasons for the revision should also now be better understood. It should thus no longer be an occasion for surprise that in their maturity both Marx and Engels referred not to the abolition of the division of labour *tout court,* but spoke instead of the need for 'the abolition of the *old* division of labour'.[35] In their mature discourse the issues of technical and natural exigencies are powerfully intertwined: it is precisely because they relinquish the notions of the abolition of labour and the abolition of division of labour as conceptualised in the early texts that they come to regard 'free time' as the real sphere of freedom, for it is only here that there is an opportunity for a diversification of interests and activities divorced from the technical and natural imperatives bound up with the satisfaction of a basic 'standard of life'.

If it is necessary now to acknowledge that the mature Marx does not believe in the complete abolition of the division of labour in future society, it is still unclear what forms he thinks the division of labour *will* take. Marx's reluctance to speculate about the precise character of a socialist reconstruction of the social order poses formidable problems of interpretation, and any attempt to provide an organisational sketch must be undertaken with some caution. Nevertheless, one broad theme consistently emerges in his mature discussions: the division between mental and manual labour and its connection with the problem of control over and participation in decision-making, both in the process of production and outside it. If anything can be confidently asserted about Marx's changing views on socialist society, it is that his attention shifts from a concern with the abolition of the division of labour as such (in the early writings), to an interest in overcoming the separation between intellectual and manual tasks (in the mature period). It is this aspect of the capitalist labour process which emerges as the dominant *motif* in Marx's analysis in *Capital*, where he emphasises at several points that the most flagrant dismemberment of the worker is accomplished by the capitalist's continuous appropriation of the scientific knowledge and technical skills essential to the process of production. It is this process above all which turns the worker simply into an appendage of the machine, transforms labour into a mindless drudgery and allows capital to reproduce the conditions of existence of its own domination.[36] Hence, too, the argument in the *Grundrisse* that labour concerned with material production can only have a 'free character' if it has 'a scientific character', thereby becoming 'the activity of a subject controlling all the forces of nature in the production process'.

Marx's interest in overcoming, as far as possible, the crippling effects of the division between mental and manual labour is also rooted in a more general prognosis of the increasing demands for variability in productive skills implicit in rapid technological change. Modern large-scale industry, Marx says in *Capital*, 'imposes the necessity of recognising as a fundamental law of production, variation of work, consequently fitness of the labourer for varied work, consequently the greatest possible development of his varied aptitudes'. 'It becomes,' Marx adds, 'a question of life and death for society to adapt the mode of production to the normal functioning of this law.'[37] Elsewhere in *Capital* Marx buttresses this with an almost Fourierist notion, claiming that 'constant labour of one uniform kind disturbs the intensity and flow of a man's animal spirits, which find recreation and delight in mere change of activity'.[38]

To what extent and in what sense did Marx believe in the possibility of completely abolishing the division between mental and manual labour? It is at least clear that the general cast of Marx's mature view goes against the idea that *every* worker could *individually* appropriate *every* possible form of scientific discipline and technical skill that is involved in diverse sectors of production in modern large-scale industry: this is intrinsic to the conception of natural necessity which has already been discussed, and also to the concept of the 'collective labourer'. The particular aim of a socialist society, given natural and technical imperatives, is not individual appropriation of all mental tasks, but *collective* appropriation such that, in relation to the instruments of labour, 'the collective labourer, or social body of labour, appears as the dominant subject, and the mechanical automaton as the object'. As Marx points out in criticism of Ure, this is very different from the capitalist labour process where 'the automaton itself is the subject, and the workmen are merely conscious organs, co-ordinate with the unconscious organs of the automaton'.[39] Even at the point where Marx discusses the urgent technical need for variability of productive skills from the worker, he does not suggest that every worker can acquire command over *every* skill: the aim is one of 'the greatest possible development of his varied aptitudes', whatever they might be.

Implicit in this injunction is the belief that every worker has the capacity to master both manual and mental skills, and therefore the ability to exercise some control over the production process. Hence Marx's very keen interest in educational schemes in the nineteenth century which combined schooling with productive work:

> From the Factory system budded, as Robert Owen has shown us in detail, the germ of the education of the future, an education that will, in the case of every child over a given age, combine productive labour with instruction and gymnastics, not only as one of the methods of adding to the efficiency of production, but as the only method of producing fully developed human beings.[40]

A little later Marx adds:

> when the working class comes into power . . . technical instruction, both theoretical and practical, will take its proper place in the working class schools . . . such revolutionary forments, the

> final result of which is the abolition of the *old* division of labour, are diametrically opposed to the capitalistic form of production, and to the economic status of the labourer corresponding to that form.[41]

Note two features of Marx's argument: first, the accent throughout is on bridging the rift between mental and manual labour; the passages contain no hint of the idea that all skills can be mastered by everyone. The aim is to produce individuals with a variety of capacities, physical, manual and mental. Second, the issue of control is central to the project of combining mental and manual abilities: a new system of education is required to transform 'the economic status of the labourer', to provide the worker with the intellectual tools and the confidence to exercise control over the process of production, and to take a full and active part in decision-making. And this proposition gives rise to one final set of considerations: the possible structure of an authority system which could enable the worker to exercise intellectual capacities at all levels of policy formation in a socialist society.

There is little doubt that for Marx socialism meant above all the extension of democracy in all areas of social life and that collective participation in decision-making at the point of production constituted for him a fundamental index of the real development of a distinctively socialist labour process. Although Marx too often leaves this point implicit in his critique of the capitalist organisation of production, at two stages in the analysis in *Capital* he states this view more clearly. For instance, when condemning the authority system of the capitalist factory as a 'caricature of that social regulation of the labour-process which becomes requisite in . . . the employment in common, of instruments of labour and especially of machinery', Marx mentions in particular the 'autocracy' of the capitalist and the absence of any 'division of responsibility' or a 'representative system' to extend the area of control downwards to the worker.[42] This concern with a genuine form of industrial democracy is further underlined in a revealing footnote worth quoting in full:

> That Philistine paper, the *Spectator*, states that after the introduction of a sort of partnership between capitalist and workman in the 'Wirework Company of Manchester', 'the first result was a sudden decrease in waste, the men not seeing why they should

> waste in their own property any more than any other master's . . .' The same paper finds that the main defect in the Rochdale co-operative experiments is this: 'They showed that associations of workmen could manage shops, mills, and almost all forms of industry with success, and they immediately improved the conditions of the men; but then they did not leave a clear place for masters.' *Quelle horreur!*[43]

Marx leaves us in no doubt about where his sympathies lie, and it can be stated with some confidence that the consistent thrust of his own views is in the direction of a form of 'worker's control'. He does acknowledge the continuing existence of 'managers' in contemporary cooperative enterprises, but immediately adds that they are paid by the workers, implying that the 'managers' are *accountable* to the workers and carrying out tasks of 'co-ordination' and 'supervision' collectively and democratically allocated and specified.[44]

This concern with the accountability of agents occupying administrative positions also emerges as a central theme in Marx's writings on the Paris Commune of 1871. There is, of course, some dispute about the precise status of Marx's remarks in this context: it is not entirely clear whether he, like Engels, regarded the Commune as an example of 'the dictatorship of the proletariat'.[45] He certainly provided differing assessments of its significance. But it cannot be doubted that Marx applauded many of the political and administrative innovations of the Communards and his reflections upon them give an interesting and genuine insight into the sorts of measures that he expected in a future socialist order, and this despite the fact that there is little agreement amongst modern historians about Marx's interpretation of the significance of the Commune.[46]

Many of the measures that Marx approved of reflect his underlying commitment to the need for transforming the character of the division of labour in future society. For example, he welcomed the replacement of a standing army by the 'armed people', and favoured the amalgamation of legislative and executive structures so that executive functions could no longer remain 'the hidden attributes of a trained caste', but had to be turned into roles that could be effectively performed by any ordinary citizen. In addition, Marx stresses the importance of the fact that all persons occupying positions of public authority – the police, magistrates, administrators and so on – were actually elected and instantly revocable agents who were, moreover, paid no more than other workers.[47]

In keeping with the views expressed in *Capital* regarding the need for coordination, Marx clearly accepted the need for the continued existence of some kind of public power, but his comments on the Paris Commune suggest very strongly that this can only have a genuinely socialist character if accompanied by widespread decentralisation and an overall structure which links separate administrative units through a system of indirect elections. He emphasised the importance of 'real self-government' and 'local municipal liberty', and welcomed a plan which made the commune principle the basis of organisation for 'even the smallest country hamlet'. Several rural communes (in the proposed plan) would have formed a district with its own assembly of delegates; this assembly in turn would elect delegates for a National Delegation, 'each delegate to be at any time revocable and bound by the *mandat imperatif* (formal instructions) of his constituents'.[48]

However, despite the writings on the Paris Commune, the precise nature of the administrative functions that would have to be performed in a socialist society is nowhere clearly specified by Marx. Thus the notion of the abolition or 'withering away' of the state remains, in the final analysis, opaque. Nevertheless, when the remarks on the uprising of 1871 are set alongside those on forms of industrial organisation, three themes stand out clearly: first, that in his mature writings Marx does not envisage the complete abolition of the division of labour or the social division of labour. Second, that his major concern at this stage is with transforming the pernicious gulf between mental and manual tasks that necessarily arises from capitalist domination of economic and political functions. Finally, that the need to overcome the crude manifestation of a division of labour which confines one whole class to manual drudgery and allows another to appropriate and monopolise skills, knowledge and expertise, together with free time in which to cultivate a variety of aptitudes and interests, is crucially connected to a desire to extend democracy and genuine popular control over decisions which affect the character and direction of social development.

2
The Socialism of the Mature Marx: Some Problems

The vision of socialism that emerges in Marx's later writings is less utopian, indeed more mature, than the one found in the early texts. It is no less compelling for that, in fact more so, for it is more credible. In abandoning his youthful belief in the possibility of completely abolishing the division of labour, Marx strengthens and widens rather than weakens and narrows the appeal of his ideas. But it would be absurdly complacent to pretend that even his mature conception can be accepted without qualification, for it contains several sets of propositions and presuppositions and implies many forms of practice that need reappraisal. This necessary process of rethinking has already begun and has its immediate roots in the unique conjuncture which gave birth to the New Left in the social formations of advanced capitalism. The inevitably controversial discussion that follows is a modest and brief contribution to the debates already under way, *confining itself to problems that arise directly out of the issues discussed in previous parts of this text.* Any theses advanced here are necessarily provisional: they represent merely an attempt to underline the need for re-evaluation and the significance of present debates in this context.

The first set of issues that demand attention may be grouped loosely under the term 'technicism': that is, Marx's tendency to ascribe both determinacy and neutrality to the forces of production. Note, in the first place, the ambiguity which haunts Marx's conceptualisation of 'large-scale production', a notion which performs a key function in disengaging 'class' from 'division of labour' in the mature texts. As indicated earlier, it is partly by way of conceptualising a necessary relationship between scale of production and the organisation of labour that Marx is able to posit the permanence of some form of division of labour under socialism. However, Marx uses a variety of terms in this context apart from 'large-scale production', 'cooperation on a large scale', 'combined social labour', and 'large-scale industry' being the most frequent. In so doing, Marx conflates a variety of historically and analytically distinct set of relationships: most especially, he conflates the geographical scale and size of the labour force in operations like the building of the pyramids and Asiatic irrigation projects, similar considerations involved in the administration of whole societies, whether ancient or modern, the complexity of technical and social processes involved in industrial production, and the 'size' of industrial organisations.[49] Thus the precise meaning and scope of 'technical' and functional exigencies leading to determinate forms of divided labour remains obscure in his writings, giving rise to considerable theoretical arbitrariness, as in the third volume of *Capital*, where the analogy of the orchestra conductor is extended to cover (and obscure the differences between) the technical functions of coordination and unity performed both by the capitalist in the factory and governments in 'despotic states'.[50]

Nevertheless, Marx's argument that there *are* limits to forms of organisational rearrangement, whether stemming from scope of production or levels of technical complexity and interdependence in production, can hardly be ignored. Indeed, it has recently been deployed by Carchedi in his theorisation of contradictory class locations in conditions of monopoly capitalism, by way of Marx's notion of the duality of the capitalist production process.[51] But it is clear that the notion of the 'technical' function of coordination and unity as the outer limit to the reorganisation of political and production processes stands in need of much greater historical and theoretical specification. The delineation of its forms and conditions of variation poses an important challenge to any analysis that locates itself in the non-class-reductionist terrain opened up by Marx in *Capital*, and has some considerable relevance for understanding the possibilities for reorganising production and administration under socialism.[52]

One of the limitations of Marx's own account in this context, and which compounds the difficulties deriving from the already noted ambiguities in his theorisation, is the tendency to view the means of production as neutral, posing organisational exigencies which are merely 'technical'. Although it is of course intrinsic to Marx's theorisation that the relations of production provide the conditions for and set determinate limits to the development of the forces of production, this form of analysis is rarely extended to include the notion that the very character of the instruments of production may be marked by the type of social relations that provide their conditions of existence and development. Thus, despite his repeated insistence that the emergence of capitalist relations of production preceded the development of industrialisation, Marx's characteristic remarks on machinery at no point imply that the presence of specifically capitalist relations and choices may be registered in the very design of these means of production. The following passage is typical of Marx's general views on their neutrality:

> machinery, considered alone shortens the hours of labour, but, when in the service of capital, lengthens them . . . in itself it lightens labour, but when employed by capital, heightens the intensity of labour . . . in itself it is a victory of man over the forces of Nature, but in the hands of capital, makes man the slave of those forces . . . in itself, it increases the wealth of the producers, but in the hands of capital, makes them paupers.[53]

And in discussing organisational exigencies stemming from modern machinery, Engels subscribes to a very similar notion concerning the essential neutrality of the means of production:

> The automatic machinery of a big factory is much more despotic than the small capitalists who employ workers ever have been. If man, by dint of his knowledge and inventive genius, has subdued the forces of nature, the latter avenge themselves upon him by subjecting him . . . to a veritable despotism independent of all social organisation. Wanting to abolish authority in large-scale industry is tantamount to wanting to abolish industry itself, to destroy the power loom in order to return to the spinning wheel.[54]

Most commentaries exaggerate the authoritarianism of Engels's 'On Authority'; it is important to remember that it was aimed at contemporary anarchism, and that the essay contains clear indications that under socialism the form of 'despotism' would alter significantly, with decisions being taken by delegates elected by workers.

Nevertheless, there is little doubt that today it is difficult to share the complacency with which Marx and Engels viewed the development of technology and its material embodiment in specific means of production. Recent studies have clearly revealed the social and political pressures involved in the choice and financing of technology, and in the design of machinery.[55] The implications for socialism are both daunting and encouraging: on the one hand, we are only just beginning to realise how gigantic a transformation will have to be accomplished to establish socialism, involving as it must now a basic re-evaluation and redesign of technologies and means of production long taken for granted; on the other hand, a recognition that many contemporary technologies and means of production are not neutral, as between contending classes and modes of production, opens up possibilities and hopes for the reorganisation of forms of production which until recently have met with incomprehension and disbelief.[56]

Within Marxism the thesis of the essential neutrality of the forces of production is closely bound up with conceptions of scarcity and abundance and their function in the construction of socialism. Historically, most Marxists have uncritically taken over Marx's youthful view that the abolition of 'scarcity' (a concept that is rarely subjected to theoretical scrutiny) is a precondition for the establishment of socialism and thus also for the abolition of the division of labour and exchange. In other words, most Marxists have accepted the idea that the forces of production must be developed first, especially as socialist revolutions have occurred under conditions of underdevelopment, before any fundamental changes can be realistically instituted in the social organisation of production. Now, I have shown earlier that Marx had begun to distance himself from an absolute notion of scarcity in his mature writings and that this 'break' played a not insignificant part in prompting a revision of his earlier belief in the irrelevance of the division of labour under conditions of socialist production. But neither of these fundamental changes in Marx's thinking have ever been fully registered in subsequent Marxist theory. Any comprehensive explanation of this phenomenon would no doubt require reference to many different conditions, but for present purposes two need to be underlined: first, Marx himself fails to rethink other aspects of his conception of socialism in the light of changes in his views on the abolition of scarcity and the division of labour; most importantly, he continues to uphold the idea of the abolition of exchange relations, a form of reorganisation predicated upon the abolition of scarcity.[57] The problems attending the notion of the abolition of exchange are explored later. Second, although in his later writings Engels also abandons the idea of the abolition of the division of labour *tout court*, Engels fails to problematise the concept of scarcity in his own discourse and most especially in the highly influential *Anti-Dühring* of 1894. Given its centrality in much subsequent Marxist theory, the concept of scarcity deserves some attention here.

In *Anti-Dühring* Engels continues to advance the proposition (which Marx had also espoused in his earlier writings) that the basic determinant of the historical emergence of classes is the existence of 'scarcity'. And not surprisingly, Engels logically derives the fateful conclusion that the abolition of classes (and, by implication, the abolition of the 'old' division of labour) can only proceed on the basis of the abolition of 'scarcity':

> The separation of society into an exploiting and an exploited class, a ruling and an oppressed class, was the necessary consequence of the deficient and restricted development of production in former times. So long as the total social labour only yields a produce which but slightly exceeds that barely necessary for the existence of all; so long, therefore, as labour engages all or almost all the time of the great majority of the members of society – so long, of necessity, this society is divided into classes. Side by side with the great majority . . . arises a class freed from directly productive labour, which looks after the general affairs of society . . . It is therefore the law of division of labour that lies at the basis of the division into classes . . . But if, upon this showing, division into classes has a certain historical justification, it has this only under given social conditions. It was based upon the insufficiency of production. It will be swept away by the complete development of modern productive forces.[58]

Before examining these propositions critically it is worth setting out their underlying logic. The basic premise here is that any one social group can only free itself from labour if the overall level of productivity can ensure the reproduction of the labour-power of the direct producers. Thus in a 'limit' situation where every able-bodied member of society must engage in productive labour to ensure bare physical survival, no part of society can free itself from this labour, for the labour of the rest of society would not be productive enough to sustain the exploiting group: presumably, the direct producers would either die off or their capacity for work would be seriously impaired.[59]

The fundamental objection to this thesis is that it operates with absolute conceptions of 'scarcity', 'needs' and 'surplus', predicated upon an implicit notion of the requisites of bare survival for the species. It therefore commits itself to an evolutionary scheme in which history is seen as a process of continually diminishing scarcities, culminating in a sort of post-industrial, scarcity-less state. In doing so, this conception obscures the relationship between scarcity, needs and surplus at both 'ends' of the historical chain. For instance, in the case of hunters and gatherers – generally regarded as one of the least developed in most evolutionary schemes including that of Engels – Sahlins has pointed out that all the available evidence suggests that in relation to their own conception of material needs they find themselves in a state of abundance, spending much less time on productive labour than most members of advanced industrial societies.[60] There exists in these societies – and it may be postulated that there existed for earlier hunters and gatherers – the possibility of a surplus, but what is conspicuously absent is the existence of a group whose reproduction depends on compelling others to perform surplus labour. Indeed, it is possible to argue that it is the development of relations of domination and subordination which actually leads to the systematic creation and appropriation of surpluses. In this context Pearson's remarks are particularly apposite:

> It is no good either to go half the distance in the surplus argument by admitting that surplus is a necessary but not sufficient cause of change, for this is to beg the question. There are always and everywhere potential surpluses available. What counts is the institutional means for bringing them to life.[61]

And at the other end of the evolutionary chain, in a highly developed industrial system of the sort presupposed by conceptions of post-scarcity socialism, the Engels thesis (deriving largely from the eighteenth century) again encounters a serious difficulty in so far as it comes up against the proposition advanced in *The German Ideology*, that the development of productive capacities generates *new* needs. Thus, while some scarcities are abolished, others are continually engendered. In *Capital*, while acknowledging this possibility, Marx does add that in so far as the bourgeoisie as a class can only survive on the basis of constantly revolutionising the means of production, capitalism generates new needs at a pace and level of intensity unlikely under socialism, a form of argument that has recently been revived by Macpherson and Leiss, and receives support in the work of Polanyi and Pearson.[62] Nevertheless, unless all technological innovation and economic growth stop it is difficult to see how scarcity *as such* can be abolished, a possibility that appears even more remote in the context of a potential crisis in the world's natural resources.[63]

Despite the difficulties that become apparent under theoretical scrutiny, the scarcity thesis in the form handed down by Engels's *Anti-Dühring* has been widely influential within Marxism, sitting snugly with the notion of a determinate 'correspondence' between the forces and relations of production, and thus receiving additional support in Marx's famous *Preface* of 1859.[64] And in encouraging the idea that the forces of production must be developed prior to fundamental changes in the relations of production, the scarcity thesis *simpliciter* has led to a species of technicism that is perhaps most clearly evident in Lenin's characteristic strategy for the establishment of socialism in Russia:

> The only socialism we can imagine is one based on all the lessons learned through large-scale capitalist culture. Socialism without postal and telegraph services, without machines, is the emptiest of phrases.[65]

> Socialism owes its origins to large-scale machine industry. If the masses of the working people, in introducing socialism, prove incapable of adapting their institutions to the way that large-scale industry should work, then there can be no question of introducing socialism.[66]

Moreover, it is well known that Lenin looked towards Taylor's notorious 'scientific management' techniques to improve productivity. Now, it must be admitted that in the aftermath of the revolution and civil war Lenin was confronted by serious problems, including the threat of complete annihilation, a fact grossly underplayed by some of Lenin's critics.[67] But even at the time, groups of dissenters emerged in Russia who expressed serious reservations about Lenin's strategy for development: Kollontai, for example, a member of the 'Workers' Opposition', picked out Lenin's veneration for experts and specialists as particularly inimical to the establishment of socialist relations of production.[68]

Indeed, the typical Marxist belief that transformations in the division of labour under socialism must necessarily await the development of productive forces – and it must be borne in mind that the 'necessary' level of development is rarely specified – must surely be reappraised.[69] Let it be said at the outset that the belief is not entirely groundless. For example, if universal literacy is a basic precondition for transforming the division between mental and manual labour, then any effort in this direction will obviously be limited by the availability of resources for this purpose: teachers, books, and so on and so forth. And without necessarily engaging in a lengthy discussion of definitions of 'productive' and 'unproductive' labour, it may be admitted that levels of productivity in the economy as a whole will set limits to the resources that can be made available for bringing about universal literacy. However, as against this it must be noted, first, that in so far as 'free time' is considered vital for the full development of individual capacities and thus for transforming the division of labour, then it is at least as likely that with increased production there will be an expansion in the social conception of 'basic needs', and that there will not necessarily be a reduction in the time that is allocated for social reproduction. In the second place, it is worth indicating that attempts to transform various aspects of the division of labour need not necessarily await a high level of productivity and technological development. In the Chinese Cultural Revolution, for example, considerable emphasis was placed on overcoming 'the three great differences': between town and country, between industry and agriculture, and between mental and manual labour. Thus various sorts of measures were implemented to alter the character of these relations. Educational facilities and industrialisation were expanded in the rural areas, while within the industrial enterprises themselves technicians, engineers and cadres were encouraged to engage in manual work and manual workers were given, by way of a variety of institutional mechanisms, greater powers of decision-making and in management.[70] Recent political changes have undoubtedly led to a reversal of many of these policies, and in any case several question marks hang over the Chinese Revolution generally, but this should not be allowed to detract from the basic point that the characteristic Marxist emphasis on developing the forces of production before transforming the division of labour is in need of serious reconsideration.[71]

Socialism for Marx, of course, implied not merely a radical transformation in the capitalist division of labour, but also in the role of the closely related phenomenon of exchange and the production of commodities. In his earlier work Marx conflated the two sets of social relations in the over-arching concept of alienation and, as shown previously in some detail, he argued that the abolition of both the division of labour and exchange was a fundamental prerequisite for the full realisation of socialism. He gradually modified his views on the abolition of the division of labour under socialism and this adjustment parallels developments in his understanding of the relationship between exchange and the division of labour: while the earlier writings imply that division of labour and exchange must necessarily coexist, the mature writings recognise that division of labour does not necessarily imply the production of commodities, and in *Capital* Marx illustrates this point by reference to 'the primitive Indian community'.[72] Paradoxically, the analytical separation of division of labour from exchange meant that modifications to his belief in the abolition of the division of labour did not lead to changes in his vision of the role of exchange in socialist society: Marx never wavered in his belief that the existence of production for exchange on any scale was fundamentally incompatible with socialism. In the 'Critique of the Gotha Programme', for example, Marx writes:

> Within the co-operative society based on common ownership of the means of production, the producers do not exchange their products; just as little does the labour employed on the products appear here as the value of these products, as a material quality possessed by them, since now, in contrast to capitalist society, individual labour no longer exists in an indirect fashion but directly as a component part of the total labour.[73]

Marx's critique of exchange relations in general is closely tied to his analysis of the irrationality of capitalism, that is, of a system completely dominated by exchange. While Marx was well aware that the existence of commodity production (production for exchange) did not lead inexorably to a system of *generalised* commodity production in which land, labour and the instruments of production became commodities to be bought and sold on the market, he always held to the view that there was an intrinsic connection between the two forms:

> The mode of production in which the product takes the form of a commodity, or is directly produced for exchange is the most general and most embryonic form of bourgeois production.[74]

To understand why Marx advances this proposition, it is important to return to a point made previously where it was argued that in Marx's usage of the term 'social division of labour' two elements were included without sufficient analytical discrimination: division of labour between agents as such, and the tendency, in systems embodying private ownership of the means of production, for separate commodities to be produced by distinct owners. The absence of a more refined analysis in this context means that Marx fails to make a rigorous enough separation between a system in which social division of labour and commodity production are embedded in relations of private ownership, and a form of social organisation in which social division of labour and production for exchange coexist with common ownership. Herein lie the roots of potential difficulties in Marx's understanding of the possible role of exchange relations under a socialist system.

Marx's unwavering hostility to production for exchange under socialism stems basically from the association between production for exchange on the one hand, and the anarchy of capitalist market relations and the consequent combination of squandered resources and unmet needs on the other. The remedy proposed by Marx is economic planning: capitalism and all other forms of commodity production are contrasted with 'a community of free individuals, carrying on their work with the means of production in common, in which the labour power of all the different individuals is consciously applied as the combined labour power of the community'.[74] And, reflecting sardonically upon the difference between the 'lawless caprice of the producers' in the capitalist social division of labour and the 'undisputed authority of the capitalist' within the factory, Marx remarks:

> The same bourgeois mind which praises division of labour in the workshop . . . denounces with equal vigour every conscious attempt to control socially and regulate the process of production . . . It is very characteristic that the enthusiastic apologists of the factory system have nothing more damning to urge against a general organisation of the labour of society, than that it would turn all society into one immense factory.[75]

One basic weakness in Marx's conception here is that he has an unacceptably complacent view of the possibilities for planning in production. While it is somewhat anachronistic to accuse Marx of not anticipating the formidable problems of socialist planning it is nevertheless important to set these out, for they have a significant bearing on Marx's views on exchange and division of labour under socialism. In this context, the fundamental thesis supported here is that the experience of state socialist societies is powerfully suggestive of the difficulties and disadvantages of operating a complex industrial economy without some room for market forces and commodity production, although large numbers of orthodox Marxists, especially in the west, continue to believe that the commodity form is fundamentally incompatible with socialism.[76]

In *The State and Revolution* Lenin himself had echoed Marx's views on the role of exchange relations under socialism, and even in 1919 was able to write that the aim of the Bolsheviks was to 'strive for the most rapid carrying out of the most radical measures preparing the abolition of money'.[77] While it is true that rampant inflation had by this time eroded the value of the Russian currency and had therefore created a favourable climate for the idea of the abolition of money, this should not be allowed to detract from the point that the notion of the abolition of commodity relations had in any case been accepted by Lenin before the revolution; Bukharin and Preobrazhensky, moreover, added their voice in the classic *ABC of Communism* (also published in Russia in 1919) and reinforced an orthodoxy which still survives in contemporary Marxism.[78] It is by now well known that after the brief period of 'War Communism' in which attempts were made to bring about a greater degree of centralisation in economic affairs and to limit the role of money and trade, Lenin and the Bolsheviks were forced to introduce the 'New Economic Policy' (NEP) which, in the wake of severe economic crises, gave much greater freedom of trade and explicitly encouraged production for exchange. The advocates of NEP, including Lenin, saw the measures as a temporary retreat occasioned by special circumstances: the ravages of civil war, famine, and the structure of Russian landownership which had saddled the new regime with millions of small-holding peasants.[79] NEP provoked fundamental theoretical and political debate, especially between those (like Preobrazhensky) who remained implacably hostile to market forces and wanted a speedy return to centralisation, and others (like Bukharin) who began to see in NEP a long-term strategy for Russian development and a useful corrective to the inefficiencies of excessive centralisation.[80]

By the 1920s and 1930s some hostile western economists had begun to challenge the claims of the socialist economic system to greater rationality and efficiency in comparison with capitalism: von Mises, in a famous paper originally published in German in 1920, argued that the absence of production for exchange and the abolition of money would make rational economic calculation impossible, while Hayek and Robbins suggested that the efficient functioning of a planned economy would require the solution of millions of simultaneous equations, which they argued was practically impossible.[81] Oskar Lange proposed a solution to these problems which is highly interesting from the perspective of later debates: he advocated a combination of market forces with a system of flexible, centrally organised prices which would alter in response to changes in supply and demand; he also emphasised the compatibility between socialism and commodity production.[82] In later years Lange pinned his hopes on the computer, though as Nove has pointed out most Soviet economists are much less convinced of the ability of the computer to eliminate market mechanisms.[83] The advent of collectivisation, centralisation and a brutal censorship under Stalin effectively blocked the debate, and it was not until the Yugoslavian reforms of the 1950s that the issues were once again publicly discussed, a trend greatly reinforced by the problems of the Soviet economy and which culminated in the attempted reforms of 1965.[84] Two interrelated themes from these debates need to be considered here: the economic drawbacks of excessive centralisation and the issue of democratisation. Both carry implications for Marx's conception of exchange and the division of labour.

The economic critique of over-centralisation in planning has concentrated in the main on the fact that it is actually wasteful, although some of the initial impetus to debates in the Soviet Union came from the increasing volume of decisions that confronted planners in a period of rapid industrialisation, and also from attempts to give greater priority to consumers' goods and agriculture which meant that imbalances could not easily be rectified by withdrawing supplies from these sectors of production. Soviet and western economists have pointed to at least three main ways in which over-centralisation has resulted in a waste of resources.[85] First, enterprises have attempted to obtain 'soft' plan targets by concealing their true productive potential in order to ensure a reserve in case of errors in central planning, unforeseen shortages in supplies, and to ensure an easy target in any subsequent plan. Second, pressures to conform to the plan target have often led to the neglect of adequate maintenance of plant and machinery, and have also discouraged technical innovation because in the short term both maintenance and innovation could involve interruptions to the flow of output. Third, rigid pricing policies have also discouraged technological innovation: if enterprises engaged in the production of machinery, for example, manage to produce more efficient machinery, this reduces their sales, but as prices cannot be altered they actually stand to lose revenue. Inflexibility in pricing has also led to acute imbalances in the production and distribution of goods for personal consumption, while a 'seller's market' has obviously led to insufficient attention to quality and taste and, in turn, has often resulted in large quantities of unsold goods.

What is particularly interesting here is that many reformers of socialist economic systems have proposed the *limited* extension of market forces and commodity production as a corrective to the defects of centralised planning as this has been implemented in the Soviet Union and eastern Europe. The first post-war proposals of this type came from Kidric in Yugoslavia, while in the Soviet Union, Liberman in 1962 also advocated a restriction of central planning and a more flexible approach to pricing and production for exchange.[86] In more recent years Šik and Brus have produced sophisticated guidelines for the introduction of market-based reforms in socialist economic systems.[87] Most advocates of 'market socialism' have been careful to stress that central planning must remain a crucial element within any socialist economic system and that market forces can only be allowed to play a subordinate role.[88] However, this has not prevented serious opposition to their ideas: in the Soviet Union the reforms of 1965 were never properly implemented, while many critics of the Yugoslav system, including the *Praxis* group, have argued that the extension of market forces has resulted in the spread of typical capitalistic problems: inflation, unemployment and rising levels of inequality.[89] There is little doubt that some of the misgivings of the critics are justified, but as Ellman has suggested neither inequality nor unemployment are inevitable consequences of decentralisation in economic planning, and it is interesting to note that after a sustained and detailed analysis of planning problems in the Soviet Union he argues clearly and persuasively for the reintroduction of market forces in well-defined areas of economic life.[90]

Nevertheless, it must be noted that despite attempts by some of the reformers to find passages in Marx and Engels in support of an extension of the role of exchange relations and commodity production under socialism, the idea of 'market socialism' (something of a misnomer because it exaggerates the actual role of the market) marks a definite departure from the classical texts. The roots of Marx and Engels's underestimation of the role of market forces under socialism appear to lie, first, in too close an identification between commodity production and private ownership, a tendency reflected in some of the confusions in the concept of social division of labour, and second, in an unwillingness to think through in any detail the measures required for the establishment of socialist relations of production.

Marx's critique of market relations is concerned not simply with the inefficiency generated by production for exchange, but also with the problem of control: the generalisation of commodity production involves loss of control by the direct producers to the owners of the means of production who, in turn, find themselves at the mercy of a system subject to periodic crises. However, it now seems likely that the complete abolition of market forces (which was Marx's solution to inefficiency) would actually produce irrationalities of its own. Moreover, it is now being increasingly argued that Marx's notion of the abolition of market forces may also conflict with his desire for economic and political control of the production process by the direct producers. This issue is central to any appraisal of Marx's views on the division of labour, for Marx always regarded the issues of power and authority as aspects of the underlying theme of divided labour.

In his writings on the Paris Commune, Marx proposes an elaborate system of representation and accountability which is crucial to his vision of a transformed division of labour under socialism. Nevertheless, Marx never explains how the decentralisation measures advanced in these writings would integrate decision-making in individual productive enterprises into an overall political system based on planned production, and it is necessary to consider seriously the argument that effective decentralisation of economic decision-making, which is a precondition for the democratisation of the work place, is unlikely without some room for market forces. Of course, it is not entirely clear how much power Marx expected individual workers to have over the running of their own enterprise: Marx has little to say, for example, about the role of workers in deciding what to produce in their own factory or farm, how much to produce, what techniques to use, pricing, levels of investment, and a host of other problems which need to be resolved in any economy. Many of Marx's remarks are almost syndicalist in tone and spirit, and it is fair to say that this aspect of his thought is never really reconciled with the centralising tendency intrinsic to his views on coherent and effective planning at a societal level.

The question of democratisation of the work-place has emerged as an important theme in discussions on 'plan and market' under socialism, and many socialists have argued that the danger of bureaucratisation at the centre under a system of common ownership can only be avoided by an extension of the role of the market. Perhaps the clearest argument along these lines has been made by Selucký; a crucial passage from his paper is thus worth quoting in some detail:

> I would like . . . to suggest that rejection of the market is, by definition, incompatible with the concept of a self-managing socialist economic system. If the market is abolished, horizontal relationships (i.e. exchange) among economic units also disappears. If the market is abolished, the information coming from the consumers is either fully cut or at least quite irrelevant for producers. Then, the central plan is the only source supplying producers with relevant information. If this is the case, the structure of the economic system must be based on the prevailing vertical type of relationship (i.e. subordination and superiority), with decision-making centralized in the planning board, without any outside

control of central decisions. A self-managing system, even if formally introduced, is a foreign body within any non-market, vertical and centralized economic structure . . . Since any workable model of self-management or workers' participation requires decentralization of microeconomic decisions, an indicative rather than a command central plan . . . control of macro-decision-making from the bottom and real autonomy of enterprises and self-managing bodies, it is quite clear that any concept of the self-managing socialist economy would require a revision of the Marxist rejection of the market socialist economy. Apart from what Marx and Engels have said about the self-government of producers or about centralized planning, their anti-market concept for a future socialist economy implicitly puts any variant of self-management out of the question.[91]

Selucký undoubtedly exaggerates his case: for example, he has little to say about forms of democratisation and accountability other than the market. Moreover, as Yugoslav Marxists have pointed out, the introduction of procedures of self-management in their country has not prevented the emergence of technocratic elites in many enterprises, nor has it ensured that the decisions of individual enterprises take adequate account of the interests of society as a whole.[92] But in the absence of concrete proposals for reorganisation from the critics, Selucký's basic thesis must be allowed to stand, albeit in a modified and less dogmatic form: the enlargement of genuine control by the direct producers over economic decisions, and thus a real transformation in the principles of authority embedded in the structure of tasks in the enterprise and in society as a whole, may well be impossible to establish without some extension of market principles, at some point, to allow individual enterprises the freedom to decide the nature and the level of production, together with the character of distribution. The challenge that faces Marxism in this context has been clearly set out by Nove in response to Bettelheim's critique of the USSR:

The New Left see the inefficiency and the waste, but tend to attribute it to the power of the bureaucracy and the lack of democratic control by those whom they like to describe as the 'direct producers'. At no point do they analyse how the direct producers are to control the economy. Bettelheim, for instance, asserts the

> dominance of politics over economics, but by what political process are the direct producers to determine social need, and to 'translate' this into literally thousands of millions of interrelated decisions on production, allocation, distribution, transport? Indeed, in what units should the necessary calculations be made?[93]

The usual orthodox Marxist response to critical reflections of the kind discussed above has been to argue that they represent merely the problems associated with a transitional order. The abolition of scarcity, it is suggested, will inaugurate a new epoch, a 'higher phase', in which division of labour, inequality and exchange will no longer exist. In relation to exchange, the reasoning that underlies this expectation is clearly set out by Bukharin and Preobrazhensky in *The ABC of Communism*:

> There will be an ample quantity of all products . . . a person will take from the communal storehouse precisely as much as he needs, no more. No one will have any interest in taking more than he wants in order to sell the surplus to others, since all these others can satisfy their needs whenever they please. Money will then have no value.[94]

Indeed, the most implacable opponents of the market under socialism have to admit that their position depends, in the final analysis, on the notion of the abolition of scarcity.[95] But once the idea of the abolition of scarcity *tout court* is problematised, as it must be, the argument that socialism must accommodate commodity production becomes difficult to resist. Add to this the propositions discussed earlier concerning the relationship between an extension of exchange relations and democratisation at the work-place under conditions of socialist production, and the argument becomes powerful enough to require from the defenders of orthodoxy a response well beyond the sloganising and dogma it appears to have provoked so far.

Note, too, that in so far as the idea of the abolition of exchange relations is problematised, so is the notion of the end of ideology and social science as enshrined in Marx's conception of the 'fetishism' of commodities.[96] It may well be that in rethinking its attitude to the complete abolition of relations of exchange, Marxism will at last settle its accounts with the philosophy of alienation that haunts Marx's early writings and which, in the guise of the thesis of the end of ideology and social science, re-emerges at the very heart of the discourse of *Capital*. In mapping out an alternative terrain for theory and practice, Marxism will be doing no more than completing a process set in motion by Marx himself when he began to reappraise the division of labour and its historical forms.

However, on at least one major issue it may well be that the task is not merely one of extending Marx's work but of breaking with it: the sexual division of labour.[97] Marx, of course, has little to say about the abolition of the sexual division of labour, while Engels appears to assume that the abolition of private ownership of the means of production would somehow automatically entail the disappearance of the nuclear family and the establishment of women's liberation.[98] Today it is impossible to share his complacency. Nor is it obvious that a complete synthesis between Feminism and Marxism is possible; indeed, the form of socialist discourse that emerges from the encounter between these two movements may well mean the end of Marxism as we have known it.[99] So be it: the abolition of the sexual division of labour is a task of altogether greater moment than the defence of Marxist orthodoxy.

Notes and References

Introduction

1. For differing interpretations of the relationship between Marx and Engels see, *inter alia*, G. Lichtheim, *Marxism: an Historical and Critical Study*, 2nd edn (London: Routledge & Kegan Paul, 1964) pp. 234–58; D. C. Hodges, 'Engels's Contribution to Marxism', in R. Miliband and J. Saville (eds), *The Socialist Register 1965* (London: Merlin Press, 1965); J. Coulter, 'Marxism and the Engels Paradox', in R. Miliband and J. Saville (eds), *The Socialist Register 1971* (London: Merlin Press, 1971); D. McLellan, *Engels* (London: Fontana, 1977) pp. 65–75. For one of the worst examples of the genre which delights in driving a wedge between Marx and Engels, see N. Levine, *The Tragic Deception: Marx Contra Engels* (Santa Barbara: Clio Press, 1975).
2. See, for example, H. Braverman, *Labour and Monopoly Capital: The Degradation of Work in the Twentieth Century* (New York: Monthly Review Press, 1974); *Technology, the Labour Process, and the Working Class*, special issue of *Monthly Review*, vol. 28 (1976); *The Labour Process and the Working Class*, special issue of *Politics and Society*, vol. 8 (1978); Brighton Labour Process Group, 'The Capitalist Labour Process', *Capital and Class*, no. 1 (1977); A. Zimbalist (ed.), *Case Studies on the Labour Process* (New York: Monthly Review Press, 1979); R. Edwards, *Contested Terrain: the Transformation of the Workplace in the Twentieth Century* (New York: Basic Books, 1979); M. Burawoy, *Manufacturing Consent: Changes in the Labour Process under Monopoly Capital* (University of Chicago Press, 1979). Two texts not usually included in such a list should also be mentioned: G. Carchedi, *On the Economic Identification of Classes* (London: Routledge & Kegan Paul, 1977); E. O. Wright, *Class, Crisis and the State* (London: New Left Books, 1978).
3. For instance, compare the usage in Braverman, *Labour and Monopoly Capital*, with that in Carchedi, *On the Economic Identification of Classes*. There have already been some attempts at conceptual clarification: cf. B. Hindess and P. Hirst, *Mode of Production and Social Formation* (London: Macmillan, 1977) p. 77, n. 19; A. Cutler *et al.*, *Marx's Capital and Capitalism Today*, vol. I (London: Routledge & Kegan Paul, 1977) pp. 243–312; A. Hunt, 'Theory and Politics in the Identification of the Working Class', in idem (ed.), *Class and Class Structure* (London: Lawrence & Wishart, 1977); T. Nichols, 'Introduction', in idem (ed.), *Capital and Labour: a Marxist Primer* (London: Fontana, 1980) pp. 25–6.
4. M. Burawoy, 'Toward a Marxist Theory of the Labour Process: Braverman and Beyond', *Politics and Society*, vol. 8 (1978). Cf. R. Edwards, 'Social Relations

of Production at the Point of Production', and S. Aronowitz, 'Marx, Braverman and the Logic of Capital', both in *The Insurgent Sociologist*, vol. 8 (1978); A. Cutler, 'The Romance of "Labour"', *Economy and Society*, vol. 7 (1978); G. Mackenzie, 'The Political Economy of the American Working Class', *British Journal of Sociology*, vol. 28 (1977).

Part I

1. See, for instance, V. Foley, 'The Division of Labour in Plato and Smith', *History of Political Economy*, vol. 6 (1974).
2. For different versions of the discontinuist thesis in the historiography of the natural and social sciences, see T. Kuhn, *The Structure of Scientific Revolutions*, 2nd edn (University of Chicago Press, 1970); M. Foucault, *The Order of Things* (New York: Random House, 1971). and *The Archaeology of Knowledge* (London: Tavistock, 1972). The contributions of Bachelard and Canguilhem are explored in D. Lecourt, *Marxism and Epistemology* (London: New Left Books, 1975). For an acute history of economic thought inspired in part by Foucault, see K. Tribe, *Land, Labour and Economic Discourse* (London: Routledge & Kegan Paul, 1978).
3. The conceptualisations of Kuhn, Bachelard and Foucault are not, of course, reducible to one another. Cf. Lecourt, *Marxism and Epistemology*, pp. 9–19; Tribe, *Land, Labour and Economic Discourse*, pp. 14–22.
4. *The Dialogues of Plato*, vol. III, trans. B. Jowett, 2nd edn (Oxford: Clarendon Press, 1875) bk IV, pp. 324–5.
5. For other translations of the same passage see, *inter alia*, Plato: *The Republic*, trans. H. Lee (Harmondsworth: Penguin, 1971) p. 196; *Republic*, trans. P. Shorey in E. Hamilton and H. Cairns (eds), *The Collected Dialogues of Plato* (Princeton University Press, 1973) p. 685.
6. That Aristotle did not possess a notion of the 'economy' in the sense assumed by modern (primarily neo-classical) historians of economic thought is argued by M. Finley in 'Aristotle and Economic Analysis', *Past and Present*, no. 47 (1970).
7. *The Republic*, bk II, p. 102. All references are to the translation by Lee. Cf. Aristotle, *The Politics*, trans. T. Sinclair (Harmondsworth: Penguin, 1967) bk I, ch. 2, p. 29. All references are to this edition.
8. *The Republic*, bk II, p. 103.
9. Ibid, p. 105.
10. *The Politics*, bk IV, ch. 4, pp. 156–68. For a discussion of Aristotle's 'functionalism' and an assessment of the influence of biological studies on his thinking, see J. H. Randall, Jr, *Aristotle* (New York: Columbia University Press, 1960) esp. pp. 65–7, 186–8, 219–71.
11. Cf. *The Republic*, bk II, p. 102.
12. Xenophon, *Cyropaedia*, trans. W. Miller (London: Heinemann, 1943) p. 33.
13. *The Politics*, bk I, ch. 9, pp. 41–2. Cf. Finley, 'Aristotle and Economic Analysis', p. 4.
14. That the thought of Plato and Aristotle represented a systematisation of anti-democratic, aristocratic ideology is argued in E. Wood and N. Wood, *Class Ideology and Ancient Political Theory* (Oxford: Blackwell, 1978).
15. R. J. Littman, *The Greek Experiment: Imperialism and Social Conflict 800–400 BC* (London: Thames & Hudson, 1974) p. 99. See also A. Gouldner, *Enter Plato: Classical Greece and the Origins of Social Theory* (London: Routledge & Kegan Paul, 1967) pp. 3–40; A. Andrewes, *Greek Society* (Harmondsworth: Penguin, 1971) pp. 97–160. On the problem of slavery, see M. Finley (ed.),

Slavery in Classical Antiquity (Cambridge: Heffer, 1960).

16. Cf: M. Finley, *The Ancient Economy* (London: Chatto & Windus, 1973) pp. 40–1.
17. *The Politics*, bk VII, ch. 9, p. 273.
18. Xenophon, *Oeconomicus*, trans. L. Strauss (Cornell University Press, 1970) p. 17. It is sometimes suggested that Plato's doctrine is essentially meritocratic. For a detailed critique of such an interpretation, see Wood and Wood, *Class Ideology and Ancient Political Theory*, pp. 144–53.
19. *The Politics*, bk IV, ch. 4, p. 158.
20. Ibid, bk IV, ch. 11, p. 173.
21. *The Republic*, bk IV, p. 182.
22. R. Bambrough, 'Plato's Political Analogies', in P. Laslett (ed.), *Philosophy, Politics and Society*, First Series (Oxford: Blackwell, 1967).
23. *The Republic*, bk IV, p. 197.
24. Ibid, bks V and VI, pp. 236–65.
25. Wood and Wood, *Class Ideology and Ancient Political Theory*, p. 133. Cf. C. Mossé, *The Ancient World at Work* (London: Chatto & Windus, 1969) pp. 25–30; 75–96.
26. Cf. G. E. R. Lloyd, *Greek Science after Aristotle* (London: Chatto & Windus, 1973) pp. 154–74, esp. pp. 166–7; E. Roll, *A History of Economic Thought*, 2nd edn (London: Faber, 1973) pp. 35–8. For the social background to Roman thought see, *inter alia*, P. A. Brunt, *Social Conflicts in the Roman Republic* (London: Chatto & Windus, 1971); D. Dudley, *Roman Society* (Harmondsworth: Penguin, 1975); P. Brown, *The World of Late Antiquity* (London: Thames & Hudson, 1971).
27. Cf. Cicero, *De Officiis*, trans. W. Miller (London: Heinemann, 1947) bk I, pp. 153–5.
28. Roll, *A History of Economic Thought*, p. 38.
29. For an important example of medieval 'economics', see the extracts from Aquinas in A. E. Monroe (ed.), *Early Economic Thought* (Harvard University Press, 1951), pp. 51–77. Cf. B. Gordon, *Economic Analysis before Adam Smith* (London: Macmillan, 1975), pp. 153–86.
30. For divergent interpretations of this fundamental restructuring of the social and intellectual order see, *inter alia*, R. Hilton (ed.), *The Transition from Feudalism to Capitalism* (London: New Left Books, 1976); M. J. Kitch (ed.), *Capitalism and the Reformation* (London: Longmans, 1967); V. L. Bullough (ed.), *The Scientific Revolution* (New York: Holt, Rinehart & Winston, 1970).
31. Cf. Tribe, *Land, Labour and Economic Discourse*, pp. 80–109. In this context Smith may be said to be a transitional figure.
32. *The Economic Writings of Sir William Petty*, ed. C. H. Hull (Cambridge University Press, 1899) vol. I, pp. 355–6; vol. II, p. 473.
33. The quotation is from his essay, 'A Search into the Nature of Society', which was included in the 1723 edition of the book. Cf. Bernard Mandeville, *The Fable of the Bees*, ed. P. Harth (Harmondsworth: Penguin, 1970) p. 368. For Francis Hutcheson, see R. L. Meek (ed.), *Precursors of Adam Smith 1750–1775* (London: Dent, 1973) p. 29; W. L. Taylor, *Francis Hutcheson and David Hume as Predecessors of Adam Smith* (Durham: Duke University Press, 1965) pp. 56–68.
34. Cf. R. L. Meek, *Studies in the Labour Theory of Value*, 2nd edn (London: Lawrence & Wishart, 1973) p. 20.
35. See R. Williams, *Keywords: a Vocabulary of Culture and Society* (London: Fontana, 1976) pp. 145–8.
36. Cf. A. McIntyre, *A Short History of Ethics* (London: Routledge & Kegan Paul, 1967) pp. 124–8.

37. C. B. Macpherson, *The Political Theory of Possessive Individualism* (Oxford University Press, 1964). Cf. L. Goldmann, *The Philosophy of the Enlightenment* (Routledge & Kegan Paul, 1973) pp. 18–20.
38. S. Lukes, *Individualism* (Oxford: Blackwell, 1973).
39. Cf. G. Therborn, *Science, Class and Society* (London: New Left Books, 1976) pp. 121–2. Goldmann is one of many who mislead by an over-extension of 'individualism': cf. Goldmann, *The Philosophy of the Enlightenment*, pp. 20–1. See also the critique of Macpherson in Tribe, *Land, Labour and Economic Discourse*, pp. 40ff.
40. P. Gay, *The Enlightenment: an Interpretation* (London: Weidenfeld & Nicolson, 1970) vol. II, p. 319.
41. The originality of some of the best-known Enlightenment schemes of evolution is painstakingly established by R. L. Meek, in *Social Science and the Ignoble Savage* (Cambridge University Press, 1976).
42. Cf. R. L. Meek (ed.), *Turgot on Progress, Sociology and Economics* (Cambridge University Press, 1973) pp. 43, 89, 121, 145.
43. Cf. G. Bryson, *Man and Society: the Scottish Inquiry of the Eighteenth Century* (Princeton University Press, 1945) p. 7. For a more detailed exploration of Scotland's changing social and economic structure during this period, see D. Kettler, *The Social and Political Thought of Adam Ferguson* (Ohio University Press, 1965) pp. 15–32.
44. J. A. Schumpeter, *History of Economic Analysis* (London: Allen & Unwin, 1954) p. 187.
45. Adam Smith, *The Wealth of Nations*, ed. E. Cannon (London: Methuen, 1961) vols I and II. All references are to this edition.
46. Ibid, pp. 7–8.
47. Ibid, pp. 11–13.
48. This critique of Smith is detailed in S. Marglin, 'What do Bosses do? The Origins and Function of Hierarchy in Capitalist Production', in A. Gorz (ed.), *The Division of Labour* (Hassocks: Harvester, 1976) pp. 18–20.
49. As we shall see, Marx insisted on the fundamental importance of the distinction between division of labour 'in society' and division of labour 'in the workshop'.
50. It is of course possible to exaggerate the extent of Smith's reliance on the 'invisible hand' of the market: as Tribe has pointed out, the absence of a notion of competition between productive units – the necessary consequence of Smith's concentration on division of labour between individual agents – led him to postulate an important regulatory role for the statesman. Cf. Tribe, *Land, Labour and Economic Discourse*, p. 104 and *passim*.
51. Smith, *The Wealth of Nations*, vol. I, p. 17.
52. Ibid, p. 18.
53. Ibid, pp. 19–20.
54. For a discussion of Smith's epistemology and its relation to Locke's writings, see D. A. Reisman, *Adam Smith's Sociological Economics* (London: Croom Helm, 1976) pp. 22–37.
55. Cf. W. C. Lehmann, *John Millar of Glasgow 1735–1801* (Cambridge University Press, 1960) p. 132. The passage illustrates, moreover, the variety of terms with which the division of labour was conceptualised ('trades', 'professions', 'employments'), and the continuing influence of Greek discriminations ('liberal' and 'mechanical') although now incorporated into a transformed theoretical structure.
56. Smith, *The Wealth of Nations*, vol. I, p. 21.
57. Ibid, pp. 21–5.
58. Ibid, p. 401. The theoretical centrality occupied by exchange and the market in Smith's work, however, prevented him from recognising the importance of

changes in the relations of production which were a prerequisite for the successful operation of his model of self-sustaining growth. That is, he failed to see the necessity of 'free' labour, labour divorced from the means of production, if the transfer of labour power between agriculture and manufacture, country and town, was to respond to market opportunities. Cf. R. Brenner, 'The Origins of Capitalist Development: a Critique of Neo-Smithian Marxism', *New Left Review*, no. 104 (1977) pp. 33–8.

59. Smith, *The Wealth of Nations*, vol. I, p. 34.
60. Ibid, p. 35. This exposition of his argument illustrates, of course, the basic confusion in Smith's theory of value, which led him to reject the notion that in a capitalist economy labour could be regarded as the sole source of value: Smith conflated the proposition that the value of a commodity was determined by the amount of labour it could purchase in the market through an exchange with other commodities, with the proposition that the value of a commodity was determined by the quantity of labour embodied in it. Cf. M. Dobb, *Theories of Value and Distribution since Adam Smith* (Cambridge University Press, 1973) pp. 43–9.
61. Ibid, p. 276. A discussion of the novelty of this class map can be found in Meek's 'Introduction' to *Precursors of Adam Smith 1750–1775*.
62. R. A. Nisbet, *Social Change and History* (New York: Oxford University Press, 1969) p. 139.
63. Cf. A. Ferguson, *An Essay on the History of Civil Society* (1767) ed. D. Forbes (Edinburgh University Press, 1966) p. 87; Meek, *Social Science and the Ignoble Savage*, pp. 37–67.
64. Commentators have often exaggerated the similarities: it is therefore necessary to insist here that, above all, there is little in the writings of the Scottish Enlightenment to allow a direct conflation with the doctrine that all history is the history of class struggles and, partly for that reason, Marx and Engels's notion of 'mode of production' is also conceptually distinct from the modes of subsistence delineated by the Enlightenment.
65. Quoted in R. L. Meek, 'The Scottish Contribution to Marxist Sociology', *Economics and Ideology and Other Essays* (London: Chapman & Hall, 1967) p. 37.
66. Ferguson, *An Essay on the History of Civil Society*, p. 81.
67. See Smith's 'Lectures on Justice, Police, Revenue and Arms', in H. W. Schneider (ed.), *Adam Smith's Moral and Political Philosophy* (New York: Harper Torchbooks, 1970) pp. 290–301. Cf. Reisman, *Adam Smith's Sociological Economics*, pp. 129–38; A. S. Skinner, 'Adam Smith: an Economic Interpretation of History', in A. S. Skinner and T. Wilson (eds), *Essays on Adam Smith* (Oxford University Press, 1975). For contemporary French versions of historical development by stages, see Meek (ed.), *Turgot on Progress, Sociology and Economics*, pp. 64–83; A. N. Condorcet, *Sketch for a Historical Picture of the Progress of the Human Mind* (1795) ed. S. Hampshire (London: Weidenfeld & Nicolson, 1955); K. M. Baker, *Condorcet: from Natural Philosophy to Social Mathematics* (Chicago University Press, 1975) esp. pp. 343ff.
68. Ferguson, *An Essay on the History of Civil Society*, p. 135.
69. Smith, 'Lectures on Justice', p. 291.
70. Cf. Ferguson, *An Essay on the History of Civil Society*, p. 157; Smith, *The Wealth of Nations*, vol. I, p. 75. In his *Early Draft* of *The Wealth of Nations* Smith was even more critical of employers, arguing at one point that 'those who labour most get least'. Cf. R. L. Meek and A. S. Skinner, 'The Development of Adam Smith's Ideas on the Division of Labour', *Economic Journal*, vol. 83 (1973).
71. All references are to the edition of 1779 reprinted in Lehmann, *John Millar of Glasgow 1735–1801*.

72. Ibid, pp. 183–93. Note the 'naturalistic' assumptions, which later reappear in the work of Marx.
73. Ibid, p. 265.
74. Ibid, p. 208.
75. Ibid, p. 302. Cf. p. 290.
76. Ferguson, *An Essay on the History of Civil Society*, p. 97. Smith regarded the accumulation of 'stock' as an important precondition for the development of the division of labour. Cf. Smith, *The Wealth of Nations*, vol. I, pp. 291–2.
77. Cf. W. C. Lehmann, *Adam Ferguson and the Beginnings of Modern Sociology* (University of Columbia Press, 1930) p. 121.
78. At one point, at least, Ferguson did make an explicit analytical distinction between inequality arising from the occupational structure and that based on differential ownership of property, but little use was made of this discrimination in the rest of his work. Cf. *An Essay on the History of Civil Society*, p. 184. See also Condorcet, *The Progress of the Human Mind*, p. 179. It must be emphasised that nothing in my argument in this context is meant to imply a simple, linear relationship between the existence of pre-capitalist modes of production and associated conceptions of class and the division of labour.
79. Smith, *The Wealth of Nations*, vol. II, pp. 302–3. There was also a group of apologists in the eighteenth century who failed to recognise any of these effects of the division of labour: cf. M. Myers, 'Division of Labour as a Principle of Social Cohesion', *Canadian Journal of Economics and Political Science*, vol. 33 (1967).
80. Ferguson, *An Essay on the History of Civil Society*, pp. 182–3. Marx had erroneously believed that Smith had been Ferguson's student and had merely echoed his critique; in fact Smith had made his observations public well before Ferguson, in his lectures at Glasgow. Cf. R. Hamowy, 'Adam Smith, Adam Ferguson and the Division of Labour', *Economica*, vol. 35 (1968). Lukács repeated Marx's error: see *The Young Hegel* (London: Merlin Press, 1975) p. 329.
81. Smith, *The Wealth of Nations*, vol. II, p. 309.
82. Cf. E. G. West, 'Adam Smith's Two Views on the Division of Labour', *Economica*, vol. 31 (1964); N. Rosenberg, 'Adam Smith on the Division of Labour: Two Views or One?', *Economica*, vol. 32 (1965). For a recent exploration of Smith's political views, see D. Winch, *Adam Smith's Politics* (Cambridge University Press, 1978) esp. pp. 113–20.
83. See, for example, Ferguson's *Essay*, pp. 63, 67, and *passim*.
84. For an analysis of Locke's views on property, see Macpherson, *The Political Theory of Possessive Individualism*, pp. 194–221. I shall demonstrate later that the relationship between scarcity and inequality plays an important role in the work of Marx.
85. Cf. Hume's *Essays Moral, Political and Literary*, quoted in Taylor, *Francis Hutcheson and David Hume as Predecessors of Adam Smith*, pp. 146ff.
86. There are by now some excellent expositions of Hegel's thought as a whole: see, especially, J. N. Findlay, *Hegel: a Re-examination* (London: Allen & Unwin, 1958); W. Kaufman, *Hegel: a Reinterpretation* (New York: Doubleday Anchor, 1966); R. Plant, *Hegel* (London: Allen & Unwin, 1973); C. Taylor, *Hegel* (Cambridge University Press, 1975). A good introduction to the phenomenology can be found in R. Norman, *Hegel's Phenomenology* (Sussex University Press, 1976).
87. Cf. Plant, *Hegel*, p. 16.
88. Quoted in ibid, p. 21.
89. Cf. H. Marcuse, *Reason and Revolution: Hegel and the Rise of Social Theory*,

2nd edn (London: Routledge & Kegan Paul, 1967) pp. 13–16. The influence of the Scottish writers on German thought is explored in Plant, *Hegel*, pp. 17–22.

90. An excellent analysis of these writings, and an argument for the continuity between them and the *Philosophy of Right* can be found in S. Avineri, *Hegel's Theory of the Modern State* (Cambridge University Press, 1972) esp. pp. 87–114.
91. This theme, of course, overlaps with his concept of alienation. For a detailed study of the various meanings of Hegel's use of 'alienation', see R. Schacht, *Alienation* (London: Allen & Unwin, 1971) pp. 30–64; Norman, *Hegel's Phenomenology*, pp. 86–104.
92. A good discussion of Hegel's notion of labour is to be found in R. Plant, 'Hegel and Political Economy', parts I and II, *New Left Review*, nos 103 and 104 (1977). See also Lukács, *The Young Hegel*, pp. 338–64; K. Löwith, *From Hegel to Nietzsche* (New York: Doubleday Anchor, 1967) pp. 262–7.
93. Quoted in Avineri, *Hegel's Theory of the Modern State*, p. 92.
94. Ibid, p. 97. Cf. Lukács, *The Young Hegel*, p. 331.
95. Hegel, *The Philosophy of Right*, trans. T. M. Knox (Oxford University Press, 1942) para. 201.
96. Ibid, para. 243.
97. Ibid, para. 195.
98. Ibid, para. 67. Nevertheless, it is worth noting that in his delineation of major classes Hegel does not use property as a criterion: he distinguishes instead between the agricultural class, the business class, and the bureaucracy or civil service.
99. Ibid. para. 207. Classes are not the only mediators between individuals and society; like Tocqueville and Durkheim many years later, Hegel advocated the development of intermediate structures – 'corporations' – based on the division of labour to link the individual to society, and especially, the state. These were seen, like the family, as entities which would counter the egoism and atomisation generated by the process of individuation in civil society, would unite members of the same profession and trade in cooperative organisations, and could even form the basis for a system of political representation. See addition to para. 255. Cf. G. Heiman, 'The Sources and Significance of Hegel's Corporate Doctrine', in Z. A. Pelczynski (ed.), *Hegel's Political Philosophy* (Cambridge University Press, 1971) pp. 111–35.
100. Hegel, *The Philosophy of Right*, addition to para. 41.
101. Ibid, addition to para. 49.
102. The implication of my remarks is definitely *not* that Hegel was simply a reactionary and chauvinistic upholder of the Prussian state. For a spirited and convincing defence of Hegel against those who would see him in this light, see the essays by Avineri and Kaufman in W. Kaufman (ed.), *Hegel's Political Philosophy* (New York: Atherton Press, 1970).
103. Cf. G. D. H. Cole, *A History of Socialist Thought*, vol. I, *The Forerunners 1789–1850* (London: Macmillan, 1953) p. 4 and *passim*.
104. G. Lichtheim, *The Origins of Socialism* (London: Weidenfeld & Nicolson, 1969) p. 31.
105. Cf. Fourier, *The Utopian Vision of Charles Fourier: Selected Texts on Love, Work and Passionate Attraction*, ed. J. Beecher and R. Bienvenu (London: Jonathan Cape, 1972) p. 44.
106. Ibid, pp. 275–6.
107. Ibid, pp. 274–5.
108. The term 'socialism' seems to have made its first appearance in 1827 in the Owenite *Co-operative Magazine*, and in the Saint-Simonian *Le Globe*: cf. Cole, *A History of Socialist Thought*, p. 1.

109. Cf. Saint-Simon, *Henri Saint-Simon 1760–1825: Selected Writings on Science, Industry and Social Organisation*, ed. K. Taylor (London: Croom Helm, 1975) pp. 194–7.
110. Manuel has suggested that this 'spiritualisation' of labour may well have contributed something to the influence of Saint-Simon's doctrine in Catholic France – as opposed to Protestant countries – for it was an 'ideal bourgeois credo for a culture that required something more positive than an affirmation of the Rights of Man'. F. Manuel, *The New World of Henri Saint-Simon* Harvard University Press, 1956) p. 253.
111. Ibid, pp. 243–61.
112. Cf. Saint-Simon, *Selected Writings on Science, Industry and Social Organisation*, pp. 111–23.
113. Cf. Saint-Simon, *The Political Thought of Saint-Simon*, ed. G. Ionescu (Oxford University Press, 1976) p. 182.
114. Saint-Simon, *Selected Writings on Science, Industry and Social Organisation*, p. 238. Taylor remarks in his introduction to these selections that for Saint-Simon 'the basic meaning of the word "class" was "occupational group", and naturally in industrial society, as in any other society, there would be fundamental group distinctions corresponding to the division of labour: for example . . . between industrialists, scientists, and artists; and within the industrial class between farmers, manufacturers and bankers'. Ibid, p. 49.
115. For Saint-Simonian views on property, see *The Doctrine of Saint-Simon*, trans. G. G. Iggers, 2nd edn (New York: Schocken, 1972) pp. 113–38. This document had its origins in a series of public lectures in 1828 and 1829 given by Enfantin, Bazard and Buchez.
116. Ibid, p. 140.
117. David Ricardo, *On The Principles of Political Economy and Taxation*, ed. P. Sraffa (Cambridge University Press, 1951) p. 5.
118. The extent to which this conclusion can be derived without destroying the discursive specificity of Ricardian economics is debatable, just as it remains unclear today whether Sraffa's neo-Ricardianism can be employed to resolve problems arising from Marxian economics.
119. Thomas Hodgskin, *Popular Political Economy* (1827) (New York: Kelley, 1966) pp. 27–8; cf. John Gray, *A Lecture on Human Happiness* (1825) (London School of Economics, 1931) p. 15; William Thompson, *An Inquiry into the Principles of the Distribution of Wealth* (1824) (New York: Kelley, 1963) pp. 6–17.
120. Gray, *A Lecture on Human Happiness*, pp. 15–21. Gray was convinced, moreover, that the contemporary organisation of society was inimical to happiness: the wealthy were tyrannised by the pressures of rivalry and fashion, retailers had constantly to resort to deceit, and most of the other unproductive and useless occupations also required actions that no rational being could engage in with sincerity and happiness. The constant appeals to, and belief in, rationality betray an Enlightenment residue which marked the discourse of all the early Owenites and came inevitably to grief when faced with political hostility and opposition from both Left and Right. Cf. E. P. Thompson, *The Making of the English Working Class*, revised edn (Harmondsworth: Penguin, 1968) pp. 857ff.
121. Hodgskin, *Popular Political Economy*, p. 245. Hodgskin's calculations led him to argue that only a fourth of the population could be regarded as productive: ibid, p. 14.
122. Cf. Hodgskin, *Labour Defended against the Claims of Capital* (1825) (New York: Kelley, 1963) p. 46; *Popular Political Economy*, pp. 79–90.

123. Ibid, pp. 112–14; 129–36.
124. Ibid, pp. 115–7.
125. Thomas Hodgskin, *The Natural and Artificial Right of Property Contrasted* (1832) (Clifton: Kelley, 1973) p. 30.
126. Hodgskin, *Labour Defended against the Claims of Capital*, p. 101; *Popular Political Economy*, pp. 108–9. Note also that Hodgskin refused to accept any fundamental distinction between mental and manual labour or the principle that the two should be differently rewarded. Cf. ibid, pp. 46ff.
127. This statement may seem surprising, but only because Fabian historiography has succeeded in glossing over the limited nature of Owen's own project. As with Saint-Simon, the real radicalisation is to be detected in some of the strands of the social movement and not in the original doctrine. For a balanced assessment of Owen, see the editor's introduction to *A New View of Society and Report to the County of Lanark*, ed. V. A. C. Gatrell (Harmondsworth: Penguin, 1969); all references are to this edition. See also, J. F. C. Harrison, *Robert Owen and the Owenites in Britain and America* (London: Routledge & Kegan Paul, 1968).
128. Owen, *A New View of Society and Report to the County of Lanark*, pp. 201, 207, 222.
129. Ibid, p. 223.
130. Ibid, pp. 223–4.
131. Ibid, p. 251.
132. Ibid, p. 252.
133. Cf. William Thompson, *Labour Rewarded* (1827) (New York: Kelley, 1969) p. 106. See also J. F. Bray, *Labour's Wrongs and Labour's Remedy* (1839) (London School of Economics, 1931) esp. pp. 154–92.
134. Gray, *A Lecture on Human Happiness*, pp. 4–5, 6–7. The pages of the articles of agreement are separately numbered in Gray's lecture despite the fact that they appear at the end of the volume.
135. Ibid, pp. 8–9.
136. Cf. A. Briggs, 'The Language of "Class" in Early Nineteenth Century England', in A. Briggs and J. Saville (eds), *Essays in Labour History* (London: Macmillan, 1960); Williams, *Keywords*, pp. 51–9.
137. Hodgskin, *Labour Defended*, pp. 21, 104. Cf. Bray, *Labour's Wrongs and Labour's Remedy*, pp. 20, 21, 60.
138. Cf. Tribe, *Land, Labour and Economic Discourse*, pp. 10–12.
139. Andrew Ure, *The Philosophy of Manufactures* (1835) (London: Frank Cass, 1967).
140. Ibid, p. 19.
141. Ibid, pp. 19–20.
142. Ibid, pp. 20–1.
143. Ibid, pp. 22–3.
144. Charles Babbage, *On The Economy of Machinery and Manufactures*, p. 131. All references are to the first edition of 1832, published by Charles Knight in London. Readers should note that the second edition of 1833 contains page numbers that are significantly at variance with the first.
145. Ibid, pp. 137–8.
146. Ibid, p. 131.
147. Ibid, pp. 153–7.
148. Ibid, pp. 157–62.
149. Ibid, pp. 240–70.

Part II

1. Lenin, 'The Three Sources and Three Component Parts of Marxism', *Selected Works*, vol. 1 (Moscow: Progress, 1975) pp. 44–8. Lenin's judgement still seems to command unqualified assent: see, for example, G. A. Cohen, *Karl Marx's Theory of History: a Defence* (Oxford University Press, 1978) p. 1.
2. Marx, *Economic and Philosophic Manuscripts of 1844*, ed. D. Struik (London: Lawrence & Wishart, 1970) p. 177.
3. Cf. D. McLellan, *The Young Hegelians and Karl Marx* (London: Macmillan, 1969); W. J. Brazill, *The Young Hegelians* (Yale University Press, 1970).
4. Marx and Engels, *The German Ideology* (London: Lawrence & Wishart, 1965) p. 45. It is worth remarking at this point that 'abolition' as in 'abolition of the division of labour' is often rendered by the (Hegelian) term *Aufhebung* in the original Marx and Engels texts. *Aufhebung* implies 'transcendence' rather than simple 'eradication'. But no amount of play on the term actually reveals its implications for the division of labour, which can only be grasped by analysing the more concrete proposals – few though they are – which appear at various points in their writings, and by placing these proposals in the context of the overall structure of Marx's theorisation in which the ethic of total emancipation, as I shall argue, appears as an overriding principle. Besides, as Evans has pointed out, both Marx and Engels use several other terms in similar contexts, none of which are simply reducible to *Aufhebung*: cf. M. Evans, 'Marx Studies', *Political Studies*, vol. 18 (1970).
5. Marx, *Capital*, III (Moscow: Progress, 1961) pp. 799–800.
6. Avineri, *The Social and Political Thought of Karl Marx*; R. Tucker, *Philosophy and Myth in Karl Marx* (Cambridge University Press, 1961); E. Kamenka, *The Ethical Foundations of Marxism*, revised edn (London: Routledge & Kegan Paul, 1972); E. Mandel, *The Formation of the Economic Thought of Karl Marx* (London: New Left Books, 1971); T. Bottomore, 'Socialism and the Division of Labour', in B. Parekh (ed.), *The Concept of Socialism* (London: Croom Helm, 1975); K. Axelos, *Alienation, Praxis and Techné in the Thought of Karl Marx* (University of Texas Press, 1976).
7. I. Mészáros, *Marx's Theory of Alienation* London: Merlin Press, 1970); R. Garaudy, *Karl Marx: the Evolution of his Thought (London: Lawrence & Wishart, 1967); R. Dunayevskaya, Marxism and Freedom*, 3rd edn (London: Pluto Press, 1971); B. Ollman, *Alienation* (Cambridge University Press, 1971); idem, 'Marx's Vision of Communism: a Reconstruction', *Critique*, no. 8 (1977).
8. D. McLellan, 'Marx and the Whole Man', in Parekh (ed.), *The Concept of Socialism*; A. Schmidt, *The Concept of Nature in Marx* (London: New Left Books, 1971); M. Evans, *Karl Marx* (London: Allen & Unwin, 1975).
9. McLellan, 'Marx and the Whole Man', p. 64.
10. Ibid, p. 69.
11. Ibid.
12. As Feurbach said of religion: 'in the nature and consciousness of religion there is nothing else than what lies in the nature of man and in his consciousness of himself and of the world'. Ludwig Feurbach, *The Essence of Christianity*, trans. C. Eliot (New York: Harper & Row, 1957) p. 22. Cf. E. Kamenka, *The Philosophy of Ludwig Feurbach* (London: Routledge & Kegan Paul, 1970); M. W. Wartofsky, *Feurbach* (Cambridge University Press, 1977).
13. Marx, *Critique of Hegel's 'Philosophy of Right'*, ed. J. O'Malley (Cambridge University Press, 1970) p. 30.
14. Ibid, pp. 46–54; 98–109.
15. Marx's remarks on private property have sometimes misled commentators to argue that Marx had already developed a class theory of state in the *Critique*: cf.

Avineri, *The Social and Political Thought of Karl Marx*, pp. 27–40. For readings of the *Critique* much closer to mine, see McLellan, *Mark before Marxism*, pp. 102–28; R. N. Hunt, *The Political Ideas of Marx and Engels*, vol. 1 (London: Macmillan, 1974) pp. 59–84.

16. *Writings of the Young Marx on Philosophy and Society*, ed. L. Easton and K. Guddat (New York: Doubleday Anchor, 1967) pp. 236–37.
17. Ibid, p. 246.
18. Ibid, pp. 257–8, 260.
19. Ibid, p. 262.
20. S. Avineri, 'The Hegelian Origins of Marx's Political Thought' in S. Avineri (ed.), *Marx's Socialism* (New York: Lieber-Atherton, 1973) p. 8.
21. McLellan, *Marx before Marxism*, p. 157.
22. The search for total solutions, and an apocalyptic vision, were a characteristic feature of Young Hegelian discourse: cf. McLellan, *The Young Hegelians and Karl Marx*, pp. 8, 18, and *passim*; Brazill, *The Young Hegelians*, pp. 56–63, 257–8, and *passim*.
23. Marx, *Economic and Philosophic Manuscripts*, p. 118.
24. Engels, 'Outlines of a Critique of Political Economy', *Economic and Philosophic Manuscripts*, p. 226. For Engels's intellectual and political formation see, *inter alia*, Hunt, *The Political Ideas of Marx and Engels*, pp. 93–131; H. Draper, *Karl Marx's Theory of Revolution*, vol. I *State and Bureaucracy* (New York: Monthly Review Press, 1977) pp. 149–60.
25. See, especially, the extended note on James Mill, which prefigures many of the themes of the *Manuscripts*: Marx, *Collected Works*, III (Moscow: Progress, 1975) pp. 211–28.
26. For detailed commentaries on the *Manuscripts* see, *inter alia*, McLellan, *Marx before Marxism*; L. Dupré, *The Philosophical Foundations of Marxism* (New York: Harcourt, Brace & World, 1966); H. Marcuse, 'The Foundation of Historical Materialism', in *Studies in Critical Philosophy* (London: New Left Books, 1972).
27. Marx, *Economic and Philosophic Manuscripts*, p. 135; cf. p. 139.
28. Ibid, p. 113.
29. Ibid, p. 117.
30. Ibid, pp. 73, 72.
31. Ibid, p. 152.
32. Ibid, p. 108.
33. Ibid, p. 67.
34. Ibid, pp. 110–11. Cf. p. 159: 'the division of labour . . . is therefore nothing else but the estranged, alienated positioning of human activity'.
35. Ibid, p. 116.
36. Ibid, p. 68. As Marx expresses it elsewhere in the *Economic and Philosophic Manuscripts*, p. 119: 'Private property . . . embraces both relations – the relation of the worker to work and to the product of his labour and to the non-worker.'
37. Ibid, p. 163. The connection between alienation and exchange, as I have pointed out, had already been firmly established in *On the Jewish Question* and was prefigured in the *Critique*.
38. Marx, *Economic and Philosophic Manuscripts*, p. 65.
39. Ibid, p. 156.
40. Ibid, p. 163.
41. Ibid, p. 117.
42. Cf. Marx and Engels, *The Holy Family* (Moscow: Progress, 1956), esp. pp. 124–5, 167–79.

43. *Writings of the Young Marx*, p. 402. Marx's disenchantment with Feurbach may well have owed something to Max Stirner's *The Ego and His Own*, where Feurbach's abstract notion of 'man' is mercilessly attacked: cf. M. Stirner, *The Ego and His Own*, ed. J. Carroll (London: Jonathan Cape, 1971); R. Paterson, *The Nihilistic Egoist: Max Stirner* (University of Hull Press, 1971) pp. 103ff.
44. In a passage that Marx subsequently crossed out, a distinction is made between fixed desires, 'namely those existing under all conditions, which only change their form and direction under different social conditions', and others, 'namely those originating in a particular social system', which under communism 'are totally deprived of their conditions of existence'. The communists, Marx had said, aimed to create an organisation 'which will make possible the normal satisfaction of all needs, i.e., a satisfaction which is limited only by the needs themselves': *German Ideology*, pp. 282–3n.
45. Mandel, *The Formation of the Economic Thought of Karl Marx*, pp. 154ff.
46. Cf. L. Althusser, *For Marx* (London: Allen Lane, 1969); L. Althusser and E. Balibar, *Reading Capital* (London: New Left Books, 1970).
47. For the concept of 'problematic' in Althusser's writings see, especially, *Reading Capital*, pp. 13–30.
48. Althusser, *For Marx*, pp. 227ff.
49. Ibid, pp. 229ff.
50. Althusser, *Reading Capital*, pp. 112, 139–40, 174–80.
51. Althusser, *For Marx*, pp. 228–9; *Reading Capital*, pp. 119–43.
52. This point is conceded, even if only implicitly, by the more sophisticated of Althusser's critics: cf. N. Geras, 'Althusser's Marxism: an Assessment', *New Left Review*, no. 71 (1972) pp. 78–9.
53. George Lukács is a good example of the first tendency: see *History and Class Consciousness* (London: Merlin Press, 1971) p. 238 and *passim*; for the second tendency, see for instance, H. Lefebvre, *The Sociology of Marx* (London: Allen Lane, 1968) pp. 51ff.
54. N. Geras, 'Marx and the Critique of Political Economy', in R. Blackburn (ed.), *Ideology in Social Science* (London: Fontana, 1972) pp. 289–91. Originally published as 'Essence and Appearance: Aspects of Fetishism in Marx's *Capital*', *New Left Review*, no. 65 (1971).
55. Cf. R. Johnson, 'Three Problematics: Elements of a Theory of Working-Class Culture', in J. Clarke *et al.* (eds), *Working Class Culture: Studies in History and Theory* (London: Hutchinson, 1979) p. 202; T. Benton, *Philosophical Foundations of the Three Sociologies* (London: Routledge & Kegan Paul, 1977) pp. 182ff.
56. L. Althusser, *Essays in Self-Criticism* (London: New Left Books, 1976) pp. 119–25.
57. Marx, *The German Ideology*, pp. 39–40.
58. Ibid, p. 41.
59. Ibid, pp. 38, 61, 62.
60. Ibid, p. 86. Cf. pp. 84, 90, 92.
61. Ibid, p. 32.
62. Ibid, p. 33. Cf. p. 44: 'Division of labour and private property are, moreover, identical expressions: in the one the same thing is affirmed with reference to activity, as is affirmed in the other with reference to the product of the activity.'
63. Ibid, p. 44.
64. Ibid, p. 32.
65. Ibid, p. 65.
66. Ibid.
67. Ibid, pp. 66–7.
68. Ibid, pp. 67–8.

69. Ibid, p. 68.
70. Ibid, pp. 70–1.
71. Cf. *inter alia*, A. Giddens, *Capitalism and Modern Social Theory* (Cambridge University Press, 1971) pp. 24–34; G. Lichtheim, *Marxism*, pp. 141–61.
72. Marx, *The German Ideology*, pp. 45–6.
73. Ibid, p. 49.
74. Ibid, p. 47.
75. Ibid, p. 46.
76. Ibid, p. 83.
77. Ibid, p. 45.
78. Ibid, pp. 79, 96, 224.
79. McLellan, 'Marx and the Whole Man', p. 67. In an earlier work McLellan had suggested that the major influence in such contexts could be traced to Max Stirner: cf. *The Young Hegelians and Karl Marx*, p. 132.
80. Marx, *The German Ideology*, p. 441.
81. Ibid, p. 443.

Part III

1. Tucker, *Philosophy and Myth*, p. 222.
2. Avineri, *The Social and Political Thought of Karl Marx*, p. 250.
3. For the reading Marx undertook during the summer of 1845 in Manchester, see Mandel, *The Formation of the Economic Thought of Karl Marx*, pp. 44–5.
4. Cf. J. H. Jackson, *Marx, Proudhon and European Socialism* (London: English Universities Press, 1958), pp. 50–70. For more recent research on Proudhon, see A Ritter, *The Political Thought of Pierre-Joseph Proudhon* (Princeton University Press, 1969); E. Hyams, *Pierre-Joseph Proudhon* (London: John Murray, 1979).
5. Marx and Engels, *Selected Correspondence* (Moscow: Progress, 1965) p. 153.
6. *Selected Writings of Pierre-Joseph Proudhon*, ed. S. Edwards (London: Macmillan, 1970) p. 46.
7. Ibid, pp. 47–8.
8. Marx, *The Poverty of Philosophy* (New York: International Publishers, 1963) p. 184.
9. Ibid, pp. 129–30.
10. Ibid, pp. 31–3.
11. Ibid, p. 33.
12. Ibid, p. 34.
13. Ibid, pp. 135–6.
14. Ibid, p. 128.
15. Ibid, p. 135.
16. Ibid, pp. 136–7.
17. Ibid, pp. 139–40.
18. Ibid, pp. 141–3.
19. Ibid, p. 144.
20. Ibid, pp. 142.
21. Ibid, pp. 172–3. Cf. Ure, *The Philosophy of Manufactures*, pp.279–81ff.
22. Ibid, p. 136.
23. Ibid, p. 109.
24. Ibid, p. 133.
25. Ibid, p. 183.
26. Ibid, p. 185.

27. Ibid, p. 154. The term 'relations of production' first makes its appearance in *The Poverty of Philosophy*, to conceptualise more or less the same social forms as previously contained in the notion of division of labour.
28. Cf. *Collected Works*, pp. 330, 319, 337. It is worth remarking here, in connection with the passage cited in the text, that Marx uses the term *Arbeitsweisen* in the original German: cf. *Werke*, Band 4 (Berlin: Dietz Verlag, 1959) p. 349. This is correctly translated in the *Collected Works*, from which I have cited, as 'conditions of work', but misleadingly given as 'occupations' in the only other English translation of this passage: cf. *Karl Marx: Selected Writings in Sociology and Social Philosophy*, ed. T. Bottomore and M. Rubel (Harmondsworth: Penguin, 1963) p. 208. The mistranslation by Bottomore and Rubel stems from an attempt to 'sociologise' Marx in the light of the conceptual vocabulary of academic sociology. (I am grateful to Roy Dunning for assistance with the translation from the German.)
29. Marx and Engels, *Selected Works*, 1 (Moscow: Progress, 1969) p. 171.
30. Ibid, p. 11.
31. In this context Marx's comment that the bourgeoisie 'has converted the physician, the lawyer, the priest, the poet, the man of science, into its paid wage labourers' is too ambiguous and underdeveloped to serve as a relevant point of reference for such an analysis. Cf. ibid, p. 111.
32. Ibid, pp. 109, 117.
33. Ibid, pp. 116–17. See also, *The Poverty of Philosophy*, pp. 172–3.
34. Ibid, pp. 110–11, 125, 127–36. Cf. *The Poverty of Philosophy*, pp. 109, 123–6.
35. Ibid, pp. 111, 114, 117, 119. Cf. *The Poverty of Philosophy*, pp. 58, 149, 193. These aspects of Marx's thought are given more detailed treatment in the next section of the book.
36. See Marx and Engels's own comments on these measures in the 1872 Preface to the *Manifesto: Selected Works*, I, pp. 98–9. It has recently been argued that a theoretical justification for the limited and tentative nature of the proposed reforms, confined as they are to the process of circulation rather than production, can be found in *Capital*; cf. Y. Wagner and M. Strauss, 'The Programme of the Communist Manifesto and its Theoretical Foundations', *Political Studies*, vol. 17 (1969). Wagner and Strauss, however, take no account of the obvious objection to their procedure, namely that the concepts of *Capital* differ significantly enough from the economic theory of the *Manifesto* to make highly problematic a justification of the political programme of the latter on the basis of the conceptual structure of *Capital*. McLellan apparently sees no problem here, uncritically referring the reader to the Wagner and Strauss paper for clarification of the theoretical basis of the *Manifesto*'s political programme: cf. McLellan, *Karl Marx: his Life and Thought*, p. 184.
37. The Communist League had evolved from the League of the Just, a secret, conspiratorial society similar to and closely linked to French secret organisations of the 1830s. The bulk of the members were German artisans, especially tailors, one of whom, Wilhelm Weitling, published in 1838 a pamphlet – *Mankind as it is and as it Should be* – which equated communism with primitive Christianity; this document, until it was replaced by Cabet's *Voyage en Icarie* (another form of Christian communism), provided the basic ideology of the League of the Just and gives some indication of the struggle Marx and Engels had to engage in to gain acceptance of their views. Engel's own account of their relations with the League can be found in 'On the History of the Communist League' (1885), *Selected Works*, III, pp. 173–90. See further, Evans, *Karl Marx*, pp. 23–7; McLellan, *Karl Marx: his Life and Thought*, pp. 155–8, 166ff.
38. *Selected Works*, I, pp. 92–3.
39. *Selected Correspondence*, p. 45.

40. It could of course be argued that there is no warrant for assuming a similar rethinking on Marx's part at this stage, but the only suggestion of a rift between Marx and Engels at this point in time in fact imputes to Engels a *more* deterministic and class-reductionist frame of interpretation: see McLellan, *Karl Marx: his Life and Thought*, p. 180.
41. Cf. E. Hobsbawm, *The Age of Revolution* (London: Weidenfeld & Nicolson, 1962) pp. 359–72; idem, *The Age of Capital 1848–1875* (London: Weidenfeld & Nicolson, 1975), pp. 9–26. For an overview of different interpretations of the 1848–9 revolutions see G. Rudé, *Debate on Europe: 1815–1850* (New York: Harper & Row, 1972) pp. 201–66.
42. For Marx's activities in Cologne during the abortive revolution, see McLellan, *Karl Marx: his Life and Thought*, pp. 189–225; B. Nicolaievsky and O. Maenchen-Helfen, *Karl Marx: Man and Fighter* (London: Allen Lane, 1973), pp. 165–210.
43. Cf. *Articles from the 'Neue Rheinische Zeitung' 1848–49* (Moscow: Progress, 1972), pp. 204–5. Subsequently Marx argued that the liberation of Ireland from British rule was essential if crippling divisions within the British working-class movement were to be removed: cf. *On Britain* (Moscow: Progress, 1971), 356–8.
44. This, of course, is a form of articulation between the economy and other levels of a social formation which Althusser has attempted to encapsulate within the concept of 'overdetermination'. Cf. 'On Contradiction and Overdetermination', in *For Marx*.
45. R. Johnson, 'Three Problematics: Elements of a Theory of Working-Class Culture', pp. 203–7.
46. For fuller expositions of the relevant texts, in keeping with the 'reading' offered here, see the superb essay by Stuart Hall, 'The "Political" and the "Economic" in Marx's Theory of Classes', in A. Hunt (ed.), *Class and Class Structure* (London: Lawrence & Wishart, 1977). See also D. Fernbach's 'Introduction' to *Karl Marx: Surveys From Exile*, Pelican Marx Library (Harmondsworth: Penguin, 1973).
47. Cf. *Selected Works*, I, pp. 421–2, 464 and *passim*. The significance of divisions within 'labour', as we shall see, was only really grasped by Marx in *Capital*.
48. In writing about Britain, Marx was confronted by an even more serious dislocation between the economic and political levels, the existence of an economically dominance bourgeoisie which, however, ruled through aristocratic, landed representatives: the Whigs. Cf. *On Britain*, pp. 109–15, 221–4.
49. *Selected Works*, I, p. 421. Much later, when Marx was struggling to understand the peculiarities of the British labour movement, he again referred to the independent effectivity of ideologies: 'The English have all the material prerequisites for the social revolution. What they lack is a spirit for generalisation and revolutionary fervour.' *On Britain*, p. 356. The manner in which this proposition is expressed, with its opposition between 'material' and 'spiritual', is indicative of the difficulties Marx constantly experienced in attempting to conceptualise the more complex form of articulation between the economy and other levels which his analysis implied.
50. Cf. *Selected Works*, I, pp. 478–84. This aspect of Marx's analysis finds characteristically insightful treatment in Hall, 'The "Political" and the "Economic"'; compare with the much more simplistic treatment in R. Miliband, 'Marx and the State', in R. Miliband and J. Saville (eds), *The Socialist Register 1965* (London: Merlin Press, 1965). It is as well to remember that at this stage Marx regarded the relative autonomy of the state as an *exceptional* feature which is explained by reference to a particular conjuncture; only in *Capital* does he provide the concepts with which to theorise the social relation-

ships which necessarily ensure a relative autonomy for the capitalist state. Cf. *Surveys from Exile*, ed. D. Fernbach (Harmondsworth: Penguin, 1973) pp. 16ff.

51. For the notion of 'smashing' the state, see *Selected Works*, I, p. 477.
52. Cf. *Selected Works*, I. pp. 433, 477.
53. *The Poverty of Philosophy*, p. 139.
54. *Selected Works*, I, p. 191.
55. *The Cologne Communist Trial*, ed. R. Livingstone (London: Lawrence & Wishart, 1971), p. 251.
56. Cf. McLellan, *Karl Marx: his Life and Thought*, pp. 226ff.
57. Summaries of these debates, although bearing very strongly the stamp of the authors' own particular interpretations, can be found in Mandel, *The Formation of the Economic Thought of Karl Marx*, pp. 154ff., and McLellan, *Marx before Marxism*, pp. 214ff.
58. M. Nicolaus, 'The Unknown Marx', in R. Blackburn (ed.), *Ideology in Social Science* (London: Fontana, 1972). The paper was originally published in *New Left Review*, no. 48 (1968).
59. K. Tribe, 'Remarks on the Theoretical Significance of the "Grundrisse"', *Economy and Society*, vol. 3 (1974). Cf. J. Mepham, 'The *Grundrisse*: Method or Metaphysics?', *Economy and Society*, vol. 7 (1978).
60. Nicolaus, 'The Unknown Marx', p. 311. Cf. *The Poverty of Philosophy*, p. 149.
61. Cf. Mandel, *The Formation of the Economic Thought of Karl Marx*, pp. 140–4.
62. *Capital*, I, pp. 175–6.
63. The limitations of the *Grundrisse* in this respect are underlined by Mepham, 'The *Grundrisse*', pp. 443–4.
64. My discussion here is greatly indebted to the work of Therborn: cf. *Science, Class and Society*, pp. 365ff.
65. Nicolaus, 'The Unknown Marx', p. 314.
66. *Capital*, I, p. 217; cf. p. 235.
67. *Capital*, III, p. 772.
68. Ibid, p. 771.
69. See, especially, N. Poulantzas, *Political Power and Social Classes* (London: New Left Books and Sheed & Ward, 1973). The best known of recent class-instrumentalist writings on the state is R. Miliband, *The State in Capitalist Society* (London: Weidenfeld & Nicolson, 1969). For a balanced commentary on the Miliband–Poulantzas debate, see E. Maclau, 'The Specificity of the Political', in his *Politics and Ideology in Marxist Theory* (London: New Left Books, 1977). It must be stressed that there is no question of an unqualified endorsement on my part of all Poulantzas's theses in the text mentioned above, or of all his writings, although this is not a matter that can be pursued here.
70. Marx attempts to express this type of determination in a passage in *Capital* which is by now very well known (or notorious, depending on the standpoint adopted); here Marx defends his views against the criticism that the economy only plays a determining role in the modern epoch but not, for example, in feudalism or antiquity: 'This much, however, is clear, that the middle ages could not live on Catholicism, nor the ancient world on politics. On the contrary, it is the mode in which they gained a livelihood that explains why here politics, and there Catholicism, played the chief part.' *Capital*, I, p. 82n.
71. For a useful discussion of post-Althusserian debates on the theorisation of modes of production, see H. Wolpe, 'Introduction', in idem (ed.), *The Articulation of Modes of Production: Essays from Economy and Society* (London: Routledge & Kegan Paul, 1980). An excellent extension of the concept of relative autonomy, especially in the field of ideologies, may be found in E. Laclau, *Politics and Ideology in Marxist Theory*, pp. 158–76.

72. See, *inter alia*, E. Terray, 'Classes and Class Consciousness in the Abron Kingdom of Gyaman', in M. Bloch (ed.), *Marxist Analyses and Social Anthropology* (London: Malaby Press, 1975).
73. *Grundrisse*, ed. M. Nicolaus (Harmondsworth: Penguin, 1973), p. 85.
74. Ibid.
75. Ibid, pp. 86, 87.
76. Ibid, p. 86.
77. Ibid, p. 99.
78. Ibid, pp. 99–100.
79. For differing interpretations of the 1857 *Introduction* and its significance see, *inter alia*, Althusser, *For Marx*, pp. 183ff.; Althusser and Balibar, *Reading Capital*, pp. 40–3, 46–8, and *passim*; D. Sayer, 'Science as Critique: Marx *vs.* Althusser', in J. Mepham and D. H. Ruben (eds), *Issues in Marxist Philosophy*, vol. III *Epistemology, Science, Ideology* (Brighton: Harvester Press, 1979); T. Carver, *Karl Marx: Texts on Method* (Oxford: Blackwell, 1975) pp. 88–158.
80. *Selected Works*, I, p. 502.
81. *Grundrisse*, p. 38.
82. *Selected Correspondence*, p. 209.
83. For an excellent account of the theory see, *inter alia*, P. Sweezy, *The Theory of Capitalist Development*, 2nd edn (New York: Monthly Review Press, 1968).

Part IV

1. *Capital*, 1, p. 177.
2. Ibid, pp. 183–4. Cf. pp. 42–3.
3. Ibid, p. 184.
4. Ibid, p. 178.
5. Ibid, p. 179.
6. Ibid, p. 178.
7. Ibid, p. 179.
8. Ibid, p. 180.
9. Ibid, n. 1. In this particular instance a charge of technicism against Marx *may* be unfair in so far as his remarks possibly stem from a belief that in the *absence* of other relevant evidence a classification based on the 'materials from which their implements and weapons were made' represent the only possible 'materialist' classification of pre-historic ages.
10. Ibid, p. 325.
11. Ibid, p. 324.
12. Ibid, p. 328.
13. Ibid, p. 42. Cf. pp. 357, 359.
14. Ibid, p. 354.
15. Ibid, pp. 354–7.
16. Ibid, p. 351. In his footnote to this passage Marx acknowledges that he has largely borrowed these distinctions from Frederic Skarbek's, *Theorie des richesses sociales*, vol. 1 (Paris, 1839).
17. *Capital*, II, pp. 33–4.
18. *Capital*, I, pp. 351–3.
19. Ibid, p. 351.
20. Ibid, p. 42.
21. *Theories of Surplus Value*, III, (London: Lawrence & Wishart, 1972) p. 268.
22. *Capital*, I, p. 351.
23. Ibid, pp. 353, 352.

24. See, for example, *Capital*, I, p. 49; *Theories of Surplus Value*, III, pp. 268ff.
25. *Results of the Immediate Process of Production*, Appendix to *Capital*, I, ed. E. Mandel (Harmondsworth: Penguin, 1976), p. 995.
26. Ibid, p. 991.
27. Ibid, pp. 991, 990.
28. Ibid, p. 981.
29. Ibid; cf. *Capital*, III, p. 861 where the point is restated.
30. Ibid, p. 998.
31. Ibid, p. 996.
32. Ibid, p. 990.
33. *Capital*, I, pp. 330–1.
34. Ibid, p. 331.
35. Ibid, p. 332.
36. For contrasting treatments see, for example, I. Gough, 'Marx's Theory of Productive and Unproductive Labour', *New Left Review*, no. 76 (1972); J. Harrison, 'Productive and Unproductive Labour in Marx's Political Economy', *Bulletin of the Conference of Socialist Economists*, no. 6 (1973); B. Fine and L. Harris, *Rereading Capital* (London: Macmillan, 1979) pp. 49–57.
37. *Capital*, I, p. 509.
38. Ibid, pp. 508–9.
39. *Theories of Surplus Value*, I, p. 152.
40. *Capital*, III, p. 376.
41. Ibid, p. 379.
42. Ibid.
43. Ibid, p. 380.
44. *Capital*, II, p. 34.
45. *Capital*, III, p. 772.
46. Althusser and Balibar, *Reading Capital*, pp. 212–16. In an excellent historical essay, Gareth Stedman Jones has shown the usefulness of distinguishing between the relations of ownership and real appropriation in understanding different forms of working-class struggle in the nineteenth century: 'Class Struggle and the Industrial Revolution', *New Left Review*, no. 90 (1975).
47. *Capital*, I, pp. 184–5; cf. pp. 510–11.
48. *Capital*, III, pp. 771–2.
49. *Capital*, I, pp. 713–16.
50. *Results*, esp. pp. 1019–23.
51. Ibid, pp. 996, 1026.
52. *Capital*, I, pp. 336–7. It is worth pointing out here that Marx's remark that manufacture is a particular form of cooperation, distinguished by the introduction of division of labour, illustrates again his practice of conceptualising production and its general forms at different levels of abstraction, while keeping these forms analytically distinct from the overall mode of production which organises them.
53. Ibid, p. 338.
54. Ibid, p. 339.
55. Ibid.
56. Ibid, p. 345.
57. Ibid, pp. 348–9.
58. Ibid, pp. 349–50.
59. Cf. *The Poverty of Philosophy*, p. 138.
60. *Capital*, I, pp. 367–8.
61. Ibid, p. 363.
62. Ibid, pp. 360–1.

63. The Moore and Aveling translation used here often employs 'modern industry' to render Marx's original term '*grosse Industrie*'; I have preferred to use the more appropriate term 'large-scale industry'.
64. *Capital*, I, pp. 382–3.
65. Ibid, pp. 383–4.
66. Ibid, pp. 444–5.
67. Ibid, p. 384.
68. Ibid, p. 451.
69. Ibid, p. 386.
70. Cf. *Results*, pp. 1023ff.
71. Ibid, pp. 1037–8.
72. Ibid, p. 1025; *Capital*, I, pp. 510–11.
73. *Capital*, I, p. 420.
74. Ibid, pp. 394–417, 461–2.
75. Ibid, pp. 422–3; cf. *Theories of Surplus Value*, I, pp. 390–2.
76. *Capital*, I, pp. 422–3.
77. Ibid, pp. 461–2, 466ff.
78. Cf. ibid, pp. 462–6, 470ff.
79. Cf. R. Samuel, 'Workshop of the World: Steam Power and Hand Technology in mid-Victorian Britain', *History Workshop Journal*, no. 3 (1977).
80. *Capital*, I, p. 630.
81. Ibid, p. 420. The significance of the term 'technical' in this context is not clear.
82. Cf., *inter alia*, C. More, *Skill and the English Working Class, 1870–1914* (London: Croom Helm, 1980); Samuel, 'Workshop of the World'.
83. Cf. *Capital*, I, pp. 617–21.
84. Ibid, pp. 423–4; cf. p. 332.
85. Ibid, pp. 394–402 and *passim*.
86. Ibid, pp. 395, 395n. 2. Cf. V. Beechey, 'Women and Production: a Critical Analysis of some Sociological Theories of Women's Work', in A. Kuhn and A. M. Wolpe (eds), *Feminism and Materialism: Women and Modes of Production* (London: Routledge & Kegan Paul, 1978) pp. 184–7.
87. *Capital*, I, pp. 628–48. Cf. Beechey, 'Women and Production', pp. 187–90; Sweezy, *The Theory of Capitalist Development*, pp. 87–92, 149–50.
88. *On Britain*, p. 357.
89. Ibid, pp. 391–4. The term 'aristocracy of the working class' was in common use in the nineteenth century; Marx also used it, in the first volume of *Capital*, p. 667. Engels used the concept to explain the absence of socialism in England: cf. *On Britain*, p. 394. Modern historians of the nineteenth-century British working class have deployed and redefined the concept in a variety of ways: see, for example, E. Hobsbawm, *Labouring Men* (London: Weidenfeld & Nicolson, 1964) pp. 272–316; J. Foster, *Class Struggle and the Industrial Revolution*, paperback edn (London: Methuen, 1977) pp. 203ff.; R. Gray, *The Labour Aristocracy in Victorian Edinburgh* (Oxford University Press, 1976); G. Crossick, *An Artisan Elite in Victorian Society* (London: Croom Helm, 1978); Stedman Jones, 'Class Struggle', pp. 61–8. For an excellent critical survey, see H. Moorhouse, 'The Marxist Theory of the Labour Aristocracy', *Social History*, vol. 3 (1978).
90. *Theories of Surplus Value*, II, p. 573.
91. *Theories of Surplus Value*, III, p. 63.
92. For other relevant discussions, see M. Nicolaus, 'Proletariat and Middle Class in Marx: Hegelian Choreography and the Capitalist Dialectic', *Studies on the Left*, no. 7 (1967); J. Urry, 'Towards a Structural Theory of the Middle Class', *Acta Sociologica*, vol. 16 (1973).

93. Cf. *Capital*, I, p. 446.
94. Cf. *Theories of Surplus Value*, I. pp. 174–5, 201, 289, 301.
95. *Capital*, III, pp. 293–4.
96. Ibid, pp. 376–82, 427–31.
97. Cf. Nicolaus, 'Proletariat and Middle Class in Marx'.
98. *Capital*, III, p. 294.
99. Ibid, p. 295.
100. Both Nicolaus and Urry in their discussion of the rise of the new middle class in Marx fail to notice the difference in conceptual vocabulary between *Theories of Surplus Value* and *Capital*.

Part V

1. Ollman, 'Marx's Vision of Communism'.
2. *Selected Correspondence*, p. 209.
3. *Capital*, I, p. 351.
4. Ibid, pp. 383, 386.
5. Ibid, p. 445.
6. Ibid, pp. 330–1.
7. Ibid, p. 331. Cf. *Capital*, III, p. 376: 'all labour in which many individuals co-operate necessarily requires a commanding will to co-ordinate and unify the process, and functions which apply not to partial operations but to the total activity of the workshop, much as that of an orchestra conductor. This is a productive job which must be performed in every combined mode of production.'
8. *Capital*, II, pp. 33–4.
9. *Capital*, I, pp. 480–503.
10. *Theories of Surplus Value*, I, p. 289.
11. Cf. *Capital*, III, p. 376: 'On the other hand . . . supervision work necessarily arises in all modes of production based on the antithesis between the labourer . . . and the owner of the means of production. The greater this antagonism, the greater the role played by supervision. Hence it reaches its peak in the slave system.'
12. *Capital*, II, p. 135.
13. *Capital*, I, p. 451.
14. *Capital*, III, p. 379.
15. *Capital*, I, pp. 513–14.
16. Ibid, p. 513.
17. Ibid, pp. 353–4.
18. .bid, pp. 505–6. Cf. Engels, *Anti-Dühring* (London: Lawrence & Wishart, 1969) p. 346.
19. Schmidt, *The Concept of Nature in Marx*, p. 139.
20. *The Poverty of Philosophy*, p. 147.
21. *Capital*, I, p. 376.
22. Ibid, p. 402.
23. Ibid, p. 349.
24. *Selected Works*, III, p. 18.
25. *The German Ideology*, p. 474.
26. Ibid, pp. 47, 224.
27. Ibid, p. 40. Agnes Heller has assembled the various contradictions in Marx's conceptualisation of 'needs', but she does not relate these difficulties systematically to Marx's propositions on scarcity: cf. *The Theory of Need in Marx* (London: Allison & Busby, 1976).

28. *Capital*, I, p. 512.
29. Ibid, p. 171.
30. Ibid, pp. 42–3.
31. Ibid, p. 364.
32. *Selected Works*, III, p. 19.
33. *Capital*, III, pp. 799–800. A similar point is made in the *Grundrisse*, p. 708.
34. *Capital*, I, p. 530. It is sometimes held that the following passage in the *Grundrisse* contradicts the passage from *Capital* cited in the text; I have preferred the translation given in D. McLellan, *Marx's Grundrisse* (London: Macmillan, 1971) pp. 141–2.

    > But as heavy industry develops, the creation of real wealth depends less on labour time . . . than on the power of mechanical agents which are set in motion during labour time . . . Real wealth develops much more . . . in the enormous disproportion between the labour time utilised and its product . . . Labour does not seem any more to be an essential part of the process of production. The human factor is restricted to watching and supervising the production process . . . The worker . . . is no longer the principal agent of the production process: he exists alongside it. In this transformation, what appears as the mainstay of production and wealth is neither the immediate labour performed by the worker, nor the time that he works – but the appropriation by man of his own general productive force, his understanding of nature and the mastery of it.

    (Cf. *Grundrisse*, pp. 704–5.) Very little in this passage actually contradicts Marx's characteristic views in *Capital*, for all that is implied in the *Grundrisse* is that the application of science results in productivity out of all relative proportion to time and physical effort employed. Nothing is implied about the disappearance or abolition of labour as such, or the disappearance of manual labour. The only implication is that manual tasks, for example, are easier and enormously productive, a view Marx reiterates in *Capital* when he points to the 'lighter' character of manual labour under conditions of industrial production and when he refers to the fact that the typical job of the worker in the modern factory consists of 'supervising' and 'feeding' the machinery. (Cf. *Capital*, I, pp. 462, 403, 420.)
35. *Capital*, I, p. 488; cf. *Anti-Dühring*, pp. 348, 349, 353, 355.
36. *Capital*,I, pp. 361, 386 and *passim*.
37. Ibid, pp. 487–8.
38. Ibid, p. 341.
39. Ibid, p. 419.
40. Ibid, pp. 483–4.
41. Ibid, p. 488. For more detailed discussions of Marx's views on 'the education of the future', see R. Price, *Marx and Education in Russia and China* (London: Croom Helm, 1977); S. Castles and W. Wüstenberg, *The Education of the Future: an Introduction to the Theory and Practice of Socialist Education* (London: Pluto Press, 1979) pp. 32–41.
42. *Capital*, I, p. 424.
43. Ibid, footnote.
44. This strand in Marx's thought goes hand in hand with his emphasis on the *self*-emancipation of the working class. Cf. H. Draper, 'The Principle of Self-Emancipation in Marx and Engels', in R. Miliband and J. Saville (eds), *The Socialist Register 1971* (London: Merlin Press, 1971).
45. See M. Evans, 'Karl Marx and the Concept of Political Participation', in G. Parry (ed.), *Participation in Politics* (Manchester University Press, 1972); H. Draper, 'The Death of the State in Marx and Engels'.

46. For differing accounts of the Paris Commune, see, *inter alia*, R. Williams, *The French Revolution of 1870–71* (London: Weidenfeld & Nicolson, 1969); idem (ed.), *The Commune of Paris, 1871* (New York: John Wiley, 1969); E. Kamenka (ed.) *Paradigm for Revolution? The Paris Commune 1871–1971* Australian National University Press, 1972).
47. *Writings on the Paris Commune* (Moscow: Progress, 1971), pp. 206–7 and *passim*.
48. Cf. Evans, 'Karl Marx and the Concept of Political Participation', p. 141.
49. For a critical examination of the concept of size of capitalist enterprise in *Capital*, see J. Tomlinson, 'Marx's *Capital* and the Analysis of the Capitalist Enterprise' (unpublished mimeo, Department of Economics. Brunel University).
50. *Capital*, III, p. 376. For a critique of Marx's use of the orchestra and conductor analogy, see R. Selucký, *Marxism, Socialism and Freedom: Towards a General Democratic Theory of Labour-Managed Systems* (London: Macmillan, 1979) pp. 72–4.
51. Carchedi, *On the Economic Identification of Social Classes*.
52. Many recent analyses of the capitalist labour process have tended to collapse the duality of the capitalist production process into the single function of control and surveillance, thereby squeezing out of consideration the problem of limits to the reorganisation of labour under socialism and obliterating the specificity of Marx's own conceptualisation of the production process.
53. *Capital*, I, p. 441. It is worth recalling in this context Marx's belief that the need for the abolition of the old division of labour stemmed, at least in part, from the (obviously neutral) character of the means of production: 'large-scale industry . . . imposes the necessity of recognising, as a fundamental law of production, variation in work, consequently fitness of the labourer for varied work, consequently the greatest possible development of his varied aptitudes. It becomes a question of life and death for society to adapt the mode of production to the normal functioning of this law.' Ibid, pp. 487–8.
54. *Selected Works*, II, p. 377.
55. For one of the very best investigations of this kind, see D. F. Noble, 'Social Choice in Machine Design: the Case of Automatically Controlled Machine Tools, and a Challenge for Labour', *Politics and Society*, vol. 8 (1978). It is of course necessary to guard against the danger of bending the stick too far the other way, as for example in the following bold statement: 'capitalist techniques cannot be copied neutrally. To follow them is to reproduce the appropriate ideological, cultural, political and production relations which sustain them': P. Corrigan, H. Ramsay and D. Sayer, *Socialist Construction and Marxist Theory: Bolshevism and its Critique* (London: Macmillan, 1978) p. 56. For more balanced assessments, see F. J. Fleron, Jr (ed.), *Technology and Communist Culture: the Socio-Cultural Impact of Technology under Socialism* (New York: Praeger, 1977). An interesting discussion of Soviet views on the subject can be found in J. Cooper, 'Technology and the Transition from Capitalism to Communism' (Unpublished mimeo, Centre for Russian and East European Studies, University of Birmingham).
56. See, for example, D. Dickson, *Alternative Technology and the Politics of Technical Change* (London: Fontana, 1974).
57. As one shrewd commentator has observed: 'The real difficulty is not that Marx refused to change his views, but that in later years such changes did not lead to concomitant modifications in his overall perspective.' Evans, *Karl Marx*, p. 164.
58. *Anti-Dühring*, pp. 333–4; see pp. 214–18 for other similar passages by Engels.
59. This logic is clearly set out in G. E. Lenski, *Power and Privilege: a Theory of*

Social Stratification (New York: McGraw-Hill, 1966) and serves as a reminder that non-Marxist theory has also found this form of explanation persuasive. For Marxist versions of this thesis see, *inter alia*, E. Mandel, *Marxist Economic Theory* (London: Merlin Press, 1968) pp. 23–48; G. Novack, *Understanding History: Marxist Essays* (New York: Pathfinder Press, 1972) pp. 44–5; G. Childe, *Social Evolution* (London: Watts, 1951) esp. pp. 34–5.

60. M. Sahlins, *Stone Age Economics* (London: Tavistock, 1974) pp. 1–39.
61. A. W. Pearson, 'The Economy has no Surplus: Critique of a Theory of Development', in K. Polanyi *et al.*, *Trade and Market in the Early Empires* (New York: Free Press, 1957).
62. Cf. *Capital*, I, p. 235: 'It is, however, clear that in any given economic formation of society, where not the exchange-value but the use-value of the product predominates, surplus-labour will be limited by a given set of wants which may be greater or less and that here no boundless thirst for surplus-labour arises from the nature of production itself.' See also C. B. Macpherson, *Democratic Theory* (Oxford University Press, 1973) pp. 24–76; W. Leiss, *The Limits to Satisfaction* (London: Marion Boyars, 1978); Pearson, 'The Economy has no Surplus'; K. Polanyi, *The Livelihood of Man* (New York: Academic Press, 1977) ch. II; Sahlins, *Stone Age Economics*, pp. 1–39.
63. Recently an interesting argument concerning the continual presence of 'social' scarcities has also been advanced: see F. Hirsch, *Social Limits to Growth* (London: Routledge & Kegan Paul, 1977). Rudolf Bahro is one of the few Marxists to have given serious thought to these issues: *The Alternative in Eastern Europe* (London: New Left Books, 1978) pp. 265ff. and *passim*.
64. Historical materialism as conceived in the 1859 *Preface* has received a lengthy defence in Cohen, *Karl Marx's Theory of History*; Cohen's text (pp. 207ff.) contains a clear exposition of the links between the thesis of correspondence between the forces and relations of productions (and thus the historical primacy of the forces of production) and a transhistorical conception of scarcity. For an excellent critique of Cohen, see A. Levine and E. O. Wright, 'Rationality and Class Struggle', *New Left Review*, no. 123 (1980).
65. Lenin, *Collected Works*, vol. 20, p. 310.
66. Ibid, vol. 27, p. 212. For critiques of Lenin's technicism in this context, see C. Claudin-Urondo, *Lenin and the Cultural Revolution* (Hassocks: Harvester Press, 1977); Corrigan *et al.*, *Socialist Construction and Marxist Theory*.
67. This is especially true of Corrigan *et al.*, *Socialist Construction and Marxist Theory*.
68. Alexandra Kollontai, *Selected Writings*, ed. A. Holt (London: Allison & Busby, 1977) pp. 159–200. Cf. M. Liebman, *Leninism under Lenin* (London: Jonathan Cape, 1975) pp. 285–95.
69. At the same time, it becomes necessary to reappraise the role of scarcity in the process by which the Russian Revolution degenerated into a form of bureaucratic authoritarianism; that is, it is essential to re-evaluate the forms of explanation privileged in Trotsky's *The Revolution Betrayed* and in subsequent Trotskyist texts, where bureaucratisation in general is reductively explained by reference to the level of development of productive forces, as for example in E. Mandel, *Bureaucracy: a Marxist Analysis* (London: IMG Publications, 1973).
70. See, *inter alia*, C. Bettelheim, *Cultural Revolution and Industrial Organisation in China: Changes in Management and the Division of Labour* (New York: Monthly Review Press, 1974); F. Schurmann, *Ideology and Organisation in Communist China* (University of California Press, 1971); S. R. Schramm (ed.), *Authority, Participation and Cultural Change in China* (Cambridge University Press, 1976); Fleron (ed.), *Technology and Communist Culture* (papers by Dernberger, Baum and Field).

71. For important left appraisals of China, see L. Maitan, *Party, Army and Masses in China* (London: New Left Books, 1976); F. Halliday, 'Marxist Analysis and Post-Revolutionary China', *New Left Review*, no. 100 (1977).
72. *Capital*, I, p. 42.
73. *Selected Works*, III, p. 17.
74. *Capital*, I, p. 78.
75. Ibid, p. 356.
76. See, for example, E. Mandel, *Marxist Economic Theory*, pp. 632ff.; C. Bettelheim, *Economic Calculation and Forms of Property* (London: Routledge & Kegan Paul, 1976); T. Cliff, *State Capitalism in Russia* (London: Pluto Press, 1974); H. Ticktin, 'Socialism, the Market and the State', *Critique*, no. 3 (1974).
77. Cited in A. Nove, *An Economic History of the USSR* (Harmondsworth: Penguin, 1970) p. 65.
78. N. Bukharin and E. Preobrazhensky, *The ABC of Communism* (Harmondsworth: Penguin, 1969). For an account of the inflation and Soviet discussions of money in this period, see Nove, *An Economy History of the USSR*, pp. 63–74; E. H. Carr, *The Bolshevik Revolution*, vol. II, *1919–1923* (Harmondsworth: Penguin, 1966) pp. 257–68.
79. For the periods of War Commission and NEP see Nove, *An Economic History of the USSR*, pp. 46–135; Carr, *The Bolshevik Revolution*, pp. 151–357; M. Dobb, *Soviet Economic Development since 1917*, 6th edn (London: Routledge & Kegan Paul, 1966) pp. 97–176.
80. For an excellent account of these debates, see M. Lewin, *Political Undercurrents in Soviet Economic Debates* (London: Pluto Press, 1975) pp. 33–96. For a discussion of Trotsky's views, see R. B. Day, *Leon Trotsky and the Politics of Economic Isolation* (Cambridge University Press, 1973). Day argues (pp. 183–6) that in exile in the 1930s Trotsky came to support a form of 'market socialism'; for relevant remarks by Trotsky, see *The Revolution Betrayed* (1936) (London: New Park Publications, 1967) pp. 65–77.
81. L. von Mises, 'Economic Calculation in the Socialist Commonwealth' and F. A. von Hayek, 'The Present State of the Debate', both in F. A. von Hayek (ed.), *Collectivist Economic Planning* (London: Routledge & Kegan Paul, 1935).
82. For Lange's 'trial and error' procedure for a socialist economy, see O. Lange and F. Taylor, *On the Economic Theory of Socialism* (1938) (New York: McGraw-Hill, 1964); for Lange's theoretical justification for the compatibility between market forces and socialism, see pp. 130–43.
83. O. Lange, 'The Computer and the Market', and A. Nove, 'Economic Reforms in the USSR and Hungary, a Study in Contrasts', both in A. Nove and M. Nuti (eds), *Socialist Economics* (Harmondsworth: Penguin, 1972).
84. For a survey of debates in Yugoslavia, see D. D. Milenkovitch, *Plan and Market in Yugoslav Economic Thought* (Yale University Press, 1971); for Soviet debates, see Lewin, *Political Undercurrents*, pp. 127–88.
85. Cf. M. Dobb, *Socialist Planning: Some Problems* (London: Lawrence & Wishart, 1970); M. Ellman, *Planning Problems in the USSR* (Cambridge University Press); A. Nove, 'The Soviet Economy: Problems and Prospects', *New Left Review*, no. 119 (1980); idem, *Political Economy and Soviet Socialism* (London: Allen & Unwin, 1979) ***passim***.
86. Milenkovitch, *Plan and Market*, pp. 77–9; Y. Liberman, 'The Plan, Profits and Bonuses', in M. Bornstein and D. R. Fusfeld (eds), *The Soviet Economy: a Book of Readings*, 3rd edn (Homewood: Richard Irwin, 1970). This volume also contains contemporary Soviet criticisms of Liberman. For a detailed discussion of Liberman and other Soviet reformers, see J. L. Felkar, *Soviet Economic Controversies: the Emerging Marketing Concept and Changes in*

Planning 1960–1965 (Harvard University Press, 1966).

87. O. Šik, *Plan and Market under Socialism* (New York: International Arts & Sciences Press, 1967); W. Brus, *The Market in a Socialist Economy* (London: Routledge & Kegan Paul, 1972).
88. See, for example, Šik, *Plan and Market under Socialism*, pp. 100–17 and *passim*; Brus, *The Market in a Socialist Economy*, p. 139 and *passim*.
89. For a discussion of the opposition to Soviet reforms, see Ellman, *Planning Problems in the USSR*, pp. 135–51; for the criticisms of the *Praxis* group, see G. S. Sher, *Praxis: Marxist Criticism and Dissent in Socialist Yugoslavia* (Indiana University Press, 1977) pp. 151–93. For an interesting 'auto-critique' which is nevertheless sympathetic to the Yugoslav experiment, see M. Drulović, *Self-Management on Trial* (Nottingham: Spokesman Books, 1978).
90. Ellman, *Planning Problems in the USSR*, pp. 134–75. For a discussion of unemployment and inequality in Yugoslavia see, for example, F. Parkin, *Class Inequality and Political Order* (London: MacGibbon & Kee, 1971) pp. 172–5. R. Moore, *Self-Management in Yugoslavia* (Fabian Research Series 281, 1970) cites examples (p. 11) where redundancy has not been allowed to result in unemployment.
91. R. Selucký, 'Marxism and Self-Management', in J. Vanek (ed.), *Self-Management: Economic Liberation of Man* (Harmondsworth: Penguin, 1975) pp. 57–8 (I have corrected some grammatical errors which marred the original text). Selucký has provided a more detailed argument in *Marxism, Socialism, Freedom*. See also, W. Brus, *The Economics and Politics of Socialism* (London: Routledge & Kegan Paul, 1973).
92. Cf. S. Stojanović, *Between Ideals and Reality: a Critique of Socialism and its Future* (New York: Oxford University Press, 1973) esp. pp. 115–34; Sher, *Praxis*, pp. 151–93; Milenkovitch, *Plan and Market*, pp. 285–91.
93. Nove, *Political Economy and Soviet Socialism*, p. 232. It is interesting to note that despite the interpenetration of 'economy' and 'polity' in state socialism, recent debates about Eurocommunism and the democratisation of state socialism have failed to address the question of the relationship between the extension of exchange relations and workers' control: see, for example, S. Carrillo, *'Eurocommunism' and the State* (London: Lawrence & Wishart, 1977); F. Claudin, *Eurocommunism and Socialism* (London: New Left Books, 1977); E. Balibar, *On the Dictatorship of the Proletariat* (London: New Left Books, 1977). The same is true of Bahro's *The Alternative in Eastern Europe*; but see R. Garaudy, *The Turning Point of Socialism* (London: Fontana, 1970) pp. 140–87.
94. Bukharin and Preobrazhensky, *The ABC of Communism*, p. 117.
95. See, for example, Ticktin, 'Socialism, the Market and the State'.
96. Cf. N. Geras, 'Marx and the Critique of Political Economy'; G. Cohen, 'Karl Marx and the Withering Away of Social Science', in his *Karl Marx's Theory of History*, pp. 326–44.
97. The same might be said of racism.
98. Engels, *Origins of the Family, Private Property and the State*, ed. E. Leacock (New York: International Publishers, 1972) p. 139. For assessments of Engels's explanation of women's subordination, see Leacock's introduction; also see K. Sacks, 'Engels Revisited: Women, the Organisation of Production, and Private Property', in R. R. Reiter (ed.), *Toward an Anthropology of Women* (New York: Monthly Review Press, 1975).
99. For some excellent recent discussions, see A. Kuhn and A. M. Wolpe (eds), *Feminism and Materialism: Women and Modes of Production* (London: Routledge & Kegan Paul, 1978); M. Barrett, *Women's Oppression Today: Problems in Marxist Feminist Analysis* (London: NLB/Verso, 1980).

Bibliography

Althusser, L., *For Marx* (London: Allen Lane, 1969).
Althusser, L. and Balibar, E., *Reading Capital* (London: New Left Books, 1970).
Althusser, L., *Essays in Self-Criticism* (London: New Left Books, 1976).
Andrewes, A., *Greek Society* (Harmondsworth: Penguin, 1971).
Aristotle, *The Politics*, trans. T. A. Sinclair (Harmondsworth: Penguin, 1967).
Aronowitz, S., 'Marx, Braverman and the Logic of Capital', *Insurgent Sociologist*, vol. 8 1978).
Avineri, S., *The Social and Political Thought of Karl Marx* (Cambridge University Press, 1968).
Avineri, S., *Hegel's Theory of the Modern State* (Cambridge University Press, 1972).
Avineri, S., 'The Hegelian Origins of Marx's Political Thought', in idem (ed.), *Marx's Socialism* (New York: Lieber-Atherton, 1973).
Axelos, K., *Alienation, Praxis and Techné in the Thought of Karl Marx* (University of Texas Press, 1976).
Babbage, C., *On the Economy of Machinery and Manufactures* (London: Charles Knight, 1832).
Bahro, R., *The Alternative in Eastern Europe* (London: New Left Books, 1978).
Baker, K. M., *Condorcet: from Natural Philosophy to Social Mathematics* (Chicago University Press, 1975).
Balibar, E., *On the Dictatorship of the Proletariat* (London: New Left Books, 1977).
Bambrough, R., 'Plato's Political Analogies', in P. Laslett (ed.), *Philosophy, Politics and Society*, First Series (Oxford: Blackwell, 1967).
Barrett, M., *Women's Oppression Today: Problems in Marxist Feminist Analysis* (London: NLB/Verso, 1980).
Beechey, V., 'Women and Production: a Critical Analysis of some Sociological Theories of Women's Work', in A. Kuhn and A. M. Wolpe (eds), *Feminism and Materialism: Women and Modes of Production* (London: Routledge & Kegan Paul, 1978).
Benton, T., *Philosophical Foundations of the Three Sociologies* (London: Routledge & Kegan Paul, 1977).
Bettelheim, C., *Cultural Revolution and Industrial Organisation in China: Changes in Management and the Division of Labour* (New York: Monthly Review Press, 1974)
Bettelheim, C., *Economic Calculation and Forms of Property* (London: Routledge & Kegan Paul, 1976).
Bornstein, M. and Fusfeld, D. (eds), *The Soviet Economy: a Book of Readings* (Homewood: Richard Irwin, 1970).
Bottomore, T., 'Socialism and the Division of Labour', in B. Parekh (ed.), *The Concept of Socialism* (London: Croom Helm, 1975).

Braverman, H., *Labour and Monopoly Capital: the Degradation of Work in the Twentieth Century* (New York: Monthly Review Press, 1974).
Bray, J. F., *Labour's Wrongs and Labour's Remedy* (1839) (London School of Economics, 1931).
Brazill, W. J., *The Young Hegelians* (Yale University Press, 1970).
Brenner, R., 'The Origins of Capitalist Development: a Critique of Neo-Smithian Marxism', *New Left Review*, no. 104 (1977).
Briggs, A., 'The Language of "Class" in Early Nineteenth Century England', in A. Briggs and J. Saville (eds), *Essays in Labour History* (London: Macmillan, 1960).
Brighton Labour Process Group, 'The Capitalist Labour Process', *Capital and Class*, no. 1 (1977).
Brown, P., *The World of Late Antiquity* (London: Thames & Hudson, 1971).
Brunt, P. A., *Social Conflicts in the Roman Republic*, (London:Chatto & Windus, 1971).
Brus, W., *The Market in a Socialist Economy* (London: Routledge & Kegan Paul, 1972).
Brus, W., *The Economics and Politics of Socialism* (London: Routledge & Kegan Paul, 1973).
Bryson, G., *Man and Society: the Scottish Inquiry of the Eighteenth Century* (Princeton University Press, 1945).
Bukharin, N. and Preobrazhensky, E., *The ABC of Communism* (Harmondsworth: Penguin, 1969).
Bullough, V. L. (ed.), *The Scientific Revolution* (New York: Holt, Rinehart & Winston, 1970).
Burawoy, M., 'Towards a Marxist Theory of the Labour Process: Braverman and Beyond', *Politics and Society*, vol. 8 (1978).
Burawoy, M., *Manufacturing Consent: Changes in the Labour Process under Monopoly Capital* (University of Chicago Press, 1979).
Carchedi, G., *On the Economic Identification of Classes* (London: Routledge & Kegan Paul, 1977).
Carr, E. H., *The Bolshevik Revolution*, vol. II, *1919–1923* (Harmondsworth: Penguin, 1966).
Carrillo, S., *'Eurocommunism' and the State* (London: Lawrence & Wishart, 1977).
Castles, S. and Wüstenberg, W., *The Education of the Future: an Introduction to the Theory and Practice of Socialist Education* (London: Pluto Press, 1979).
Childe, G., *Social Evolution* (London: Watts, 1951).
Cicero, *De Officiis*, trans. W. Miller (London: Heinemann, 1947).
Claudin, F., *Eurocommunism and Socialism* (London: New Left Books, 1977).
Claudin-Urondo, C., *Lenin and the Cultural Revolution* (Hassocks: Harvester Press, 1977).
Cliff, T., *State Capitalism in Russia* (London: Pluto Press, 1974).
Cohen, G. A., *Karl Marx's Theory of History: a Defence* (Oxford University Press, 1978).
Cole, G. D. H., *A History of Socialist Thought*, vol. I, *The Forerunners 1789–1850* (London: Macmillan, 1953).
Condorcet, A. N., *Sketch for a Historical Picture of the Progress of the Human Mind* (1795), ed. S. Hampshire (London: Weidenfeld & Nicolson, 1955).
Cooper, J., 'Technology and the Transition from Capitalism to Communism' (unpublished mimeo, Centre for Russian and East European Studies, University of Birmingham).
Corrigan, P., Ramsay, H. and Sayer, D., *Socialist Construction and Marxist Theory: Bolshevism and its Critique* (London: Macmillan, 1978).
Coulter, J., 'Marxism and the Engels Paradox', in R. Miliband and J. Saville (eds), *The Socialist Register 1971* (London: Merlin Press, 1971).

Crossick, G., *An Artisan Elite in Victorian Society* (London: Croom Helm, 1978).
Cutler, *et al.*, *Marx's 'Capital' and Capitalism Today* (London: Routledge & Kegan Paul, 1977).
Cutler, A., 'The Romance of "Labour"', *Economy and Society*, vol. 7 (1978).
Day, R., *Leon Trotsky and the Politics of Economic Isolation* (Cambridge University Press, 1973).
Dickson, D., *Alternative Technology and the Politics of Technical Change* (London: Fontana, 1974).
Dobb, M., *Soviet Economic Development since 1917*, 6th edn (London: Routledge & Kegan Paul, 1966).
Dobb, M., *Socialist Planning: some Problems* (London: Lawrence & Wishart, 1970).
Dobb, M., *Theories of Value and Distribution since Adam Smith* (Cambridge University Press, 1973).
Draper, H., 'The Death of the State in Marx and Engels', in R. Miliband and J. Saville (eds), *The Socialist Register 1970* (London: Merlin Press, 1970).
Draper, H., 'The Principle of Self-Emancipation in Marx and Engels', in R. Miliband and J. Saville (eds), *The Socialist Register 1971* (London: Merlin Press, 1971).
Draper, H., *Karl Marx's Theory of Revolution*, vol. I, *State and Bureaucracy* (New York: Monthly Review Press, 1977).
Drulović, M., *Self-Management on Trial* (Nottingham: Spokesman Books, 1978).
Dudley, D., *Roman Society* (Harmondsworth: Penguin, 1975).
Dunayevskaya, R., *Marxism and Freedom*, 3rd edn (London: Pluto Press, 1971).
Dupré, L., *The Philosophical Foundations of Marxism* (New York: Harcourt, Brace & World, 1966).
Edwards, R., 'Social Relations of Production at the Point of Production', *The Insurgent Sociologist*, vol. 8 (1978).
Edwards, R., *Contested Terrain: the Transformation of the Workplace in the Twentieth Century* (New York: Basic Books, 1979).
Ellman, M., *Planning Problems in the USSR* (Cambridge University Press, 1973).
Engels, F., *Anti-Dühring* (London: Lawrence & Wishart, 1969).
Engels, F., *Origins of the Family, Private Property and the State*, ed. E. Leacock (New York: International Publishers, 1972).
Evans, M., 'Marx Studies', *Political Studies*, vol. 18 (1970).
Evans, M., 'Karl Marx and the Concept of Political Participation', in G. Parry (ed.), *Participation in Politics* (Manchester University Press, 1972).
Evans, M., *Karl Marx* (London: Allen & Unwin, 1975).
Felkar, J. L., *Soviet Economic Controversies: the Emerging Marketing Concept and Changes in Planning 1960–1965* (Harvard University Press, 1966).
Ferguson, A., *An Essay in the History of Civil Society* (1767), ed. D. Forbes (Edinburgh University Press, 1966).
Feuerbach, L., *The Essence of Christianity*, trans. C. Eliot (New York: Harper & Row, 1957).
Findlay, J. N., *Hegel: a Re-examination* (London: Allen & Unwin, 1958).
Fine, B. and Harris, L., *Rereading Capital* (London: Macmillan, 1979).
Finley, M. (ed.), *Slavery in Classical Antiquity* (Cambridge: Heffer, 1960).
Finley, M., 'Aristotle and Economic Analysis', *Past and Present*, no. 47 (1970).
Finley, M., *The Ancient Economy* (London: Chatto & Windus, 1973).
Fleron, Jr, F. J. (ed.), *Technology and Communist Culture: the Socio-Cultural Impact of Technology under Socialism* (New York: Praeger, 1977).
Foley, V., 'The Division of Labour in Plato and Smith', *History of Political Economy*, vol. 6 (1974).
Foster, J., *Class Struggle and the Industrial Revolution*, paperback edn (London: Methuen, 1977).

Foucault, M., *The Order of Things* (New York: Random House, 1971).
Foucault, M., *The Archaeology of Knowledge* (London: Tavistock, 1972).
Fourier, C., *The Utopian Vision of Charles Fourier: Selected Texts on Work, Love and Passionate Attraction*, ed. J. Beecher and R. Bienvenu (London: Jonathan Cape, 1972).
Garaudy, R., *Karl Marx: the Evolution of his Thought* (London: Lawrence & Wishart, 1967).
Garaudy, R., *The Turning Point of Socialism* (London: Fontana, 1970).
Gay, P., *The Enlightenment: an Interpretation*, vols I and II (London: Weidenfeld & Nicolson, 1970).
Geras, N., 'Marx and the Critique of Political Economy', in R. Blackburn (ed.), *Ideology in Social Science* (London: Fontana, 1972). Originally published as 'Essence and Appearance: Aspects of Fetishism in Marx's *Capital*', *New Left Review*, no. 65 (1971).
Geras, N., 'Althusser's Marxism: an Assessment', *New Left Review*, no. 71 (1972).
Giddens, A., *Capitalism and Modern Social Theory* (Cambridge University Press, 1971).
Goldmann, L., *The Philosophy of the Enlightenment* (London: Routledge & Kegan Paul, 1973).
Gordon, B., *Economic Analysis before Adam Smith* (London: Macmillan, 1975).
Gough, I., 'Marx's Theory of Productive and Unproductive Labour', *New Left Review*, no. 76 (1972).
Gouldner, A., *Enter Plato: Classical Greece and the Origins of Social Theory* (London: Routledge & Kegan Paul, 1967).
Gray, J., *A Lecture on Human Happiness* (1825) (London School of Economics, 1931).
Gray, R., *The Labour Aristocracy in Victorian Edinburgh* (Oxford University Press, 1976).
Hall, S., 'The "Political" and the "Economic" in Marx's Theory of Classes', in A. Hunt (ed.), *Class and Class Structure* (London: Lawrence & Wishart, 1977).
Halliday, F., 'Marxist Analysis and Post-Revolutionary China', *New Left Review*, no. 100 (1977).
Hamowy, R., 'Adam Smith, Adam Ferguson and the Division of Labour', *Economica*, vol. 35 (1968).
Harrison, J., 'Productive and Unproductive Labour in Marx's Political Economy', *Bulletin of the Conference of Socialist Economists*, no. 6 (1973).
Harrison, J. F. C., *Robert Owen and the Owenites in Britain and America* (London: Routledge & Kegan Paul, 1968).
Hayek, F. von, 'The Present State of the Debate', in idem (ed.), *Collectivist Economic Planning* (London: Routledge & Kegan Paul, 1935).
Hegel, G. W. F., *The Philosophy of Right*, trans. T. M. Knox (Oxford University Press, 1942).
Heiman, G., 'The Sources and Significance of Hegel's Corporate Doctrine', in Z. A. Pelezynski (ed.), *Hegel's Political Philosophy* (Cambridge University Press, 1971).
Heller, A., *The Theory of Need in Marx* (London: Allison & Busby, 1976).
Hilton, R. (ed.), *The Transition from Feudalism to Capitalism* (London: New Left Books, 1976).
Hindess, B. and Hirst, P., *Mode of Production and Social Formation* (London: Macmillan, 1977).
Hirsch, F., *Social Limits to Growth* (London: Routledge & Kegan Paul, 1977).
Hobsbawm, E., *The Age of Revolution* (London: Weidenfeld & Nicolson, 1962).
Hobsbawm, E., *Labouring Men* (London: Weidenfeld & Nicolson, 1964).
Hobsbawm, E., *The Age of Capital 1848–1875* (London: Weidenfeld & Nicolson, 1975).

Hodges, D. C., 'Engels' Contribution to Marxism', in R. Miliband and J. Saville (eds), *The Socialist Register 1965* (London: Merlin Press, 1965).
Hodgskin, T., *Labour Defended against the Claims of Capital* (1825) (New York: Kelley, 1963).
Hodgskin, T., *Popular Political Economy* (1827) (New York: Kelley, 1966).
Hodgskin, T., *The Natural and Artificial Rights of Property Contrasted* (1832) (New York: Kelley, 1973).
Hunt, A., 'Theory and Politics in the Identification of the Working Class', in idem (ed.), *Class and Class Structure* (London: Lawrence & Wishart, 1977).
Hunt, R. N., *The Political Ideas of Marx and Engels*, vol. I (London: Macmillan, 1974).
Hyams, E., *Pierre-Joseph Proudhon* (London: John Murray, 1979).
Jackson, J. H., *Marx, Proudhon and European Socialism* (London: English Universities Press, 1958).
Johnson, R., 'Three Problematics: Elements of a Theory of Working-Class Culture', in J. Clarke *et al.* (eds), *Working Class Culture: Studies in History and Theory* (London: Hutchinson, 1979).
Kamenka, E., *The Ethical Foundations of Marxism*, revised edn (London: Routledge & Kegan Paul, 1972).
Kamenka, E. (ed.), *Paradigm for Revolution? The Paris Commune 1871–1971* (Australian National University Press, 1972).
Kaufman, W., *Hegel: a Reinterpretation* (New York: Doubleday Anchor, 1966).
Kaufman, W. (ed.), *Hegel's Political Philosophy* (New York: Atherton Press, 1970).
Kettler, D., *The Social and Political Thought of Adam Ferguson* (Ohio University Press, 1965).
Kitch, M. J. (ed.), *Capitalism and the Reformation* (London: Longmans, 1967).
Kollontai, A., *Selected Writings*, ed. A. Holt (London: Allison & Busby, 1977).
Kuhn, A. and Wolpe, A. M. (eds), *Feminism and Materialism: Women and Modes of Production* (London: Routledge & Kegan Paul, 1978).
Kuhn, T., *The Structure of Scientific Revolutions*, 2nd edn (University of Chicago Press, 1970).
Laclau, E., 'The Specificity of the Political', in *Politics and Ideology in Marxist Theory* (London: New Left Books, 1977).
Lange, O. and Taylor, F., *On the Economic Theory of Socialism* (1938) (New York: McGraw-Hill, 1964).
Lange, O., 'The Computer and the Market', in A. Nove and M. Nuti (eds), *Socialist Economics* (Harmondsworth: Penguin, 1972).
Lecourt, D., *Marxism and Epistemology* (London: New Left Books, 1975).
Lefebvre, H., *The Sociology of Marx* (London: Allen Lane, 1968).
Lehmann, W. C., *Adam Ferguson and the Beginnings of Modern Sociology* (Columbia University Press, 1930).
Lehmann, W. C., *John Millar of Glasgow 1735–1801* (Cambridge University Press, 1960).
Leiss, W., *The Limits to Satisfaction* (London: Marion Boyars, 1978).
Lenin, V. I., *Collected Works* (London: Lawrence & Wishart, 1960–1972).
Lenin, V. I., 'The Three Sources and Three Component Parts of Marxism', in *Selected Works* (Moscow: Progress, 1975) vol. I.
Lenski, G. E., *Power and Privilege: a Theory of Social Stratification* (New York: McGraw-Hill, 1966).
Levine, A. and Wright, E. O., 'Rationality and Class Struggle', *New Left Review*, no. 123 (1980).
Levine, N., *The Tragic Deception: Marx Contra Engels* (Santa Barbara: Clio Press, 1975).
Lewin, M., *Political Undercurrents in Soviet Economic Debates* (London: Pluto Press, 1975).

Liberman, Y., 'The Plan, Profits and Bonuses', in M. Bornstein and D. Fusfeld (eds), *The Soviet Economy: a Book of Readings* (Homewood: Richard Irwin, 1970).
Lichtheim, G., *Marxism*, 2nd edn (London: Routledge & Kegan Paul, 1964).
Lichtheim, G., *The Origins of Socialism* (London: Weidenfeld & Nicolson, 1969).
Liebman, M., *Leninism under Lenin* (London: Jonathan Cape, 1975).
Littman, R. J., *The Greek Experiment: Imperialism and Social Conflict 800–400 BC* (London: Thames & Hudson, 1974).
Lloyd, G. E. R., *Greek Science after Aristotle* (London: Chatto & Windus, 1973).
Löwith, K., *From Hegel to Nietzsche* (New York: Doubleday Anchor, 1967).
Lukács, G., *History and Class Consciousness* (London: Merlin Press, 1971).
Lukács, G., *The Young Hegel* (London: Merlin Press, 1975).
Lukes, S., *Individualism* (Oxford: Blackwell, 1973).
MacIntyre, A., *A Short History of Ethics* (London: Routledge & Kegan Paul, 1967).
Mackenzie, G., 'The Political Economy of the American Working Class', *British Journal of Sociology*, vol. 28 (1977).
Macpherson, C. B., *The Political Theory of Possessive Individualism* (Oxford University Press, 1964).
Macpherson, C. B., *Democratic Theory* (Oxford University Press, 1973).
Maitan, L., *Party, Army and Masses in China* (London: New Left Books, 1976).
Mandel, E., *Marxist Economic Theory* (London: Merlin Press, 1968).
Mandel, E., *The Formation of the Economic Thought of Karl Marx* (London: New Left Books, 1971).
Mandel, E., *On Bureaucracy: a Marxist Analysis* (London: IMG Publications, 1973).
Mandeville, B., *The Fable of the Bees: or, Private Vices and Publick Benefits* (1714), ed. P. Harth (Harmondsworth: Penguin, 1970).
Manuel, F., *The New World of Henri Saint-Simon* (Harvard University Press, 1956).
Marcuse, H., *Reason and Revolution: Hegel and the Rise of Social Theory*, 2nd edn (London: Routledge & Kegan Paul, 1967).
Marcuse, H., 'The Foundation of Historical Materialism', in *Studies in Critical Philosophy* (London: New Left Books, 1972).
Marglin, S., 'What do Bosses do? The Origins and Function of Hierarchy in Capitalist Production', in A. Gorz (ed.), *The Division of Labour* (Hassocks: Harvester Press, 1976).
Marx, K., *Capital*, vols I, II, III (Moscow: Progress, 1961).
Marx, K., *The Cologne Communist Trial*, ed. R. Livingstone (London: Lawrence & Wishart, 1971).
Marx, K., *A Contribution to the Critique of Political Economy*, ed. M. Dobb (London: Lawrence & Wishart, 1971).
Marx, K., *Critique of Hegel's 'Philosophy of Right'*, ed. J. O'Malley (Cambridge University Press, 1970).
Marx, K., *Economic and Philosophic Manuscripts of 1844*, ed. D. Struik (London: Lawrence & Wishart, 1970).
Marx, K., *Grundrisse*, ed. M. Nicolaus (Harmondsworth: Penguin, 1973).
Marx, K., *The Poverty of Philosophy* (New York: International Publishers, 1963).
Marx, K., *Results of the Immediate Process of Production*, Appendix, in *Capital*, vol. I, ed. E. Mandel, Pelican Marx Library (Harmondsworth: Penguin, 1976).
Marx, K., *Selected Writings in Sociology and Social Philosophy*, ed. T. Bottomore and M. Rubel (Harmondsworth: Penguin, 1963).
Marx, K., *Surveys from Exile*, ed. D. Fernbach, Pelican Marx Library (Harmondsworth: Penguin, 1973).
Marx, K., *Texts on Method*, ed. T. Carver (Oxford: Blackwell, 1975).
Marx, K., *Theories of Surplus Value*, vols I, II, III (London: Lawrence & Wishart, 1972).

Marx, K., *Writings of the Young Marx on Philosophy and Society*, ed. L. Easton and K. Guddat (New York: Doubleday Anchor, 1967).
Marx, K. and Engels, F., *Collected Works* (Moscow: Progress, 1975).
Marx, K. and Engels, F., *The German Ideology* (London: Lawrence & Wishart, 1965).
Marx, K. and Engels, F., *The Holy Family* (Moscow: Progress, 1956).
Marx, K. and Engels, F., *Articles from the 'Neue Rheinische Zeitung' 1848–49* (Moscow: Progress, 1972).
Marx, K. and Engels, F., *On Britain* (Moscow: Progress, 1971).
Marx, K. and Engels, F., *Writings on the Paris Commune* (Moscow: Progress, 1971).
Marx, K. and Engels, F., *Selected Correspondence* (Moscow: Progress, 1965).
Marx, K. and Engels, F., *Selected Works*, vols I, II, III (Moscow: Progress, 1969).
McLellan, D., *The Young Hegelians and Karl Marx* (London: Macmillan, 1969).
McLellan, D., *Marx before Marxism* (London: Macmillan, 1970).
McLellan, D., *Marx's Grundrisse* (London: Macmillan, 1971).
McLellan, D., *Karl Marx: his Life and Thought* (London: Macmillan, 1973).
McLellan, D., 'Marx and the Whole Man', in B. Parekh (ed.), *The Concept of Socialism* (London: Croom Helm, 1975).
McLellan, D., *Engels* (London: Fontana, 1977).
Meek, R. L., *Studies in the Labour Theory of Value*, 2nd edn (London: Lawrence & Wishart, 1973).
Meek, R. L., 'The Scottish Contribution to Marxist Sociology', in *Economics and Ideology and Other Essays* (London: Chapman & Hall, 1967).
Meek, R. L. (ed.), *Precursors of Adam Smith 1750–1775* (London: Dent, 1973).
Meek, R. L. and Skinner, A. S., 'The Development of Adam Smith's Ideas on the Division of Labour', *The Economic Journal*, vol. 83 (1973).
Meek, R. L., *Social Science and the Ignoble Savage* (Cambridge University Press, 1976).
Mepham, J., 'The *Grundrisse*: Method or Metaphysics?', *Economy and Society*, vol. 7 (1978).
Mészáros, I., *Marx's Theory of Alienation* (London: Merlin Press, 1970).
Milenkovitch, D. D., *Plan and Market in Yugoslav Economic Thought* (Yale University Press, 1971).
Miliband, R., 'Marx and the State', in R. Miliband and J. Saville (eds), *The Socialist Register 1965* (London: Merlin Press, 1965).
Miliband, R., *The State in Capitalist Society* (London: Weidenfeld & Nicolson, 1969).
Mises, L. von, 'Economic Calculation in the Socialist Commonwealth', in F. A. von Hayek (ed.), *Collectivist Economic Planning* (London: Routledge & Kegan Paul, 1935).
Monroe, A. E. (ed.), *Early Economic Thought* (Harvard University Press, 1951).
Moore, R., *Self-Management in Yugoslavia* (London: Fabian Research Series 281, 1970).
Moorhouse, H., 'The Marxist Theory of the Labour Aristocracy', *Social History*, vol. 3 (1978).
More, C., *Skill and the English Working Class 1870–1914* (London: Croom Helm, 1980).
Mossé, C., *The Ancient World at Work* (London: Chatto & Windus, 1969).
Myers, M., 'Division of Labour as a Principle of Social Cohesion', *Canadian Journal of Economics and Political Science*, vol. 33 (1967).
Nichols, T. (ed.), *Capital and Labour: a Marxist Primer* (London: Fontana, 1980).
Nicolaievsky, B. and Maenchen-Helfen, O., *Karl Marx: Man and Fighter* (London: Allen Lane, 1973).
Nicolaus, M., 'Proletariat and Middle Class in Marx: Hegelian Choreography and the Capitalist Dialectic', *Studies on the Left*, no. 7 (1967).

Nicolaus, M., 'The Unknown Marx', in R. Blackburn (ed.), *Ideology in Social Science* (London: Fontana, 1972). Originally published in *New Left Review*, no. 48 (1968).
Nisbet, R. A., *Social Change and History* (New York: Oxford University Press, 1969).
Noble, D. F., 'Social Choice in Machine Design: the Case of Automatically Controlled Machine Tools, and a Challenge for Labour', *Politics and Society*, vol. 8 (1978).
Norman, R., *Hegel's Phenomenology* (Sussex University Press, 1976).
Novack, G., *Understanding History: Marxist Essays* (New York: Pathfinder Press, 1972).
Nove, A., *An Economic History of the USSR* (Harmondsworth: Penguin, 1970).
Nove, A., 'Economic Reforms in the USSR and Hungary, a Study in Contrasts', in A. Nove and M. Nuti (eds), *Socialist Economics* (Harmondsworth: Penguin, 1972).
Nove, A., *Political Economy and Soviet Socialism* (London: Allen & Unwin, 1979).
Nove, A., 'The Soviet Economy: Problems and Prospects', *New Left Review*, no. 119 (1980).
Ollman, B., *Alienation* (Cambridge University Press, 1971).
Ollman, B., 'Marx's Vision of Communism: a Reconstruction', *Critique*, no. 8, (1977).
Owen, R., *A New View of Society and Report to the County of Lanark*, ed. V. A. C. Gatrell (Harmondsworth: Penguin, 1969).
Parkin, F., *Class Inequality and Political Order* (MacGibbon & Kee, 1971).
Paterson, R., *The Nihilistic Egoist: Max Stirner* (University of Hull Press, 1971).
Pearson, A. W., 'The Economy has no Surplus: Critique of a Theory of Development', in K. Polanyi *et al.*, *Trade and Market in the Early Empires* (New York: Free Press, 1957).
Petty, W. P., *The Economic Writings of Sir William Petty*, ed. C. H. Hull (Cambridge University Press, 1899) vols I and II.
Plant, R., *Hegel* (London: Allen & Unwin, 1973).
Plant, R., 'Hegel and Political Economy', parts I and II, *New Left Review*, nos 103 and 104 (1977).
Plato, *The Dialogues of Plato*, vol. III, trans. B. Jowett, 2nd edn (Oxford University Press, 1875).
Plato, *The Republic*, trans. H. D. P. Lee (Harmondsworth: Penguin, 1971).
Plato, *The Republic*, trans. P. Shorey in E. Hamilton and H. Cairns (eds), *The Collected Dialogues of Plato* (Princeton University Press, 1973).
Polanyi, K., *The Livelihood of Man* (New York: Academic Press, 1977).
Poulantzas, N., *Political Power and Social Classes* (London: New Left Books and Sheed & Ward, 1973).
Price, R., *Marx and Education in Russia and China* (London: Croom Helm, 1977).
Proudhon, P. J., *Selected Writings of Pierre-Joseph Proudhon*, ed. S. Edwards (London: Macmillan, 1970).
Randall, Jr, J. H., *Aristotle* (Columbia University Press, 1960).
Ricardo, D., *On the Principles of Political Economy and Taxation*, ed. P. Sraffa (Cambridge University Press, 1951).
Reisman, D. A., *Adam Smith's Sociological Economics* (London: Croom Helm, 1976).
Ritter, A., *The Political Thought of Pierre-Joseph Proudhon* (Princeton University Press, 1969).
Roll, E., *A History of Economic Thought*, 4th edn (London: Faber, 1973).
Rosenberg, N., 'Adam Smith on the Division of Labour: Two Views or One?', *Economica*, vol. 32 (1965).

Rudé, G., *Debate on Europe: 1815–1850* (New York: Harper & Row, 1972).
Sacks, K., 'Engels Revisited: Women, the Organisation of Production, and Private Property', in R. R. Reiter (ed.), *Toward an Anthropology of Women* (New York: Monthly Review Press, 1975).
Sahlins, M., *Stone Age Economics* (London: Tavistock, 1974).
Saint-Simon, H., *Henri Saint-Simon 1760–1825: Selected Writings on Science, Industry and Social Organization*, ed. K. Taylor (London: Croom Helm, 1975).
Saint-Simon, H., *The Political Thought of Saint-Simon*, ed. G. Ionescu (Oxford University Press, 1976).
Saint-Simon, H., *The Doctrine of Saint-Simon*, trans. G. Iggers, 2nd edn (New York: Schocken, 1972).
Samuel, R., 'Workshop of the World: Steam Power and Hand Technology in mid-Victorian Britain', *History Workshop Journal*, no. 3 (1977).
Sayer, D., 'Science as Critique: Marx *vs*. Althusser', in J. Mepham and D. H. Ruben (eds), *Issues in Marxist Philosophy*, vol. III, *Epistemology, Science, Ideology* (Brighton: Harvester Press, 1979).
Schacht, R., *Alienation* (London: Allen & Unwin, 1971).
Schmidt, A., *The Concept of Nature in Marx* (London: New Left Books, 1971).
Schramm, S. R. (ed.), *Authority, Participation and Cultural Change in China* (Cambridge University Press, 1976).
Schumpeter, J. A., *History of Economic Analysis* (London: Allen & Unwin, 1954).
Schurmann, F., *Ideology and Organization in Communist China* (University of California Press, 1971).
Selucký, R., 'Marxism and Self-Management', in J. Vanek (ed.), *Self-Management: Economic Liberation of Man* (Harmondsworth: Penguin, 1975).
Selucký, R., *Marxism, Socialism, Freedom: Towards a General Democratic Theory of Labour-Managed Systems* (London: Macmillan, 1979).
Sher, G. S., *Praxis: Marxist Criticism and Dissent in Socialist Yugoslavia* (Indiana University Press, 1977).
Šik, O., *Plan and Market under Socialism* (New York: International Arts & Sciences Press, 1972).
Skinner, A. S., 'Adam Smith: an Economic Interpretation of History', in A. S. Skinner and T. Wilson (eds), *Essays on Adam Smith* (Oxford University Press, 1975).
Smith, Adam, *The Wealth of Nations*, ed. E. Cannan (London: Methuen, 1961) vols I and II.
Smith, Adam, 'Lectures on Justice, Police, Revenue and Arms', in H. W. Schneider (ed.), *Adam Smith's Moral and Political Philosophy* (New York: Harper Torchbooks, 1970).
Stedman, Jones, G., 'Class Struggle and the Industrial Revolution', *New Left Review*, no. 90 (1975).
Stirner, M., *The Ego and His Own*, ed. J. Carroll (London: Jonathan Cape, 1971).
Stojanović, S., *Between Ideals and Reality* (New York: Oxford University Press, 1973).
Sweezy, P., *The Theory of Capitalist Development*, 2nd edn (New York: Monthly Review Press, 1968).
Taylor, C., *Hegel* (Cambridge University Press, 1975).
Taylor, W. L., *Francis Hutcheson and David Hume as Predecessors of Adam Smith* (Durham: Duke University Press, 1965).
Technology, the Labour Process, and the Working Class, special issue of *Monthly Review*, vol. 28 (1976).
Terray, E., 'Classes and Class Consciousness in the Abron Kingdom of Gyaman', in M. Bloch (ed.), *Marxist Analyses and Social Anthropology* (London: Malaby Press, 1975).

The Labour Process and the Working Class, special issue of *Politics and Society*, vol. 8 (1978).
Therborn, G., *Science, Class and Society* (London: New Left Books, 1976).
Thompson, E. P., *The Making of the English Working Class*, revised edn (Harmondsworth: Penguin, 1968).
Thompson, W., *An Inquiry into the Principles of the Distribution of Wealth* (1824) (New York: Kelley, 1963).
Thompson, W., *Labour Rewarded* (1827) (New York: Kelley, 1969).
Ticktin, H., 'Socialism, the Market and the State', *Critique*, no. 3 (1974).
Tomlinson, J., 'Marx's *Capital* and the Analysis of the Capitalist Enterprise' (unpublished mimeo, Department of Economics, Brunel University).
Tribe, K., 'Remarks on the Theoretical Significance of the "Grundrisse"', *Economy and Society*, vol. 3 (1974).
Tribe, K., *Land, Labour and Economic Discourse* (London: Routledge & Kegan Paul, 1978).
Trotsky, L., *The Revolution Betrayed* (1936) (London: New Park Publications, 1967).
Tucker, R., *Philosophy and Myth in Karl Marx* (Cambridge University Press, 1961).
Turgot, A. R. J., *Turgot on Progress, Sociology and Economics*, ed. R. L. Meek (Cambridge University Press, 1973).
Ure, A., *The Philosophy of Manufactures* (1835) (London: Frank Cass, 1967).
Urry, J., 'Towards a Structural Theory of the Middle Class', *Acta Sociologica*, vol. 16 (1973).
Wagner, Y. and Strauss, M., 'The Programme of the Communist Manifesto and its Theoretical Foundations', *Political Studies*, vol. 17 (1969).
Wood, E. and Wood, N., *Class Ideology and Ancient Political Theory* (Oxford: Blackwell, 1978).
West, E. G., 'Adam Smith's Two Views on the Division of Labour', *Economica*, vol. 31 (1964).
Williams, R., *Keywords: a Vocabulary of Culture and Society* (London: Fontana, 1976).
Williams, R. (ed.), *The Commune of Paris, 1871* (New York: John Wiley, 1969).
Williams, R., *The French Revolution of 1870–71* (London: Weidenfeld & Nicolson, 1969).
Winch, D., *Adam Smith's Politics* (Cambridge University Press, 1978).
Wolpe, H. (ed.), *The Articulation of Modes of Production: Essays from Economy and Society* (London: Routledge & Kegan Paul, 1980).
Wright, E. O., *Class, Crisis and the State* (London: New Left Books, 1978).
Xenophon, *Cyropaedia*, trans. W. Miller (London: Heinemann, 1943).
Xenophon, *Oeconomicus*, trans. L. Strauss (Cornell University Press, 1970).
Zimbalist, A. (ed.), *Case Studies on the Labour Process* (New York: Monthly Review Press, 1979).

Index